Anglo-Japanese Financial Relations

Anglo-Japanese Financial Relations

A Golden Tide

SIR FRED WARNER

Basil Blackwell

First published 1991

Basil Blackwell Ltd
108 Cowley Road, Oxford, OX4 1JF, UK

Basil Blackwell, Inc.
3 Cambridge Center
Cambridge, Massachusetts 02142, USA

British Library Cataloguing in Publication Data
A CIP catalogue record for this book is available from the British
Library.

Library of Congress Cataloging in Publication Data
Warner, Frederick, Sir, 1910–
    Anglo-Japanese financial relations: a golden tide/Sir Fred Warner.
    p.   cm.
    ISBN 0–631–17628–4
    1. Great Britain—Foreign economic relations—Japan.   2. Japan—
Foreign economic relations—Great Britain.   3. Finance—Great
Britain—History.   4. Finance—Japan—History.   5. International
finance.   I. Title.
HF1534.5.J3W37   1991
332'.042'0941—dc20
91–7752 CIP

Typeset in 11 on 13 pt Sabon
by Graphicraft Typesetters Ltd, Hong Kong
Printed in Great Britain by TJ Press Ltd., Padstow, Cornwall

This book is dedicated to Raymond Carr and Nobutoshi Hagihara, without whose invitation to me to lecture on the subject it would never have been written.

CONTENTS

Part III: Past, Present and Future

PREFACE

Early in 1988 I gave the second Richard Storry Memorial Lecture at St Antony's College, Oxford. I chose the subject of financial relations between Japan and the United Kingdom because it seemed to me that the emergence of Japan as the world's greatest exporter of capital – or as the richest country in the world – was one of the most significant historical developments of the 1980s. In the course of preparing the lecture I could draw on a great deal of earlier work in the field – British, Japanese, and American – but I was surprised to discover that there was no general account of the subject running from the opening up of Japan in 1858 to the state of affairs today. I therefore decided to write this book. Not having a great deal of time for the task I was fortunate to secure the collaboration in research of Thomas Nelson and the two of us have worked at it since July 1988.

This is not an academic work and is not intended for academics. Nor is it a handbook on banking in London or Tokyo, of which a number of excellent ones exist. It is intended as an introduction to the subject for executives in Britain, and we hope Japan and other countries, who will be working alongside each other or dealing with each other in London or Tokyo. It may help them to understand the problems faced by their predecessors, to learn about the past roles of some of the companies by which they may be employed or with which they may have contact, and to recognize certain patterns which may recur in the story.

I would particularly like to thank the Bank of England, the

National Westminster Bank, the Hong Kong and Shanghai Banking Corporation, Messrs Jardine Matheson and Co., Messrs Baring Brothers & Co., Messrs N. M. Rothschild and Sons, and Messrs J. Henry Schroder Wagg & Co. for giving me access to their libraries and archives and for the guidance and assistance I have had from their archivists. I am also grateful to all those members of the staffs of British and Japanese banks or securities companies who have been so willing to discuss the subject and to provide material. I owe particular thanks to Dr Geoffrey Jones, to Dr R. Roberts, and to Professor Hisahiko Saito for allowing me to see and draw on as yet unpublished work on which they were engaged. I owe a special debt to Mrs Drue Heinz for having so generously allowed me to spend several weeks at the retreat for writers at Hawthornden Castle while writing the text. Finally, both Thomas Nelson and myself would like to thank our respective families for their encouragement and understanding.

Fred Warner

PART I

1853–1946

1

HISTORICAL BACKGROUND
1853–1868

The first British companies to establish themselves in Japan arrived immediately after the signing of the Yedo Treaty between the two countries in 1858 and its ratification in the following year. This treaty opened up Japan to British commerce after more than two centuries of self-imposed isolation. To take advantage of this new situation, British trading companies flooded into the newly opened 'Treaty Ports'. Before studying their activities, it may be helpful for those readers who have only a sketchy knowledge of Japan's history to describe briefly how this revolutionary change in her relations with the outside world came about, and what were the conditions in which the new arrivals would have to carry on their businesses.

Between 1635 and 1639, for reasons not relevant to this book, the Shogun Iemitsu Tokugawa issued a series of instructions to provincial governors making it illegal on pain of death for any Japanese ship or person to leave the country. At the same time it also became illegal for any foreign ship or person to enter a Japanese port, except as specifically permitted by the Shogun's government (generally referred to as the *Bakufu*).[1] This exemption became limited to a handful of Chinese ships carrying silk imports (a trade reserved to the Shogun) and to a small annual quota of Dutch ships. The foreigners engaged in this trade were confined to the island of Dejima in the Bay of Nagasaki. This state of affairs continued for 220 years.

By the middle of the nineteenth century such a position had become completely anomalous. The wealth of the East Indies had been exploited by the Dutch for more than two centuries and the islands had fallen under Dutch sovereignty. India had been open to European traders for a similar time; a large part of the country was now under the rule of the East India Company and would soon, after the Mutiny, pass to the British Imperial Crown. As a result of the Opium Wars, China too had been opened to foreign trade. In the Far East, only Japan and Korea remained closed, and countries such as the United States, Russia, and Great Britain were particularly keen, for a number of different reasons, to establish themselves in Japan.

The first to arrive were the Americans. With the settlement and development of their West Coast on the Pacific, they were concerned to open up a regular trade route with the Far East, and Japan lay across its path. They were also much annoyed by the harsh treatment given to sailors from American whaling boats, driven by bad weather into Japanese ports or wrecked ashore. In 1845 they sent Commodore Biddle with two ships to demand the opening of relations, but without success. It was not until 8 July 1853 that Commodore Perry sailed into the Bay of Yedo (now Tokyo) with his squadron of 'black ships' and in an audience with the Shogun (who came to be known to foreigners as the 'Great Tycoon'[2]) he presented letters from the President of the United States requesting that Japan be opened to American trade. Leaving the Japanese to reflect on this, Perry returned early in 1854 and, after difficult negotiation, the Treaty of Amity and Friendship between Japan and the United States was signed on 31 March. However, this document was not in itself sufficient to regulate the conditions and facilities needed for the exercise of Trade. So in August 1856 the first American diplomatic representative, Townsend Harris, arrived to negotiate a detailed Treaty of Commerce, which was finally signed and ratified by the summer of 1858, after many months of wearisome argument and obstruction.[3]

It was only to be expected that the British would be hot on the heels of the Americans, keen to ensure that the United States did not try to establish a trading monopoly. An equally important consideration was the conduct of the Russians. After its defeat in the Crimean War, the Imperial Russian government set about securing its position on the Pacific seaboard against any further confrontation with Britain and France. It therefore occupied the island of Sakhalin to the north of Japan – which was known to contain coal deposits – and began to exploit these for its Far Eastern Fleet. This, in turn, increased the need for Britain to secure coaling stations of its own in the area and Japan was the obvious place.[4] Perry's original Treaty of Amity and Friendship was followed by similar treaties with Britain (in October 1854), with Russia (in February 1855), and with Holland (in November 1855).[5] Within one month of the completion of Harris's more extended Treaty, Lord Elgin arrived to negotiate a similar agreement on behalf of the British government. Japanese opposition had been broken by the Americans and it took him only two weeks to achieve what had taken Harris two years.

One small circumstance may be noted in view of what follows in this book. So little was known about the habits of the Japanese that Elgin brought with him a 318-ton steam yacht as a present from Queen Victoria to the Tycoon. The Tycoon was, however, virtually a prisoner of tradition and ceremonial and would never have been allowed to venture out to sea in such a newfangled and foreign contraption. As Oliphant, who accompanied the Mission, wrote: 'It was a cruel satire on this unhappy potentate to present him with a yacht; one might as well request the Pope's acceptance of a wife.'[6] The British had not done their 'prep' – an omission often to be repeated.

The treaties which had now been concluded with the Americans, the British, and others were onerous for the Japanese. Article IV of the Anglo-Japanese Treaty of Yedo,[7] for example, stated that:

> All questions in regard to rights, whether of property or person, arising between British subjects in the dominions of His Majesty the Tycoon of Japan shall be subject to the jurisdiction of the British authorities.

Article X provided that:

> All foreign coin shall be current in Japan and shall pass for its corresponding weight in Japanese coin of the same description. British and Japanese subjects may freely use foreign or Japanese

coin in making payments to each other ... Coins of all description (with the exception of Japanese copper coin) as well as
foreign gold and silver uncoined, may be exported from Japan.

Article xvi, designed to avoid internal tolls and tariff barriers,
stipulated that:

All goods imported into Japan by British subjects and which have
paid the duty fixed by this treaty, may be transported by the
Japanese into any part of the Empire without the payment of any
tax, excise or transit duty whatever.

The duty 'fixed by this treaty' was the regular customs duty and
was laid down in an annexe to the agreement. The treaties signed
with the Americans and the other European powers were similar
and, in any case, contained 'most favoured nation' clauses. Thus,
Japan was stripped of essential parts of its economic and legal
sovereignty and it is not surprising that such agreements came to
be known by the Japanese as 'Unequal Treaties'. Certainly,
although the *Bakufu* had accepted them in face of what they felt
to be overwhelming *force majeure*, some of the feudal clan chiefs
(*Daimyo*) and their military followers (*Samurai*), in whose hands
lay effective local power within the country and who felt the very
presence of foreigners to be insupportable, considered the concessions contained in the treaties a national disgrace.

This situation gave rise to certain consequences for foreigners
in Japan. In some quarters the feeling against them was so intense
that their lives were in danger. Whereas the population as a
whole showed themselves either courteous or indifferent to the
new arrivals, those who were engaged in a struggle with the
Bakufu found the slogan '*Sonno Joi*' ('Revere the Emperor: Out
with the Barbarians') a powerful rallying-cry. It appealed particularly to certain elements in the Samurai class. A series of
murderous attacks were made on foreign businessmen and their
servants. Even diplomatic missions were in danger. On one occasion the British Consul General Alcock and his staff only surviv-
ing an attack on their quarters by jumping over the back wall of
the garden. In August 1862, after the murder of an Englishman
by a retainer of the *Daimyo* of Satsuma near Yokohama, and
Japanese refusal of any satisfaction, British warships bombarded

Kagoshima in reprisal. All foreign ships then became targets and in 1863 and 1864 Japanese shore batteries in the fief of Choshu, fired on a number passing through the straits of Shimonoseki.[8] These batteries were eventually put out of action by bombardment from a combined squadron of British, French, American, and Dutch ships. But even in face of such retaliation, further assassinations followed and the foreign communities continued to be guarded by their own troops. It was some years (and not until after the overthrow of the Shogunate) before foreigners could go safely about their business.

The presence of foreigners helped exacerbate the conflicts already existing inside Japan and which would eventually lead to the downfall of the Shogunate. It was not the case that the whole Japanese ruling class was opposed to contact with foreigners. For many years before the arrival of Commodore Perry there had been demands for the relaxation of the policy of seclusion. Some 'intellectuals' had believed that foreign knowledge, particularly in the scientific fields, was essential for the future of Japan and had suffered for their views, while some military leaders had wanted to adopt foreign military technology.[9] Nor was it true that the Shogun was in undisputed control of his realm. Some of the most powerful fiefs were intriguing against him and seeking to enhance the influence of the Emperor in Kyoto. The two questions became interlinked so that, with the acceptance of the 'Unequal Treaties', the *Bakufu* found themselves obliged to defend the opening up of Japan while the Emperor's circle and the clan leaders who supported him were demanding the expulsion of foreigners.

As this power-struggle intensified, foreigners became inevitably involved. The Americans and French viewed the Shogun's unstable administration as the only legitimate government, while the French Minister, Léon Roches, hoped to secure France's position by allying himself with the *Bakufu*. The French helped in the construction of a naval dockyard in Yokosuka and supplied weapons for the Shogun's campaign against the dissident clan of Choshu.[10] The British, on the other hand, gradually reached a more realistic assessment of the situation. Ernest Satow, then a junior member of the British Legation, playing an active interventionist role, later described the situation in 1864 after the bombardment of Shimonoseki as follows: 'Having beaten the Choshu people we had come to respect them, while a feeling of dislike began to arise in our minds for the Tycoon's men on account of their weakness and double-dealing.'[11] Representatives of the Satsuma fief, who visited London in 1865, held discussions with the Foreign Office and at these and other meetings a spirit of friendship developed between the British authorities and the future rulers of Japan.

As the position of the *Bakufu* in confrontation with the Western clans declined, British businessmen who could foresee its inevitable fall were as quick as their government to follow the signs and to ensure a good position for themselves with the rising stars of the Japanese world. Both Satsuma and Choshu, which were about to play a crucial part in the overthrow of the Shogunate, and whose men would have leading positions in the successor regime, received large shipments of arms from the British firm of Glover and Co. at Nagasaki.[12] Even as early as September 1863, Jardines instructed their agent in Nagasaki to give a credit of up to 130,000 dollars[13] to the *Daimyo* of Satsuma for the purchase of silk and other goods to be shipped to them in Shanghai.[14] For the first (and happily the last) time in the history of Japan – until 1946 – foreigners had intervened decisively in the country's internal affairs. By the time that armed rebellion had finally taken place in 1868, that the Shogun had given up power, and that the Emperor Meiji had been installed as the constitutional ruler of Japan,[15] British traders had achieved a very favourable situation.[16]

A final matter arising from the 'Unequal Treaties' was that from an early stage, particularly after they had resolved their internal disputes and the new Meiji government had become master in its own house, the Japanese began furiously to press for revision. Indeed, the treaties themselves contained clauses providing for revision after an initial period. This became almost the leading issue in Japan's relations with foreigners, who came to be judged according to their attitude to the question. It will be seen in the next chapter that the British were to take the more difficult side. The activities, problems, and successes of the first British businessmen in Japan can be assessed against the background of this brief historical survey.

NOTES

1 Sir George Sansom, *A History of Japan* (Cresset Press, London, 1964), Vol. III, pp. 36–9.
2 Transliteration of the Japanese word '*Taikun*', meaning 'Great Lord'.
3 Elizabeth Barr, *The Coming of the Barbarians: The Story of Western Settlement in Japan 1853–1870* (Macmillan, London, 1967), pp. 19–54.
4 Shin'etsu Suiyama, 'Trends of Japan's Coal Exports to the Shanghai Coal Market 1859–1860', in *Kindai Ikoki no Nihon Keizai*, ed. Hiroshi Shinbo and Yasukichi Yasuba (MS copy kindly supplied by Cambridge University Library).
5 Sir George Sansom, *A History of Japan*, p. 234.
6 Elizabeth Barr, *The Coming of the Barbarians*, p. 234.
7 Foreign Office Treaty Series, Bodleian Library, Oxford.
8 H. S. Williams and Hiroshi Naito, *The Kamakura Murders* (n.p., 1971).
9 Donald Keene, *The Japanese Discovery of Europe 1720–1830* (Stanford University Press, Stanford, Calif., 1969).
10 W. G. Beasley, *Select Documents in Japanese Foreign Policy* (Clarendon Press, Oxford, 1967).
11 Ernest Satow, *A Diplomat in Japan*, p. 391, quoted in W. G. Beasley, *The Modern History of Japan* (Weidenfeld and Nicholson, London, 1981), p. 94.
12 Suiyama, *Gurabaa Shokai Bakumakki no Nagasaki Bocki* (MS copy kindly supplied by Cambridge University Library).
13 The word dollar, as used in this chapter and chapter 2, refers to the Mexican silver dollar.
14 Grace Estelle Fox, *Britain and Japan, 1858–1883* (Clarendon Press, Oxford, 1969), p. 319.
15 These events are usually described as the 'Meiji Restoration'.
16 There is just a possibility that the British were not quite as much in control of events as they thought. The Japanese historian, Nobutoshi Hagihara, in a lecture delivered to the Japan Society in London, made the intriguing suggestion that the rebel leader Saigo Takamori, at a crucial point in the revolution, made a cat's-paw out of Ernest Satow by playing on British rivalry with the French.

2

EARLY DAYS
1858–1868

The British Trading Companies

The earliest British businessmen to arrive in Japan were the representatives of the trading companies, and the first among these was William Keswick, who came from Hong Kong to Yokohama in July 1854 to open a branch of Jardine Matheson. The company was immediately known as *'Ichiban'* (number one) because it established itself on the first building lot on the sea front of the Treaty area. It was also to become the first in importance.[1] Others soon followed, not only in Yokohama but also in the other Treaty Ports of Nagasaki, Hakodate, Hyogo, and Niigata as they were opened to foreign trade. By the early winter of 1860, thirty foreign firms had rented land in Yokohama, of which the majority were British and at the Meiji Restoration in 1868 British firms numbered at least forty.[2]

The connection between such trading houses and the City of London was a tenuous one since they were primarily Eastern companies, operating from Hong Kong, the China Treaty Ports, or India, but they did usually have head offices or partnerships resident at home. Their activities set the scene for future financial relations between Japan and the United Kingdom. For many years, British trading houses handled the largest single share of Japan's foreign trade, rising to a peak of over one-half in 1880 and declining only to well over a quarter by the outbreak of the First World War.[3] Not only did they meet their own financial requirements in the early years, but they also provided finance for

Japanese merchants and entrepreneurs, thus establishing the pattern for the future Japanese system of trade finance. For the first twenty years after 1859, British companies and Chinese merchants were to finance the bulk of Japanese trade.

In the earliest days, there was some doubt as to whether it would really be possible to undertake any profitable trade. In a letter dated 6 January 1859, Mr Whittal, of the Shanghai branch of Jardine Matheson, wrote that it was becoming increasingly clear that there seemed little point in trying to compete with the Chinese as far as exports to Japan were concerned, but that he was nevertheless interested in the prospects for exporting commodities to Britain.[4] In spite of his doubts, he dispatched a cargo of cloth and medicines in the ship *Troas*, which coincidentally was bringing Keswick to Yokohama. Jardine's encountered doubts on the Japanese side also, for although it struck up a profitable bargain on the cargo with a local merchant, this person wished to keep the matter secret and unofficial for fear of arousing the wrath of the local authorities.[5]

Such problems took time to overcome. K. R. Mackenzie, who had accompanied Keswick aboard the *Troas* to Yokohama, complained that Japanese merchants set up their shops in the port but had imported almost nothing.[6] In the circumstances it was remarkable just how quickly the two biggest traders, Jardine Matheson and Dent and Company, were able to take advantage of the new opportunities. The Japanese were certainly more than willing to sell and offered stocks of seaweed, *shiitake* (mushrooms), and silk. It was upon this trade in Japanese exports that the early arrivals flourished. Between 1859 and 1865 Jardine Matheson alone controlled one-sixth of the trade of the entire country and, since the majority of their competitors were still also British, the position of companies was unrivalled.[7]

There were, as yet, no banking facilities in Japan for such trade, so the trading companies had to devise ways of financing their own deals. Foreign firms had not had time to build up a network of purchasing agents and they relied to a great extent on the help of native merchants. These men had little capital, and to enable them to buy goods from outside the Treaty Ports the trading companies made them advances of cash. The way in which the system worked is clearly shown in the records of

Jardine Matheson. In a letter of 6 May 1860, William Keswick wrote: 'I have expectations of securing a fair quantity [of silk] on very reasonable terms by making a moderate advance to enable the man to purchase it.'[8] He explained the need for Japanese merchants to be supplied with capital in a further letter to the Shanghai branch dated 20 May of the same year:

> There is still a good deal of silk in these parts and I can only account for the silk not arriving more freely from the opening of the port from the fact that the merchants were at first very poor. They could not enter into a series of operations but had to close one before arranging another.[9]

A significant, though certainly not unique, recipient of this treatment was a merchant called Takasuya, who between 1860 and 1862 was given 760,000 dollars' worth of credit. In a letter of 20 June 1860, Keswick described the optimism with which he viewed such business. He claimed that as a result of these loans exports of silk were likely to leap to 20,000 *piculs*.[10] His enthusiasm was encouraged by the Shanghai branch, who were finding that supplies of this commodity from within China were being interrupted by the activities of rebels; Jardine Matheson hoped that credit-financed exports from Japan would make up the shortfall. Whittal accordingly replied from Shanghai that, if it were not too dangerous, he would like to engage boldly in the extension of credit to the silk-producing areas.[11]

The experience of the tea traders was quite different. Most of their local contacts were wealthy merchants attached to the households of the great Daimyos. These men had enough capital to buy large stocks of tea without the need for credit and offers of loans were rarely necessary.[12]

Credit business could be risky. A plan formulated by Jardine Matheson in 1860 to finance the purchase of silk at a fixed exchange rate of 270 Mexican dollars for 100 Japanese *wakin*[13] went awry when the authorities in July suddenly discontinued the exchange of Japanese *bu*[14] against the silver dollar and allowed the latter coinage to circulate freely. So great was the demand for this foreign specie that its value in terms of Japanese coin rose steeply, making the agreed dollar price for the goods uneconomic. The whole venture was to fail disastrously and Takasuya, who had received advances from Jardine's, was sued by that company for non-performance. This particular incident illustrates one of the difficulties met with by merchants on both sides in these early deals. Neither side had sufficient experience of the market, while communication was difficult between parties who had as yet little knowledge or experience of each other's trading practices.

Jardine Matheson and other companies were also prepared to make direct loans to some of the semi-independent feudal domains. For example, credit was extended on three occasions to 'Prince Minokami', as he was styled in company correspondence, Lord of Morioka, for a total of 150,000 dollars. S. J. Gower, who had replaced William Keswick at the Yokohama office, signed a contract with the *Daimyo*'s representatives whereby he engaged to take the entire silk production of the domain for three years. In return, cash was advanced, at an interest rate of 2 per cent a month, the principal to be repaid in silk.[15] The issue of a huge credit to Satsuma in September 1863 has already been noted in chapter 1 (p. 6).

When Jardine Matheson had more cash on hand than was required for the purchase of available goods, it would often buy the promissory notes issued by other merchants and send them back to London at a profit. By the latter half of 1862 it had begun to conduct this form of financial business on a large scale. In July of that year it bought 9,975 dollars' worth of promissory notes; in August, owing to exceptional circumstances, the figure rose to 348,058 dollars. The grand total for the months July – November was 545,123 dollars. The merchants who issued these notes were all foreign traders, rather than Japanese merchants. The exceptionally high figure for August was accounted for by the fact that E. Clarke of Dent and Co., the principal rivals of Jardine Matheson, had sold it two promissory notes of 100,000 dollars each. Most of the issuers had head offices or agencies in Shanghai and the promissory notes were usually transmitted to that city for repayment and thence sometimes back to London. In this way the first rather tenuous connections were made between the Japan trade and British banks at home.[16]

Jardine Matheson seems to have been pushed into this kind of

activity by the unsatisfactory nature of the Japanese export market as it developed. The company was not disposed to buy
produce at what it believed to be unreasonable rates, even though
money was regularly sent from Shanghai to fund its trading.
Consequently, as prices rose in response to foreign buying, it
often found itself with an excess of cash, which it turned to good
use by playing the part of the banker to other merchants. Mr
Gower of the Yokohama branch wrote to the company's Head
Office at Hong Kong on 18 October 1862:

> The *Lancefield* brought over about 4 tons and a half of treasure
> but, a large portion of this being already due for produce purch-
> ased, has had little or no effect on exchange, the rate for Shanghai
> bills having still 5 to $5\frac{1}{2}$% discount. Silk, however, has advanced
> 15 dollars a *picul*, tea continues to be firmly held by the teamen at
> other rates.[17]

In other words, the margins on physical trade continued to be
squeezed. At the same time there was a constant demand for
dollars to satisfy the shortage of capital in the foreign community. It was therefore more profitable for Jardine Matheson to use
its dollars in buying promissory notes, even at not a very exciting
rate of interest.

Another recipient of loans at this time was the Japanese government. In the absence of proper financial institutions, the trading companies could fill the gap when the authorities needed
foreign exchange. For example, on 22 January 1862 a delegation
left Shinagawa headed by a Mr Takeuchi to try to negotiate with
foreign governments an agreement postponing the opening of
further Treaty Ports. Dent and Co. provided the facilities whereby funds were assured for the party in Paris. The Japanese
government gave Mr Clarke 30,000 dollars and received a promissory note for 165,000 French francs, to be drawn on Rothschild
Frères of Paris. The obligation to draw pocket-money from a
merchant cannot have been very acceptable to the Japanese and,
as soon as more regular arrangements were available, they would
have recourse to them. In 1864, when a similar delegation led by
Messrs Kawatsu and Ikeda left Yokohama, the arrangements
were made through the Central Bank of Western India, whose
arrival on the scene will shortly be discussed.

There were two other ways apart from carrying on and financing the silk and tea trades, in which the trading companies were active (or sought to be active) in these early days and which are worth noting. In chapter 1 it was pointed out that one of the chief reasons why the Western Powers had forced Japan to open her doors was because they needed coaling ports for their steamers or warships. It was this which prompted Alcock, the British Minister, to ask the Japanese authorities if British companies might search for coal in Kyushu. The request was refused. In the following years there were repeated British complaints about the slow rate at which the Japanese coal industry was developing, with anxious but vain urgings for the participation of foreign companies. In fact, it was not until 1866 that Japanese coal, mainly from the mines at Takashima in Kyushu, began to make an impression in the Far East, but by this time the boot was on the other foot. A British commercial report pointed out that Japanese and Australian coal was likely to drive the British product from the China market. In the mid-1860s Japanese coal accounted for only 10 per cent of total sales in Shanghai but during the next decade it leapt to 90 per cent. At first the trade had been handled by Glover and Co. of Nagasaki but with the export of coal from the Miike mines by the Mitsui Trading Co. the British share was to dwindle away.[18] This provides one of the earliest but clearest examples of the limitations set upon foreign capital participation in Japan, a matter which will be fully examined in the next chapter.

Second, it was inevitable that the foreign trading companies should play an important part in providing training and opportunity within the Treaty Ports for some of the young men who would be the future businessmen, technicians, or leaders of Japan. Furthermore, while the policy of seclusion had been abandoned to the extent of allowing foreigners into the country, and while Japanese were now beginning to be sent abroad to learn foreign methods, the controls on exit from the country were still strict, and some adventurous spirits looked to foreign companies to help them get round the prohibition. A famous case was that of the young Prince Ito and three of his student friends who besought William Keswick to help them to reach Britain. They were smuggled out of Yokohama by night to Shanghai and thence sent on to England in the clipper *White Adder*.[19] They thus probably became the first Japanese ever to be introduced to the City of London. And although Ito's experiences in America years later were to play a more formative part in his views on banking when he became responsible for that sector of the economy in 1872, many first ideas on financial regulation must have been planted in the minds of these Japanese through the trading companies.

It can be seen from the foregoing that trade financing developed on an *ad hoc* basis to fill a vacuum. Without proper instruments of credit, trading companies had to transport huge quantities of coin from their head offices in India or China. A succession of ships had to be chartered to make the run from China to Japan, carrying at least twenty caskets, each containing four or five thousand Mexican silver dollars. For example, in July 1862 the *Fiery Cross* arrived carrying no less than 200,000 dollars.[20] Even companies with large stocks of capital could find themselves in difficulties when their head offices happened to be suffering from a temporary shortage of cash while, needless to say, the smaller firms had no facilities for this kind of thing at all. Small firms were obliged to see their profits eroded by borrowing from their larger competitors. In any case, the length of time it took to ship goods from one place to another and the fluctuations in the market made it almost impossible for small merchants to survive for long. Nor was this state of affairs satisfactory to the Japanese as it represented a kind of off-shore financing, totally outside their control. The time soon came for the development of regular banking operations.

THE ARRIVAL OF THE BRITISH BANKS

The British banks began to arrive four years after the trading companies. Doubtless, information and above all complaints coming back to Hong Kong and Shanghai from Yokohama and Nagasaki convinced them of the need for their presence. Both the Central Bank of Western India and the Chartered Mercantile Bank of India, London, and China are said to have been the first but the more convincing evidence supports the former. According to J. R. Black, the Central Bank, whose head office was in Bombay, was on the spot before any other and placed its Japan office at Yokohama under the authority of an Acting Agent called Charles Rickerby. Further support for the Central Bank's claim is given in a letter from C. S. Hope of Jardine Matheson's Yokohama office, who wrote on 25 August 1865 that the Bank: 'was established in Yokohama a considerable time before any other and an account was opened with it about two and a half years since'.[21] The Chartered Mercantile Bank of India, London, and China followed in April 1863, the Commercial Bank of India and the East in October 1863, the Bank of Hindustan, China, and Japan in 1864, and the Oriental Banking Corporation, then the largest bank in Asia, in the same year. The Hong Kong and Shanghai Banking Corporation arrived in 1866, the Chartered Bank of India, Australia, and China did not appear until fourteen years later in 1880.[22] All opened their first offices in Yokohama. No other foreign bank of any nationality was present until the Russo-Chinese Bank arrived in 1898, to be followed by the International Banking Corporation (US) in 1902 and the Deutsche Asiatische Bank in 1905.[23] It was a clear run for the British, but not an easy one. Two banks failed in 1866 because of the Overend Gurney crisis in England. The Chartered Mercantile Bank eventually found the circumstances uncongenial and withdrew in 1886. These were all 'Imperial banks' rather than London banks, carrying on most of their business in and from offices overseas.

THE STRENGTH OF THE BRITISH PRESENCE IN JAPAN

At this point, one might begin to ask why it was that British trading companies and banks dominated the scene for so long. After all, it was the American naval squadron led by Commodore Perry which had forced Japan to open its doors to the West and it was likewise the American Consul, Townsend Harris, who had negotiated the first of the 'Unequal Treaties'. Considering how active the Americans were at this time on the China coast, it is surprising that the British should have taken an absolute lead.

They would have argued that they were more experienced in the
Eastern trade and better organized than their American rivals and
there was some truth in this, but the most important reason
must be, without any doubt, that the American government
wished to direct as much investment as possible towards its own
new Western frontier on the Pacific seaboard. This led to the
passage of the Federal Reserve Act, which forbade American
banks from establishing branches overseas. Private entrepreneurs
in the United States were also overwhelmingly concerned with
exploiting the new opportunities in their own West. A second
factor of great importance was the American Civil War which
engaged much of the country's available shipping and with its
extraordinarily destructive consequences absorbed so much of
the nation's resources. Nevertheless, a few American companies
and individuals did manage to find a way round. Sale Frazer, for
one, was able to engage in banking in Yokohama as a supplement to its main business of commodity trading.[24] The first two
building lots on the sea front had gone to British companies but
the third was taken by a citizen by the name of Mr Peru. He
seems to have engaged in financial activities, but it is hard to say
whether his business should be classified as a bank since he
operated in an individual capacity.[25]

   On the continent of Europe, too, conflict was distracting the
attention of other competitors. France was either preparing for or
recovering from her war against the Austrians in Italy in 1863
and would soon be engaged in the disastrous Franco-Prussian
war of 1870. Germany was similarly tied up in her own struggle
for unification. The British, by contrast, were on an expansionary
imperial wave and suffered from none of these disabilities of their
rivals.

EARLY BANKING ACTIVITIES

The British banks were now to take over the financial functions
which had hitherto been exercised, although at times inad-
equately, by the leading trading companies. As has been discussed, these functions were limited to the provision of import and
export finance and the arranging of small amounts of extraordinary credit for the Japanese government. The profits to be made

from such activities were unexciting but sufficient to justify a presence and there was an expectation, to be realized in the event, that the Japan trade would eventually expand so considerably as to offer a great volume of business. Conditions were at first difficult; two British officers were murdered nearby in Kamakura in July 1864 and the chaotic state of the exchange markets was a serious problem.[26] Nevertheless, the banks quickly established a leading position within the foreign community. Mr Rickerby, presumably because he had been the first banker to arrive, seems to have been accepted as a leader, for it was he who called a conference in September 1864 to discuss the validity of the various currencies, other than the Mexican dollar, circulating in the Treaty Ports. Representatives of most of the other banks and trading companies attended. Sadly, however, he lost his position when the Commercial Bank of India was closed after the financial crisis of 1866. Jardine Matheson, characteristically, had foreseen this and had already moved its account to the Oriental Banking Corporation.

EARLY JAPANESE CREDIT SYSTEMS

Before closing this description of the first years it is worth considering the condition of Japan's own financial institutions. Though these could hardly be described as 'banks' in the Western sense of the term, some of them were of long standing. Throughout the Tokugawa Period,[27] merchants had lent money to farmers on the security of their rice crops and to *Daimyo* against income deriving from their fiefs – sometimes a rather dangerous activity. The domestic trade in cotton and silk goods was also credit-financed and involved the formation of *ryogae* or money shops to handle the exchange between the silver coin used in the West of Japan and Edo gold coin. Credit notes circulated freely. Thus, the Japanese entered the international market-place with some experience of credit finance and exchange dealings and it was to such well-established merchant houses as Mitsui and the Onogumi that the *Bakufu* turned for help in dealing with the first disturbing effects of foreign trade. They were charged with such tasks as issuing currency notes, handling customs dues, and transmitting tax revenues to the capital.[28] However, as a Japanese commentator, Yukichi Fukuzawa, was to point out, the system then in operation was in no way sufficient to cope with the demands suddenly being made of it.[29] Long years of isolation had left Japan ill equipped to understand the complexities of foreign trade and it was here that the British banks were to make their most valuable contribution – as the 'New Japan' set about building a modern financial system of its own.

NOTES

1 *Jardine Matheson and Company ... A Historical Sketch* (Jardine House, Hong Kong), pp. 53–5.
2 Grace Estelle Fox, *Britain and Japan, 1858–1883*, (Clarendon Press, Oxford, 1969), p. 313.
3 Ibid, p. 365.
4 Kanji Ishii, *Bakumatsu ni okeru Gaikoku Shosha 1859–1865*, in the Supplementary Volume to *The History Of Yokohama City* (MS copy kindly supplied by Cambridge University Library).
5 Jardine Matheson Archives (available on microfiche in Cambridge University Library).
6 Ishii, *Bakumatsu ni okeru gaikoku shosha*, p. 6.
7 Ibid, p. 10.
8 Jardine Matheson Archives.
9 Ibid.
10 A *picul* was a Chinese weight of about 60 kg, current for the measurement of raw silk.
11 Ishii, *Bakumatsu ni okeru gaikoku shosha*, pp. 28–30.
12 Ibid., pp. 75–86.
13 The *wakin* was one of the many Japanese coins of the time.
14 Another hitherto standard Japanese coin to which the *wakin* was linked.
15 Ishii, *Bakumatsu ni okeru gaikoku shosha*, pp. 42–3.
16 Jardine Matheson Archives.
17 Ibid.
18 Suiyama, 'Trends of Japan's Coal Exports to the Shanghai Coal Market 1859–1860', in *Kindai Ikoki no Nihon Keizai*, ed. Hiroshi Shinbo and Yasukichi Yasuba (MS copy kindly supplied by Cambridge University Library).

19 *Jardine Matheson and Company* ... *A Historical Sketch* (Jardine House, Hong Kong), pp. 53–5.
20 Ishii, *Bakumatsu ni okeru gaikoku shosha*, p. 146.
21 Ibid., p. 148.
22 Fox, *Britain and Japan*, ch. 4.
23 R. P. T. Davenport-Hines and Geoffrey Jones (Draft MS kindly provided by the authors).
24 Hikomatsu Kamikawa, *Japanese–American Cultural Relations in the Meiji–Taisho Era* (Pan-Pacific Press, Tokyo, 1958), p. 435.
25 Ibid., p. 432.
26 H. S. Williams and Hiroshi Naito, *The Kamakura Murders* (n.p., 1971).
27 The period of effective rule of the Tokugawa Shogunate from 1603 to 1868.
28 *The Mitsui Bank: A History of the First 100 Years* (Mitsui Bank, 1976), pp. 33–6.
29 Michio Nagai, *Chishikijin no seisanruuto in kindai Nippon Shisoshi Koza*, Vol. IV (Chikuma Shobo, Tokyo, 1959), pp. 202–3.

3

THE NEW JAPAN
1868–1873

THE MEIJI RESTORATION: VIEWS AND POLICIES

The governments which succeeded to the demise of the Shogunate, and which were to carry Japan forward in the Meiji period, approached their task with the overall conviction that only by rivalling the West would they be able to ensure their independence and their national destiny. Those forces were now unleashed which had seen the need to adopt Western science and Western methods if Japan were not, like other Asian countries, to fall a victim to Western Imperialism. For some of the leaders, this was to prove a dangerous pursuit and in the years that followed a number of ministers were to die at the hands of assassins because of their commitment to Westernization. Nevertheless, it was generally accepted that political independence required the building of a new, modern, industrial economy which would support the necessary up-to-date military power. This faced the regime with very great problems, but the new rulers showed remarkable confidence in their ability to surmount them. A clear view of the task is given by Tomomi Iwakura, who was designated in 1873 to lead a delegation which included most of Japan's leading political figures on what was virtually a Grand Tour to inspect at first hand the technology, institutions, and financial systems which lay behind the imperial power of the Occident. On the eve of departure he wrote a letter to the President of the United

States, in slightly romantic terms, which was to remain an accurate statement of Japanese policy for a very long time:

> We expect and intend to reform and improve [the 'Unequal Treaties'] so as to stand upon a similar footing with the most enlightened nations and to attain the full development of public rights and interests. The civilization and institutions of Japan are so different from those of other countries that we cannot expect to attain the desired end at once. It is our purpose to select, from the various institutions prevailing among enlightened nations, such as are best suited to our present conditions and adopt them in gradual reforms and amendment of our policy and customs so as to be on an equal footing with them.[1]

Such a policy included the notion that wars, or at least struggles for national supremacy, were fought as much in the market-place as on the battlefield. Yukichi Fukuzawa, one of Meiji Japan's most influential thinkers, summed up the situation by writing: 'Japan's prospects for success in trade [at present] are very poor ... In these days when battles are fought with commerce, if we do not study commerce we cannot hope to compete with foreigners.'[2]

The greatest achievement of the new regime, in one way, lay in establishing a very wide consensus that national policy should follow this path and the success of that policy rested to a large extent on the whole-hearted support it received from the bulk of the population. Within twenty years the results were plain for all to see and Japanese people, viewing their progress, could feel satisfaction or even euphoria. The liberal writer Yukio Ozaki, while on a visit to Britain in 1889, wrote for the *Western Times* of Exeter on 18 June 1889:

> If you [British] think you can spare such a little friend as Japan, it is a great mistake. An empire of 40 million inhabitants cannot be despised, especially when she is on the sure road to eventual wealth and prosperity and to a civilization unparalleled probably in the history of the world.[3]

This prophecy, so astonishing for its time, was to be part realized and part betrayed in the century ahead. It is still in the process of fulfilment today.

As is clearly expressed in the earlier quotation from Iwakura, the idea was not just to swallow Western ideas and methods wholesale but to select, adapt, and even improve on them. One of the main results of this strictly national approach was that Japanese industry, commerce, and banking would develop in a very different way from what was happening in the rest of the world. In the view of Japanese leaders, political and military independence could only be secured if founded on an independent economy. In all dealings with the outside world their aim was to establish as quickly as possible an independent industrial base to match and support an independent military power. Such a view generally excluded direct foreign ownership of industry. We have already noted in chapter 2 how British attempts to obtain ownership in the coal industry were frustrated. The whole economic infrastructure was to be a Japanese infrastructure. For example, whereas in Latin America and Africa the railways were almost entirely developed and owned by foreigners, in Japan they were to be owned by State or private Japanese corporations. This pattern was universal and allowed for few joint ventures or multinational enterprises, and very little change in this respect took place in the next 100 years. Thus, for foreigners, Japan was to be a loan economy and not an equity economy. This feature greatly restricted the business which could be carried on by the British banks and meant that they were largely confined to trade-finance and raising loans.

It was inevitable that this approach to economic development should profoundly affect financial policies. The purchase from abroad of military goods, industrial plant and equipment, raw materials, and ships gave rise to a massive demand for foreign exchange which was to plague the authorities for many years. Indeed, like so many other features of the time, it would recur regularly until the 1970s. The obvious long-term solution was to develop a strong export trade. In the financial sector it would require the creation of a modern banking system and a stable currency. Before looking at these developments, however, it is necessary to examine some of the instant problems with which the new regime was faced. First among these was the teaching and dissemination of foreign ideas in the New Japan, a process in which the British community would play a significant part.

SCHOOLING, TRAINING AND TUTORS

The stream of Japanese students, teachers, and managers going to receive training abroad grew very rapidly, many of them (like the hero of 'A Conservative' in Lafcadio Hearn's '*Kokoro*') coming to Europe and Britain. Establishments and universities teaching the new knowledge were also rapidly set up in Japan. The need for commercial and financial skills was paramount. Mori Arinori, Japan's first Education Minister, invested his personal fortune in setting up a commercial academy, which later grew into the internationally renowned Hitotsubashi University.[4] A few young Japanese were getting a practical introduction to the same skills by working in the offices of the foreign companies in the Treaty Ports. But the main way in which the Japanese sought to spread the new knowledge was by the recruitment of foreign tutors, experts, and managers. The view taken of such foreigners was affected by the preceding centuries of isolation, by traditional attitudes, and by the drive to maintain independence and self-sufficiency. Their skills were essential to the country's own success but, once understood and mastered, those skills had to be independently exercised by the Japanese themselves. The first experts hired by the Meiji government were welcomed as *Okakae* (tutors); their successors were soon viewed as *Oyatoi* (subordinate employees) – to be dispensed with as soon as no longer needed. H. J. Jones has aptly described their situation in the following words: 'These live machines and books provided the manual tools and instruments of knowledge for the new Japan.'[5]

This disembodiment was encouraged by the lofty attitude of many foreigners. The British expatriate communities in the Far East were particularly notorious for their arrogance and condescension. Lord Elgin himself, who had considerable experience of conditions in India, complained that his compatriots there had reduced the native inhabitants to the status of 'salaaming machines'.[6] Again, the British community in Japan at this time was put at a special disadvantage by the home government's attitude towards revision of the 'Unequal Treaties'. Revision became an understandable obsession of the Japanese, and foreigners tended to be judged, treated, or employed according to their government's attitude to the problem. The British Minister, Alcock, was strongly opposed to any change, while the French sought to steal a march by claiming to be in favour. Add to all this that the foreigners themselves often found it hard to bear with the conditions under which they had to work and the people with whom they had to deal, in addition to the serious language problems. There were numerous failures; time and time again, progress was only made thanks to the efforts and capabilities of exceptional people on both sides.

A particularly good illustration is the case of Alexander Allan Shand. He came to Japan in 1869 as manager of the Yokohama office of the Chartered Mercantile Bank. He very quickly acquired personal standing with Japanese officials, writers, and even Ministers that went far beyond that of his employment. His influence arose from his willingness to guide and tutor young men who were soon to become important in the history of their country. Among those who were influenced by him and who helped to shape the Japanese economy were Taguchi, the Sasaki brothers (the earliest of modern Japanese bankers), Kobayashi, Uemura, and the future Finance Minister and Prime Minister, Korekiyo Takahashi.[7] While Shand and others of his kind could not always persuade the Japanese to adopt British models, they could certainly teach them how to operate new systems. Thus, he acquired considerable influence in the field of book-keeping, and the treatise which he published on the subject was treated as a textbook in Japan.[8] In 1874 a Banking Bureau was established and Shand was asked to give advice and guidance on how it should spread knowledge of good financial practice. In his work 'On Banking' he explained the workings of the English banking system. This was widely read in financial circles in Japan and its influence was considerable.[9]

The relationship between Shand and Taguchi illustrates very well the prestige of British economic theory in Japanese circles. Taguchi was the founder of an influential weekly magazine, the *Tokyo Economist*. The economic liberalism current in Britain in the nineteenth century was the first of a series of foreign concepts to be imported into Japan and popularized by this journal. Economic liberalism held sway for a long time and one of its chief protagonists was Fukuzawa, already quoted at the start of this chapter (p. 21). By the 1880s, other ideas had begun to penetrate, some of them also British. In 1886 Tameyuki Amano published a work entitled *Keizai Riron: the Theory of Economics*. This book was extremely influential. It was divided into three parts which corresponded closely with the three parts of J. S. Mill's *Principles of Political Economy* (1848).

The influence of Shand will be seen again in a number of important developments discussed in this book. But any early lead got by the British in the importation of ideas was immediately challenged by other nations. The Japanese were eager to look at anything on offer, to take it to pieces and decide on its merits. For example, although it was resolved to use British models for the development of the Japanese Navy, a recognizably German model was used for the country's political constitution. In finance, as in many other spheres, Continental and American ideas began to win prestige and, as already noted, this process was distorted by the wretched dispute over revision of the 'Unequal Treaties', which sometimes led Ministers to make deliberate decisions against British proposals, personnel, or commercial bids. Shigeki Nishimura summed up this change in attitude well: 'Those who clamorously support free trade probably see Britain as flourishing by free trade and believe that we should follow suit. But the trade of the two countries has nothing in common.'

This conflict was to become particularly apparent in the development of a central banking system in Japan, which will be discussed in the next chapter. But a somewhat absurd example of what could happen is that of the attempt to set up a Japanese Stock Exchange. Although the man entrusted with the task was a Frenchman named Monsieur Boissonade, the regulations he drafted were inspired directly by the British model, which he much preferred to his own Bourse. It was generally conceded that they were nothing more than a translation of the rules of the London Exchange and, since they were totally unadapted to local conditions, the original venture failed. The reformed Tokyo Stock Exchange, which eventually opened at Kabuto-cho on 4 May 1878, was set up at the initiative of a group of Japanese businessmen who traded at a sugar warehouse in Sakaimachi.[10]

Within three years, 137 stock exchanges had been opened, many of them ephemeral. But in little more than 100 years the Tokyo market would represent the largest capitalization in the world.

The First Foreign Loans

The first Meiji administrations were faced with a large potential trade deficit and little prospect of closing the gap in the foreseeable future. Since they were set against direct foreign investment, the most obvious way of financing capital requirements for the new infrastructure was to follow the example of other developing countries and raise loans abroad. There was, however, a division in the leadership about this. A faction led by Saigo Takamori believed that Japan would be dangerously dependent on the Western Powers if she were to ask them for money. The other faction, led by Hirobumi Ito and Shigenobu Okuma, the Finance Minister, realized that domestic resources were plainly insufficient and that the need for an industrial and transport infrastructure was so pressing that money must be found abroad without delay. In less than two years the question came to a head over the issue of railway construction and the pro-loan party won the day.[11]

There were several good reasons why it should have been the British, rather than others, who raised Japan's first loan. The French and Americans had entered into agreements to lend money to the previous Tokugawa authorities for railway development, but on terms which did not appeal to the new government.[12] Ministers resented the pressure now put upon them by the would-be lenders to honour the lapsed agreements. Sir Harry Parkes, the new British Minister, was keen to see railway development, feeling that British technology and industry were particularly well placed to undertake the task. In collaboration with Henry Brunton, an engineer working in Japan, he suggested to Ito a scheme for a railway along the southern coast which would eventually link Tokyo with Yokohama, Kyoto, Hyogo, and Tsuruga. At this point, a gentleman turned up in Tokyo who had been prospecting for railway ventures in China. He was called Horatio Nelson Lay and his manner appears to have accorded with the flamboyance of his name. Undeterred by this, Parkes introduced him to Japanese Ministers as a man who would be able to raise money privately on the London market.[13]

The ensuing events were unfortunate, to say the least. The Japanese were inexperienced in such matters and Sir Harry Parkes also showed a notable lack of insight in choosing a man like Lay. Lay claimed to have been sent by a group of London Banks to offer the governments of China or Japan a loan of up to £3 million, specifically for railway development. The Japanese accepted his assurances at face value. On 14 December 1869 an agreement was signed giving Lay the right to raise £1 million from private sources in England on behalf of the Japanese government, for construction of the first stretch of the railway, the section from Tokyo to Yokohama. Interest and commission were to be secured against the customs revenues and the net earnings of the railway. For this reason it became known as the 'Customs Loan of 1870'. The contract defined Lay's powers in the broadest terms:

> Wherefore, for the purpose aforesaid, we do by this our Imperial edict constitute and appoint the British subject, Horatio Nelson Lay ... to raise and negotiate the said loan, upon which terms as to the time and manner of repayment of the same and at such rate of interest as he, the said Horatio Nelson Lay, shall deem fit.[14]

In a separate agreement of the same date, which made no reference to the first, Lay persuaded the Japanese authorities to give him even greater powers – virtually *carte blanche* – on the grounds that this was 'a necessary adjunct' and 'was required to prove to his friends that he had received full power from the Japanese government to borrow and receive money'.[15] Yet a third arrangement, concluded several days later, took the extraordinary step of appointing him as prime contractor for the purchase of equipment and construction of the line. Thus, the man who had come to Tokyo to offer a loan had now been given powers as Commissioner to raise the money, as well as authority to spend it. Lay was almost certainly aiming, by this irregular arrangement, to deceive the Japanese and line his own pockets, for a Bill of Chancery later filed against him by two of his partners reveals the full scale of the profits which he was hoping to make out of his dual role.[16]

Lay had none of the financial connections which he claimed. Instead he went to Paris, where he propositioned Baron Emil Erlanger. The Baron was preparing to transfer his interests to England under the shadow of the Franco-Prussian War and referred Lay to his friends at Schroders Bank in London. So it was Schroders who, in the City of London in 1870, launched the first public institutional loan for the government of Japan, the Customs Loan of 1870. The rate of interest and commission obtained was unusually high (12 per cent) and it was enthusiastically subscribed on the London Market. But when Lay reappeared in Tokyo to announce the terms, the Japanese Ministers were furious. They had counted on his assurance that the money would be raised privately and were mortified by the public exposure of their low credit-rating. They swiftly decided to get rid of Lay and the letter of dismissal included the following passage:

> Lay hath made use of the powers thus improperly obtained from us and hath in our name and on our behalf solicited subscriptions to a loan of one million pounds sterling from the general public in London.[17]

The Japanese public was also indignant about what had occurred and the ministers responsible came in for a good deal of criticism for having attached national revenues. The government's first reaction was to try to give back to the subscribers all the money that had been raised, an attempt surely unmatched in the history of international lending. This proved to be impractical and so the Japanese government resolved to honour the obligations into which they had entered with Schroders and the lenders, in order to preserve their international standing. They replaced Lay by transferring their trust to more responsible hands, those of the Oriental Banking Corporation in Yokohama. This determination to abide by an agreement, however unsatisfactory to themselves, was important to their future relations with the City and immediately increased their credit-worthiness. *The Times* of London announced that Japan was 'emerging from centuries of fanaticism to take a prominent place among the commercial nations'.[18] Thereafter the railway project went well. Construction as far as Yokohama was successfully concluded and the line was opened by the Emperor Meiji himself at the end of 1872. The loan was fully redeemed in August 1882 and the then Minister of Finance, Masayoshi Matsukata, wrote to thank Schroders for their trouble. The bank still refers to this in its advertising today.

So successful had been the role of the Oriental Banking Corporation in straightening out the muddle, that they were entrusted with the task of raising the next Japan Loan. The *Daimyos* and their *Samurai*, the whole feudal class which had been disestablished by the events of 1868, were to be pensioned off with money to be raised by an issue of government bonds. The loan was floated in London in 1873 and raised £2,400,000. Japan's vastly improved standing as a borrower was reflected in the rate of interest of only 7 per cent (5 percentage points lower than the Customs Loan three years earlier) and the fact that it was oversubscribed to a total of £9,644,900 of applications. The relationship of the Oriental Banking Corporation with the Japanese government was also growing in importance. It was now the leading foreign bank in Japan and enjoyed a quasi-official position. Giving evidence a few years later, in 1877, to a Committee of the British Parliament, Major Kinder remarked that 'The Oriental Bank continue[s] in the position of foreign bankers and agents of the [Japanese] Government'.[19]

Parkes was keen for the bank to raise a third loan in 1874 but by then the Japanese view had radically changed. They now sensed that servicing further loans would put too heavy a strain on their frail resources. The Government, therefore, raised no further foreign loan for twenty-five years. Commercial loans, however, were made by British banks to Japanese businesses or to individuals for business purposes. For example, the Hong Kong and Shanghai Banking Corporation lent $700,000 to Mitsui Bussan in 1876 and $250,000 to Yanosuke Iwasuku, co-founder of the Mitsubishi Bank, in 1888.

NOTES

1 S. Lane-Poole, *The Life of Sir Harry Parkes* (Macmillan, London, 1894), Vol. II, p. 199.

2 Michio Nagai, 'Chishikijin no Seisanruuto', in *Kindai Nippon no Shisoshi Koza*, Vol. IV, (Chikuma Shobo, Tokyo, 1959) pp. 202–3.
3 *Western Times* (18 June 1889).
4 Ivan Parker Hall, *Mori Arinori*, (Harvard East Asian Series, Cambridge, Mass., 1968), p. 232.
5 H. J. Jones, *Live Machines: Hired Foreigners in Meiji Japan* (University of British Columbia Press, Vancouver, 1980), p. 126.
6 Ibid.
7 Umekichi Yoneyama, 'A Banker's Reminiscences', Japan Times Pamphlet.
8 Grace Estelle Fox, *Britain and Japan, 1858–1883* (Clarendon Press, Oxford, 1969), p. 395.
9 Yoneyama, 'A Banker's Reminiscences'.
10 Fox, *Britain and Japan*, p. 386.
11 Information kindly provided by Dr R. Roberts of J. Henry Schroder Wagg.
12 Ibid.
13 Schroders Archives.
14 Ibid.
15 Ibid.
16 Ibid.
17 Ibid.
18 *The Times* (22 Aug. 1870), quoted in Fox, *Britain and Japan*, p. 392.
19 *Minutes Taken before the Select Committee on the Depreciation of Silver* (London, 1878), p. 158.

4

A MODERN CAPITALIST ECONOMY
1873–1894

PROBLEMS OF TRADE

At the time that the Meiji regime took over the reins of government in 1868, Japan's annual foreign trade was running at only 26 million yen (£5.5 million, say). After that, it was to rise very rapidly indeed, reaching over 500 million yen (£95 million) by 1890. But during the earlier years, until well into the eighties, it could fairly be said that the Japanese themselves had no foreign trade at all, for export goods were normally sold to foreign merchants at the Treaty Ports and were thence sent abroad by them. The same system was used in the other direction – goods were brought into the country by foreign middlemen and sold by them to Japanese merchants who were only able to get their hands on imports in this indirect manner. The system was known as 'settlement trade' and meant that, in so far as Japanese merchants were concerned, commerce in foreign goods functioned only as internal trade. In the early 1880s, 90 per cent of the Japan trade was handled in this way by foreign companies – the Chinese and the British accounting for nearly half the total volume.[1] With the arrival of the British imperial banks from 1863 onwards, the smaller trading companies could obtain adequate and cheap supplies of working capital and were no longer dependent on Jardines or Dents. Their numbers consequently mushroomed and this eventually led to growing competition and declining profits.

The new foreign trade proved damaging to the frail but emerging Japanese economy. In the first place, the sudden demand for export goods brought about a rapid inflation. Second, imports greatly exceeded exports in value, producing a serious shortage of specie. Third, 'settlement trade' ensured that the payments' mechanism was almost entirely in the hands of the foreign community and it gave the British banks a monopoly of foreign exchange. This situation was obviously unacceptable to the Japanese. The removal of Okuma from office in 1881 and his replacement by Matsukata marked a major change in Japan's economic policies. The new Finance Minister claimed that the need to service foreign loans and the country's persistent balance of payments deficit were draining specie out of Japan and that this was undermining her currency. His solution was a stringent policy of financial retrenchment. The demand for imports was reined in and exports were encouraged. The decision, noted in chapter 3, not to raise any further foreign loans formed part of the same package. In general, these measures met with a good deal of success. A huge deficit was converted into a net surplus for the overall period 1881 to 1885.[2]

Matsukata's aim, of course, was to secure large reserves of specie and thus stabilize the Japanese currency. However, as I have explained above, the system of 'settlement trade' had hitherto kept most of the available specie in the hands of British banks and British and Chinese traders. To remedy this situation and to establish the financial independence of Japan in line with its industrial and military independence, the government made every effort to oust foreign banks and trading houses from the marketplace. British and other foreign companies experienced in the most forceful way, and certainly not for the last time, the ability of the Japanese authorities to limit their activities in favour of those of their own citizens.

As a first step, the government itself now began to engage actively in the export trade in rice and *Kombu* (dried kelp). The payments made for these goods, largely in Chinese *taels*, went to the exchequer. At the same time it took steps to encourage Japanese firms to trade directly with foreign countries without recourse to intermediaries or British banks. It lent to Japanese exporters' funds in yen at preferential rates which made them very competitive with foreign firms. In repayment of these loans, the exporters deposited their earnings of foreign currency with Japanese consulates abroad, which in turn transferred them to reliable banks in those countries. These steps effectively broke the monopoly position of the foreign banks in Yokohama and it was shortly afterwards in 1886 that the Chartered Mercantile Bank withdrew from Japan, judging the game no longer worth the candle. However, this process also introduced a new and close relationship between Japan and the City of London. The money now being deposited around the world was almost invariably remitted to London, where it was lodged with the Oriental Banking Corporation. When this went into receivership in 1884, the funds were transferred to the London Joint Stock Bank.[3]

A BANKING SYSTEM FOR JAPAN

The development of this modern trading economy required parallel financial institutions – designed to serve the interests and independence of the country in the same way as all the other features of the economy. As was noted in chapter 2, the traditional banking functions which had developed in Tokugawa times were not up to the new tasks and the first Meiji government immediately set about replacing them with something better. In 1868 a Commerce Department (*Shihoshi*) was set up and it was intended that this should in some ways act like a bank, giving loans to Japanese businesses. This venture met with little success. In 1869 the Trade Department (*Tsuhoshi*) helped to establish fledgling banks, provisionally referred to as 'exchange firms', in eight cities. It was hoped that these would be able to take over the lucrative exchange business which had hitherto been handled entirely by the foreign banks and trading companies. Loans were extended to them to finance the export trade but, despite the government's backing, this venture also failed. The exchange firms were all liquidated when the Trade Department itself was abolished in 1871.[4]

The first fully modern Japanese bank was the Dai Ichi Kokuritsu Ginko (Number One National Bank), founded in 1873. It soon ran into problems and the Ministry of Finance put in

Alexander Shand to overhaul its management and institute proper accounting systems.[5] By 1876 there were still only four licensed banks, including the Mitsui and the Yasuda (now Fuji) banks, both still extant today. A relaxation of the rules governing the formation of banks then led to an explosion in their number, and by the end of the decade the figure had risen to 239. The peak was reached in 1901 with no fewer than 1,867 banks in operation.[6]

These new financial institutions were to be fitted into a legal and regulatory system. Ito was charged with this task, and after a visit to the United States recommended adoption of the American system. This was based on a number of 'National Banks', each empowered to issue its own notes. The necessary regulations were promulgated in 1872. At first there were only four such banks, those referred to in the preceding paragraph, but the number soon multiplied, with a consequent flood of issues of paper banknotes. Neither the skills nor the experience were yet available to work such an open-ended system, nor was it in tune with Japanese concepts of central authority. From the beginning there was sharp criticism of the arrangements. Particularly strong opposition was voiced by Alexander Shand, who had earlier been invited by the Ministry of Finance to take up a junior position teaching book-keeping to the Ministry's employees. He was soon transferred to the Banking Department, where his influence grew. In an article commemorating the invaluable services which Shand had rendered to Japan, Umekichi Yoneyama, President of the Mitsui Trust Company, wrote in later years:

> [Shand] strongly objected to the American system of banking, pleading the advantages of the English pattern, based on a central bank. His opinion caused much heated discussion and disagreement in the Treasury [Ministry of Finance]. Yoshida, who had advocated the American plan like Ito, changed front. He was won over to the Shand camp.[7]

The very nature of the article that Yoneyama was writing, possibly led him to overstate Shand's influence. But there can be no doubt that in this matter, as in many others, his opinions carried great weight. Kiyonari Yoshida (referred to in Yoneyama's quotation) had made a study of England's financial and economic institutions and he now echoed Shand's arguments against the wholesale adoption of the American system. He insisted that the national bank system could not solve Japan's financial difficulties. Indeed he feared that it might make them worse, for it would mean the introduction of yet other kinds of convertible paper, the circulation of which had already had such a pernicious effect on the economy. He argued that the solution lay in the establishment of a convertible currency as had been done in England.[8]

Shand left Japan and returned to London to take up a post with the Alliance Bank before these issues were resolved. By the end of the 1870s, the Japanese government was facing increasingly serious difficulties with the economy. There had been a dangerous rebellion in the south-west of the country led by Saigo Takamori, a disaffected member of the leadership. To pay for the campaign against the insurgents, the government itself had issued a large number of inconvertible banknotes. Okuma, as Finance Minister, wrongly diagnosed the problems and, as we have seen in the previous section (p. 32), in 1880 he resigned and was replaced a year later by Matsukata, who brought a more realistic view. Shortly after assuming office, in October 1882, the new Minister presented a memorandum to the government in which he insisted that the issue of inconvertible banknotes had to be terminated and specie accumulated to support the currency. Next, the national banks were prohibited from issuing further notes and a term was placed on the future validity of those already in circulation. Matsukata's deflationary policies, as we have seen, were a success. Out of the government's surplus of 40 million yen, 14 million was used for redemption of paper and 26 million for the purchase of specie. In addition, 11 million yen in notes was retired.[9]

In turning his attention immediately to reform of the banking system, Matsukata was influenced by a growing feeling of caution in the country about the impact of Westernization. The setting up at this time of a number of Shinto academies bore witness to the fear of many conservatives that Japan was in danger of sacrificing too much of her traditional identity.[10] Matsukata believed that more careful and critical thought should be given to the modernization of banking and its impact on local conditions. In his memorandum he wrote:

> That the system, as thus established, has proved so imperfect was perhaps unavoidable, owing to the fact that the Government was urged on by the pressure of circumstances hastily to establish a system of banking, not having had sufficient time given them, not only for studying the American system, but also for comparing and studying the different systems now in vogue in Europe.[11]

The system which Matsukata envisaged was based on a Central Bank with a variety of functions. It could smooth irregularities in the markets by keeping the various national banks in communication with each other and, should the money supply falter, by advancing loans to those banks. Should imports exceed exports, it could restrain an outflow of funds by raising the discount rate and, by lowering interest rates, it could also preserve the liquidity of the national banks. These proposals had many of the features of the British system which Shand had been so strongly urging, but Matsukata's own personal experiences in Belgium played at least as important a part. Indeed, in his writings concerning the founding of the Bank of Japan, he explicitly cited the Société Générale de Belgique as his model.[12]

In June 1882 the new Bank of Japan Act, laying down regulations for the Central Bank, was published and in October it commenced operations. At the same time, measures were enacted to bring some order into the chaos which had developed in the private banking system. Members of the public had become much more willing to make bank deposits now that they were no longer liable to receive inconvertible paper in exchange. In 1882 rules were laid down concerning bills of exchange and promissory notes and the Bank of Japan likewise began to publish ordinances relating to the use of cheques and discounting bills. In the same year approval for the foundation of further banks was placed in the hands of the Ministry of Finance. In 1888 it was decreed that all National Banks should make an annual report to the government. Finally, in 1890 the 'Bank Regulations' were published, together with a Commercial Code. These remained essentially valid until 1928.[13]

FOREIGN EXCHANGE: THE YOKOHAMA SPECIE BANK

In the first part of this chapter, attention was drawn to the monopoly in foreign exchange exercised by foreign firms at the beginning of the Meiji era and to certain measures designed to enable the government and private Japanese companies to earn foreign specie themselves. Although these measures were successful within their own limits, throughout the 1870s most foreign exchange transactions remained in the hands of foreigners. Indeed, the Hong Kong and Shanghai Bank was acting almost as a national foreign exchange bank for Japan. In due course, the authorities decided that the only satisfactory solution would be to take all such transactions into the control of their own agents. Following an interval during which Mitsui Bussan (i.e. Mitsui Trading Company) was charged with the task, the government in 1880 set up a semi-official organization named the Yokohama Specie Bank.[14] This was in part modelled on the Hong Kong and Shanghai Bank. It was given preferential powers to finance foreign trade. The Banking Act of 1882 (referred to in the previous section) also ensured it close links with the Bank of Japan, which was empowered to advance loans at privileged rates.[15]

At the same time the new bank was appointed to deal in foreign exchange, a right which was enshrined in the Foreign Exchange Banking Act of 1882. This right was to become a monopoly, in so far as Japanese banks were concerned, in 1887. However, powers were passed on from time to time to the principal private banks, which would be designated as 'Foreign Exchange Banks'. The Sumitomo Bank, for example, acted in this capacity in 1901.

It took some time for the management of the Yokohama Specie Bank to acquire the skills needed to operate such advanced financial machinery and the organization was not an early success. By 1881 the Yokohama Specie Bank stood on the verge of bankruptcy, but after a series of management shake-ups it had recouped its losses by 1885.

Although improved management ability contributed to the success of this bank, its survival was chiefly due to the highly preferential treatment which it received from the State. The government charged no interest on the funds it deposited with the bank, which was left free to retain the whole commission. The bank itself was obliged to discriminate heavily in favour of native institutions. Article xi of 'The Rules for Transacting Foreign Exchange' ran as follows:

> It being the aim for this whole scheme to encourage the foreign trade of this country, the bill of exchange shall under all possible circumstances be discounted for a Japanese merchant. When, however, for reasons of necessity it is to be discounted for a foreign merchant, a representation shall be made to the Finance Department and special permission secured.[16]

No doubt permissions were slow in coming and this naturally served to drive foreigners out of the market, or at least to make trading much more difficult for them. The rules were reinforced in 1884 when the Yokohama Specie Bank was allowed to increase the amount charged to discount bills of exchange for particular transactions, making it too expensive for some foreign merchants to operate.

The foreign loans which Japan had previously contracted still had to be serviced. Responsibility for this had been exercised by the Oriental Banking Corporation. Matsukata's attitude to foreign banks was basically that they should become redundant as Japan mastered the financial machinery to perform the same functions. The Yokohama Specie Bank now proposed to the Ministry of Finance that it should take over responsibility for all payments to service the foreign loans.[17] For this purpose it would require representation abroad, specifically in London where the loans had been raised. In 1884 it opened an office at 84 Bishopsgate Street Within, under a Mr Tokuda as manager. Thus, the first Japanese Bank ever to go abroad started its career in London. Interestingly, a Mr Hihara, residing at the same address, had opened an account in his own name three years earlier with the Alliance Bank. Why the Alliance Bank? No doubt because Alexander Shand was now a manager of its London Office. In March of 1885 the Yokohama Specie Bank itself opened an account with the Alliance and in March 1886 they introduced the Bank of Japan which also opened an account.[18]

A New Japanese Currency

While all the above events were in progress the authorities had been faced with numerous problems in trying to establish a stable currency, suitable for international trade as well as domestic use. It is necessary to go right back to early days to appreciate the difficulties and serious handicaps under which the Japanese had to labour. For one thing, the 'Unequal Treaties' had stipulated that all foreign coins should be légal in the Treaty Ports (see p. 5) and, for another, the fiscal system which it had inherited from its predecessor could at best be described as chaotic. Moreover, right from the outset, the Western Powers, particularly Britain, were hostile to the idea of treating any new Japanese currency as the legal equal of coins minted by their own governments. At the time of the Meiji Restoration there were gold and silver Japanese coins and public and private note issues, all in circulation together. The Spanish silver dollar had been widely in favour in the Far East until the middle of the century, the Hong Kong 'trade dollar' had appeared through the Treaty Ports in 1866, and other such 'trade currencies' were to follow. But by far the most popular instrument of exchange was the Mexican dollar. By 1867 it was the only foreign coin passing currently in Yokohama and, according to a report of the British Consul, had become the standard measure of value, displacing the Japanese *ichibu*.[19]

The Meiji administration's first attempt to introduce an effective national currency simply added to the confusion. They resorted to issuing millions of paper notes called *Kinsatsu*, which were to be redeemed in thirteen years. The general public had little confidence in the venture and the new money had to be exchanged for debased local coinage at a heavy discount of as much as 55 per cent. Notes amounting to the equivalent of 48 million gold *ryo* were in circulation by the end of 1869. The foreign community reacted angrily to this behaviour, saying that it contravened the commercial treaties. In reply, the authorities responsible could make only the most meagre excuses. In the circumstances they had no choice but to recognize the Mexican dollar as legal tender.[20]

To deal with this situation, it was decided to call in British help. The Japanese *ichibu* in circulation had fluctuating metal content. If a standard new currency were minted by British professionals, then surely it must win the approval of the foreign governments. In 1868 the Japanese purchased the old mint in Hong Kong. It was set up in Osaka, but the building almost immediately caught fire and the machinery was destroyed. In 1869 a new mint was ordered from England and Major William Kinder, the Master of the Hong Kong Mint, arrived with a team to become its director for five years. These proceedings were managed on behalf of the Japanese authorities by the Oriental Banking Corporation. At last, in 1871, the new Japanese national currency appeared as the silver yen.

The choice of a silver coinage was not hard to explain. It is true that the ultimate aim was to be able to adopt the gold standard; from the start, Ito had favoured such a course on the grounds that the major Western nations were moving in that direction. But the immediate problem was to have a currency which could readily participate in the trade of East Asia, on which Japan still so greatly depended. This trade was completely dominated by silver in all the forms of coinage already described. In the Far East, silver was mined, minted, circulated, exchanged, debased, clipped, melted down, or turned into jewellery, but it was, above all, the primary means for the settlement of trade. This state of affairs was to continue well into the next century. A Japanese consular report from Hong Kong on 29 August 1897 ran:

It should be noted that every year, about the end of autumn, the Mexican dollar rises in price and the demand for its importation increases. This is owing to the fact that around this time of year there is a strong call for capital for the purchase of raw silk ... Such being the state of things, the Chinese bankers are vying with each other in drawing out specie from the Hong Kong and Shanghai Banking Corporation and the Chartered Bank and forwarding it to Hong Kong with great activity. In consequence, the amount of the New Mexican Dollars drawn out of the conversion reserve of the Hong Kong and Shanghai Banking Corporation during the last five or six weeks is thought to be over two million dollars.[21]

Compared to this prevalence of the Mexican dollar, the silver yen would (for most of its life) have only a rather secondary role to play. But it had one great advantage over other silver currencies. The worth of the Mexican dollar corresponded only to the value of the silver contained in it. From 1870 onwards, the price of silver in Europe tended to fall so that, despite fluctuations, the Mexican dollar also tended to depreciate. The yen, on the other hand, went half-way towards a gold standard for, although minted in silver, it was backed by gold. It could, therefore, instantly be changed for gold, thus putting a heavy strain on Japanese reserves, or it could provide a satisfactory way of holding silver for the long term. This became its ultimate strength.

To return to the date of its first issue in 1871, the silver yen was not an early success. Initially its standing appeared doubtful and most holders preferred to take the gold option and change their yen into that metal. In the circumstances of the current trade deficit this led to a massive outflow of gold from Japan. Between 1871 and 1877, no less than 51.3 per cent of all gold coin in the country was exported.[22] Lack of confidence in the new yen was also shown by the fact that foreign trading houses in the Treaty Ports were still improperly issuing notes backed by Mexican dollars.

Eventually, it was the British banks which most clearly saw the need for a national currency and did their best to bring about its general acceptance in international trade. Townsend, the representative of the Hong Kong and Shanghai Bank in Yokohama, received a decoration from the Japanese government for his part in promoting the new currency.[23] But foreign banks were not solely motivated by good will. In order to guard against fluctuations in the demand for capital, the banks in Treaty Ports all over the Far East were in the habit of keeping very large stocks of the metal. Hence the Hong Kong and Shanghai Bank, the Chartered Bank of India, Australia, and China, and the Oriental Banking Corporation shipped quantities of silver yen from Japan to other parts of Asia. With its gold backing and relatively fixed value, it was becoming a most attractive form of specie. In addition, trade between the Crown Colonies in the East and Japan was growing and this created a powerful requirement for traders outside Japan to accept the yen.[24]

In circumstances such as these it is odd that the British government should have refused to recognize the silver yen in the Crown Colonies and especially in Hong Kong, which was the largest trading entrepôt in the Far East. When in 1880 the Governor sought to reverse the policy, he enjoyed the active encouragement of Thomas Jackson, General Manager of the Hong Kong and Shanghai Bank, as well as that of the Hong Kong Chamber of Commerce and of the Chinese bankers. Nevertheless, the home government used its reserve currency powers to veto the proposal.[25]

This impediment did little to restrict demand for an attractive currency and, whatever the *de jure* edict, silver yen became *de facto* legal currency all over East Asia. In 1897, prior to proposing the Coinage Act of that year which brought the silver yen to an end, the Finance Minister dispatched telegrams to Japanese Consuls at places throughout the region asking for information on its distribution. Their reports showed that whereas only small numbers of yen were in general circulation in China (Tsientsin 5,000 yen, Chefoo 1,900, Shanghai none at all) the Hong Kong and Shanghai Bank held around 550,000 yen, the Chartered Bank around 350,000, and other British banks kept various large amounts. The Consul reporting from Singapore on 7 May 1897 stated that the silver yen was making 'a triumphant entry into the neighbouring countries such as the Malay Archipelago, Siam, Annam, Burma, Borneo, Sumatra, etc., being welcomed everywhere.'[26] In that year Japan realized its long-term aim and followed the major nations of the West on to the gold standard. The United States, Russia, and India had done away with the free minting of silver coins and it was no longer possible to estimate the future value of silver, which had been falling steadily now for years. The decision of the Japanese to make the change from silver to gold was inevitable; it also reflected a large measure of confidence on their part that they could now hold their own with the West on equal terms. But there were considerable problems to be faced in making this move and, once again, British firms were to play an important part in solving those problems.

Although the silver yen now ceased to be legal tender in Japan, it proved extremely difficult to withdraw from circulation elsewhere in Asia. Some of it, as we have seen, was in the hands of the Western banks and trading houses with their branches and associates all over the Far East. These were initially confused by the new Japanese regulations and in July 1897 informed their clients that they might make specie payments in either Japanese gold or silver. Matsukata took immediate action to counter this. The exchange of all domestic yen was placed in the hands of the Bank of Japan. At the same time the Bank was ordered to ask foreign banks to exchange all their holdings of yen silver coins for gold coins of the same denomination through the Yokohama Specie Bank, and co-operation was encouraged by offering preferential rates. The banks were only allowed to keep chopped or defaced silver for use outside Japan. Unfortunately, the world price of silver was at such a low level that many people were buying coins cheap and hoarding them in expectation that the price would surely rise again. A memo at the Hong Kong and Shanghai Bank went so far as to say that: 'especially the more shrewd among the bankers are declaring that the greatest money-making scheme in the world would be to corner the market in Japanese yen'.[27] Surprisingly, however, circumstances changed to the advantage of the Japanese government. There was such a scarcity of British trade dollars and Mexican silver dollars on the market that some Japanese yen found their way back on to it. This produced a chain reaction among hoarders who, for reasons they may have not clearly understood, followed the trend and quickly released the yen they had been holding. Thomas Jackson and other British managers in the area played a leading part in collecting these and selling them back to the Japanese government. Nevertheless, of all the coins that had left Japan, only 10 per cent were returned home by this operation. It was concluded that the remainder had been debased, melted down by the Chinese, or turned into silver ornaments, for they never reappeared in the market. Thus, the government was able successfully to withdraw the silver yen from currency and replace it with the new coinage.[28]

The Shift of Financial Power

The events described in this chapter show two things very clearly. First, the Japanese had laboriously mastered the skills to carry out modern trading and financial transactions and to run the necessary trading and banking institutions. Second, they had used this knowledge and skill to establish national independence from foreign companies. Japan now had all the machinery she needed to finance and carry on her own financial trade. She was no longer a trainee. The main sufferers in this were the resident British banks and trading houses which lost the great predominance which they had enjoyed in the early years of Japan's opening to the West. While the banks never recovered their former level of activity, there was still a remunerative volume of business for the British trading houses. Such was the rate at which Japanese trade grew that, even with a much diminished share of the market, they were still able to increase the volume of their transactions.

These developments were reflected in the political field. In 1894 a 'Commercial Agreement', replacing the 'Unequal Treaty' between Japan and Britain, was signed in London. It provided for all rights of extraterritoriality to lapse in five years' time and for the customs privileges to lapse at a later date. Similar agreements with other nations followed. It was ironic, but perhaps typical of the 'pragmatic' British, that they were the first to lay this ghost, which had haunted their own relations with Japan for more than twenty years.

Notes

1 R. P. T. Davenport-Hines and Geoffrey Jones (Draft MS kindly provided by the authors).
2 *Banking in Modern Japan* (Fuji Bank Ltd., Tokyo, 1967), p. 15.
3 Hiroshi Saito, *The Origins of Japanese Specie Abroad* (MS kindly provided by the author).
4 *Banking in Modern Japan*, p. 15.
5 Ibid., p. 16–17.

6 *The Banking System of Japan*, (Federation of Bankers' Associations of Japan, 1982).
7 Umekichi Yoneyama, 'A Banker's Reminiscences', Japan Times Pamphlet.
8 Ibid.
9 *Banking in Modern Japan*, p. 23.
10 Michio Nagai, 'Chishikijin no seisanruuto' from *Kindai Nippon Shisoshi Koza*, Vol. IV, pp. 224–5.
11 Thomas Adams and Iwao Hoshii, *A Financial History of Modern Japan* (Research Japan Ltd., Tokyo, 1964). Cf. also Meiji Taishō Zaiseishi.
12 Ibid.
13 *Banking in Modern Japan*, pp. 32–4.
14 It was renamed Bank of Tokyo after the Second World War.
15 *Banking in Modern Japan*, pp. 34–6.
16 Saito, *The Origins of Japanese Specie Abroad*.
17 Ibid.
18 Archives of the National Westminster Bank.
19 Takeshi Hamashita, 'A History of the Silver Yen', in F. H. H. King (ed.), *Eastern Banking* (Athlone Press, London, 1983), p. 325.
20 Ibid.
21 Ibid., p. 328.
22 Ibid., p. 325.
23 Ibid., p. 325.
24 Ibid., pp. 327–30.
25 Ibid., p. 325.
26 Ibid., p. 330.
27 Ibid., p. 332.
28 Ibid., pp. 333–5.

5

THE COST OF EMPIRE
1895–1914

JAPAN AS A NEW WORLD POWER

Japanese political movements often express themselves through slogans. Usually of four syllables, as compressed yet resonant as a line from a haiku, these calls to action embody the aspirations of the moment in a form to which all can respond. One of those which enshrined a particularly strong aspect of Meiji policies was *'Fukoku Kyohei'*, which can be roughly translated as 'Rich country, strong army'. Towards the end of the nineteenth century it could certainly not be said that Japan, with its chronic lack of natural resources, was yet a rich country, though she had now learnt the skills and established the machinery for eventually becoming so. On the other hand, her naval and military forces had been fast growing, in size, armaments, and proficiency, to the point where they would be used to achieve, first, military supremacy and territorial expansion in East Asia and, second, recognition as an emerging great power on the world stage.

Although Japan referred to itself as an 'Empire' ruled by an Emperor, this was a rather misleading translation of the situation into European terms. Japan was a strictly homogeneous country (if one excepts the Ainu and, marginally, the Okinawans) and had known no external territorial ambitions for 300 years. Meiji leaders and thinkers had assumed that the creation of New Japan as an independent Eastern power of great industrial and military strength would give them a natural moral and political leadership in Asia, and there was a school which believed that Japan would thus rally all its neighbours, and particularly China, to follow the same path. This was not what happened and Japan found herself increasingly involved in fighting her way to an overseas empire. For reasons which are not relevant to this book she entered into a war with China in 1895 and with Russia in 1904–5. Japan annexed Formosa in 1895 and Korea in 1910. This was the path that was eventually to lead to the seizure of Manchuria in 1932, to the attempt to overrun the whole of China, and to the Great Asian Co-Prosperity Sphere of the Second World War.

The Western Powers were undoubtedly slow to notice the rapid growth of Japanese military power and were quite taken by surprise when they saw Japanese successes on the Chinese mainland in 1895. Indeed, they were alarmed by what they saw. France, Germany, and Russia mounted a 'Triple Intervention' which deprived Japan of most of the expected fruits of her crushing victory over China. However, Americans and Europeans were glad enough to have Japanese troops marching alongside their own to lift the siege of the foreign legations in Peking during the Boxer Rebellion of 1900. They were delighted by what were described as the 'pluck, heroism and reserve' of Japanese troops. In 1902 Japan was brought into the balance of power. Britain was now in the initial stages of the 'Anglo-German Naval Race'. It was no longer possible to maintain an adequate home fleet to defend Britain against the growing German menace while policing most of the rest of the world, so the British government decided to share the task with the Japanese in the Pacific. The resultant agreement was the first equal treaty of alliance signed between an Eastern and a Western power. In the ensuing war against Russia, Japanese sailors trained by the British fought in ships built by the British, and under the terms of the alliance Britain would have been called upon to go to war on the side of the Japanese had any other power intervened on the side of the Russians.[1]

Anglo-Japanese relations were generally cordial and even enthusiastic throughout this period. All the elements we have just described – the fact that Britain had been the first to replace its 'Unequal Treaty' in 1894, her refusal to join the Tripartite Intervention in 1895, and the conclusion of the Alliance in 1902 – made her respected and popular in Japan. This, naturally enough, had repercussions on the financial sector. The next section will examine the need for foreign loans which arose out of Japan's policy of aggrandizement. The British government wished to see the requirements of its ally satisfied with funds at reasonable rates. In a letter to Lord Rothschild dated 22 September 1902, Francis Bertie of the Foreign Office wrote: '[Lord Lansdowne (the Foreign Secretary)]' authorizes me to say that His Majesty's Government regard it as a matter of political necessity that Japan should be able to raise in this country, rather than elsewhere, the money which she requires.'[2]

Political factors also played a part in discouraging London's competitors on the Continent from seeking business in Japan. It was Kaiser Wilhelm II who took up the phrase 'yellow peril' (die gelbe Gefahr). As for the French, on 22 September 1902, the Banque de Paris et des Pays Bas wrote to Baring Brothers: 'it is necessary for them to call Baring Brothers' attention to the fact that [if the Banque were to help the Japanese government to raise capital] they might not encounter a favourable response from their [own] government'.[3]

In the private sector it was now for Japanese businessmen to make their own decisions as to where they would go for overseas sources of finance for their operations. With the independence and competence which they had established, they could afford not only to choose but often to call the tune. Such confidence is shown in the following often-quoted passage from a circular instruction sent by the Chief of the Mitsui Bank to his subordinates:

> Do not bow down before the Hong Kong and Shanghai Banking Corporation, but hold your head up high and associate with them on equal terms. When you need to buy exchange, do not worry; I shall send you as much as fifty or one hundred thousand yen as soon as I receive your telegram. In this way the Hong Kong and Shanghai Banking Corporation will recognize the strength of the Mitsui family and will make finance available to us.[4]

Thus, the Japanese government's new-found confidence on the international stage was reflected in the Japanese private sector.

JAPANESE STATE LOANS 1897–1910

Although the China War was short, the costs were heavy. Every-thing possible was done to raise the money at home. Bonds worth 84 million yen were sold on the internal market. In order to free capital, all railway construction was halted and the discount rate was raised to 2.1 *sen*[5] per diem to discourage borrowing. But these measures were not enough. Government expenditure and revenue for the year 1893 had been balanced at 84 million yen, but the war was to cost 200 million in a few months.[6] As the price of defeat, the Japanese government was able to extract an indemnity of 230 million silver taels[7] from the Chinese, which went a long way to alleviate the situation. It was not enough, however, to meet the continuing need for specie to plug the persistent trade gap. Following the decision to go over to the Gold Standard, further reserves were needed to underpin the new gold currency. In 1897 the Japanese government decided on a radical change of direction. They abandoned Matsukata's rigorous policy of self-financing, and, after an absence of twenty-five years, they returned to the London Market in search of loans.

The Oriental Banking Corporation had failed in 1884 and it was now the Hong Kong and Shanghai Bank which was invited to take its place as the principal London agent of the Japanese authorities. It joined with the Yokohama Specie Bank and the Chartered Bank of India, Australia, and China to raise the Japan Government Loan, 1897 for 43 million yen at 5 per cent, repay-able in gold.[8]

The next loan was raised two years later, in 1899. The Minis-try of Finance acted through the Yokohama Specie Bank in London, whose first contact was Parr's Bank. This was originally a banking partnership in Warrington which had grown rapidly throughout the nineteenth century by absorbing many small local banks, at first in Cheshire and Lancashire and then in other parts of the country.[9] In 1882 it swallowed the Alliance Bank, thereby gaining the services as a manager of Alexander Shand, who had been with the Alliance for fourteen years. His importance as a

link with Japanese finance had been greatly enhanced by a sur-
prising twist of fate. During his period as branch manager of the
Chartered Mercantile Bank in Yokohama, he had hired as a
general office boy and messenger a young man called Korekiyo
Takahashi.[10] Although at first performing very subordinate tasks,
Takahashi became a bright trainee in banking skills. In time, as
Viscount Takahashi, he was to become five times Minister of
Finance, to serve as Prime Minister, and to die at the hands of an
assassin. At this stage he had risen to be Vice-President of the
Yokohama Specie Bank and the Bank of Japan. This explains
why the business of raising loans in London was now brought to
Parr's Bank, an otherwise extremely unlikely choice. A syndicate
was formed with Parr's Bank, the Yokohama Specie Bank, and
the Hong Kong and Shanghai Bank as co-managers. Together
they raised the Japanese Government Loan, 1899 for £10 million
at 4 per cent, an issue again reflecting (both in its size and
favourable rate of interest) the great improvement in the credit-
rating of Japan since the early 1870s. The issue went off well and
it was not difficult to find underwriters.[11]

In 1902 a third loan was raised in a remarkable and totally
different way. The Hong Kong and Shanghai Bank and Baring
Brothers agreed with the government of Japan to buy, through
the Industrial Bank of Japan, 50 million yen of an internal loan,
the Japan Government 5 per cent Consolidated Bonds, and to
place them in London, New York, and on the Continent. While
this provided foreign currency as if the loan had been raised
abroad, it meant that the managers were selling Japanese domestic paper in foreign markets for the first time in history.[12]

This bold experiment, though successful, would not bear re-
peating, for Japan was now steadily and visibly heading for a war
with Russia. Both countries were deeply suspicious – and with
reason – of the other's intentions in Korea and Manchuria. Japan
had been particularly angered by the 'Triple Intervention'. A
slogan was adopted to express this: '*Gashin Shotan*' ('struggling
for revenge in the face of adversity'). Japanese aspirations would
only be satisfied by a showdown with Russia. The requirements
of the military machine were paramount.

Takahashi turned repeatedly to the Parr – Yokohama – Hong
Kong and Shanghai syndicate, which became known as the

London Group. In 1904 they raised £10 million at 6 per cent, and, in a second series in the same year and at the same rate they raised a further £12 million. Once again, these loans were popular with investors. The General Manager of Parr's Bank reported that applications of £80 million had been received by the managers for the £6 million of bonds, which formed that half of the second series reserved for London. In 1905 there were two more series of Japanese bonds. The first was for £30 million at 4.5 per cent and the second was for £55 million, in two tranches at 4.5 per cent and 4 per cent respectively, all again heavily over-subscribed. Of this, £25 million was to be used for converting the earlier 6 per cent loan and the other half for redeeming internal loans. In 1907 £23 million was raised at 5 per cent and a final issue for £11 million and Fr. francs 450 million at 4 per cent was made in 1910, largely for conversion of earlier amounts. In all, the London Group had raised about £200 million over the period. No other financial centre at the time could have handled these transactions.[13]

This is the last occasion on which Alexander Shand appears in this book. His pivotal role in these arrangements is shown by the fact that, on completion of the 1899 loan, the Yokohama Specie Bank sent him a gift of £1,000 in reward for his services. In a minute dated 17 August of that year the Board of Parr's Bank noted this and voted him a similar amount, a favour which they repeated in respect of each succeeding issue of bonds. The Bank also marked the importance which they attached to their relations with Japan by a series of charitable donations. In 1904 £250 was donated to a fund for the widows and orphans of Japanese soldiers, while in 1906 £1,000 went to relieve the victims of famine.[14]

JAPANESE CREDIT IN THE INTERNATIONAL MARKETS

Although such an outstandingly successful series of loans had been launched through the London Market, the risk had been spread to other financial centres as well. This suited the Japanese authorities who wished to extend their borrowing capacity world-wide. For the two series of 1904 and the first series of 1905, half the total amounts were placed in New York by Kuhn Loeb, though underwritten by Baring Brothers. For the second 1905 series, £10 million was placed in New York through the same channels, £10 million in London, and £10 million in Germany by M. M. Warburg of Hamburg. This bank, which was particularly close to Kunh Loeb, also brought in the Deutsche Asiatische Bank and eleven smaller banks, with Barings underwriting 25 per cent of this German risk. For the third loan of 1905, N. M. Rothschild joined the London Group and placed £24 million through Rothschild Frères in Paris, the remaining £26 million being spread between London, New York, and Germany, as before. This distribution was repeated with the 1907 loan.[15]

There was now a wide international market in Japanese bonds but, not surprisingly, many people had had their doubts, both about the stability of the Japanese economy and about the likelihood of Japan winning the war. The British government remained staunch on these issues. Five days after Francis Bertie had written to reassure Rothschilds in the terms quoted on page 48, the Foreign Secretary himself replied to a letter from Lord Revelstoke, the Senior Partner of Baring Brothers, who had asked for an assurance of Japanese ability to repay. While declining to give this, on grounds of established practice, he wrote on 27 September:

> I am, however, myself strongly impressed with the belief that they [the Japanese] mean to conduct their affairs honestly and on sound principle ... they are very shrewd and they know perfectly well that it will be to their advantage to establish their credit and to get classed as something better than a semi-barbarous power.[16]

Barings, in fact, was in a delicate position. Because of its association with the 1902 domestic Japan Loan and their current attempts to arrange railway loans, they were tempted to become members and co-managers of the London Group. The partners of Barings eventually decided, however, that their close relationship with the Imperial Russian government, for whom they acted as agents in Great Britain, tilted the scales against taking such an active sponsorship of what were obviously War Loans for Japan. Instead, as recorded earlier in this chapter, they chose to underwrite some of the placings outside London.[17] Even then, towards the end of the proceedings, Lord Revelstoke noted his opinion that: 'The wave of enthusiasm for Japanese securities seems to have carried the markets beyond any reasonable limits . . . In my judgement, there are many directions in which money could be more profitably employed.'[18]

Even after Japan had won the war, James and Edouard de Rothschild in Paris were made nervous by newspaper reports of budgetary mismanagement or of famine in the remoter islands of Japan. Lord Rothschild, on the other hand, remained a clear supporter of the Japanese connection, frequently pointing out that whereas Russian Imperial Bonds were at a considerable discount, Japanese Bonds were nearly always at par or showing a small premium. In a letter to his cousins, dated 26 January 1906, he observes: 'They [the Japanese] are just as proud about good financial measures as they are about successes on land and water.'[19] Again, he wrote them a chiding letter on 2 December 1906 which runs: 'What you say about the Japanese Treasury Bills is not exactly complimentary, but this evil will soon be cured . . . Their dense and intelligent population will bring them to the front rank, both in commerce and in finance.'[20]

Lord Rothschild had a particular regard for the wisdom and abilities of Viscount Takahashi; as did everyone who met that remarkable man. The public as a whole received a good impression of the reliability of Japan, the London *Standard*, for example, reported on 21 March 1900 that Japan's improved credit-rating was thanks both to her military prowess and 'to the skill with which the finances of the country are handled'.

THE ROLE OF THE LONDON GROUP

The existence of the London consortium limited the manner in which loans could be raised and gave the management banks all the powers of decision as to placing. It does seem, however, to have suited both the British and Japanese governments. Lord Lansdowne (as the architect of the Anglo-Japanese Treaty) and the government to which he belonged, were obviously keen to see their ally receive all the financial support it needed. At the same time, by originating the transactions in London, they hoped to have a unique influence over the Japanese. It was therefore quite natural that, as we have seen, they should have encouraged British banks to advance loans at good rates. Besides that, the British Empire was the world's leading exporter to Japan and the huge Chinese War indemnity had been deposited with the Bank of England. In fact, the Bank appears to have given the London Market considerable assistance in supplying Japan with money. In a telegram to Yokohama on 4 October 1902, Baring Brothers reported that the co-operation of the Bank of England was vital in ensuring the success of the proposed 5.5 per cent loan. Finally, as already seen, a number of the most influential figures among London Bankers were strongly in favour of such a reliable customer as Japan. By forming a syndicate they could hope to freeze out any competition.

From the Japanese side, the existence of a regular consortium, of which their foreign-exchange bank was a lead member, meant that they were dealing with people who had an intimate knowledge of their requirements and who could be absolutely relied upon. In a letter to the Hong Kong and Shanghai Bank, Lord Revelstoke insisted (as a prospective underwriter) that a precondition for membership of the consortium must be that: 'each member should apply for the full amount of their subscription and be prepared to take their full proportion of the allotment'.[21] On the other hand, despite the security given by these arrangements, the Japanese must have seen that they excluded open competition.

Certainly there were banks which, given the opportunity, would have been more than willing to break the monopoly of the London Group and its associates. Each time that the Japanese government decided to raise a new foreign loan, Speyers Brothers of New York sought to undercut the consortium by approaching the authorities in Tokyo directly. This provoked great annoyance, both in London and New York. Initially the member banks tried to freeze out this competition by refusing themselves to have any part in any loan which Speyers might contract. Such was the persistence of this rival, however, that eventually it was decided to give them a share of the New York allotments.[22]

More dangerous by far was the growing interest shown by some German bankers who were not covered by M. M. Warburg's arrangements. After the Japanese victory in 1905 the Kaiser seems to have been less inclined to discourage financial support for Japan. These banks proceeded to form a rival consortium of their own. The London *Standard* reported on 20 March 1905: 'There seems to be a certain amount of truth in the report that a powerful financial syndicate has been formed to take up the loan, subject to the approval of official quarters in Berlin.' Thus, in a telegram sent on the same day from New York to Baring Brothers, Kuhn Loeb cabled:

> Strong competition must be expected from [Germany] ... [The] German Chancellor has declared [that] the Government of Germany will acquiesce if [a] public issue is made in Germany ... We cannot imagine that the Japanese Government, by whom the English Syndicate and us have stood while others have remained aloof, to be [sic] willing to subject us to the mortification of having the financing go to others.[23]

The Japanese were, however, as capable of *Realpolitik* as anyone else. It must be supposed that the gradual extension of the loans, first to Kuhn Loeb in New York, then to Warburg and its associates in Germany, and finally to Rothschild Frères in Paris, was as much due to the urgings of the Yokohama Specie Bank on behalf of the Japanese government as to any fears of the British banks and the Bank of England that London was carrying too much risk. Indeed, Kuhn Loeb was given its first share of the 1904 loan only after Mr Takahashi had met Mr Schiff of that bank in London.[24] Nevertheless, some British sources may have aroused Japanese doubts as to whether the City of London was as keen as it might have been to meet the full requirements of Japan. In a letter dated 12 July 1905 the Managing Director of Baring Brothers warned that it was the 'very general opinion in Europe that the Japanese Government should not, for the time being, make any further appeal to the money markets of the world ... [since] fresh borrowing in the near future would only damage their credit'.[25]

Further evidence is supplied by Kuhn Loeb which wrote to Lord Revelstoke urging that their friends at Warburgs should be admitted to the second series of the 1905 issues so as 'not to see the Anglo-American Market overloaded by making it the sole recipient of the proposed loan ... [and also because it was] the desire of the Japanese Government'.[26]

In view of the enormous popularity of the Japan issues, such fears appear, with hindsight, to have been groundless. All requirements were quite easily satisfied through the London Group and the threatened new German syndicate was frustrated. Nevertheless, Japanese borrowing tailed off rapidly after 1905, with only the issues of 1907 and 1910 to come at much longer intervals.

BRITISH LOANS FOR JAPANESE INDUSTRIAL DEVELOPMENT

At first sight it is rather strange that during this active period of lending to the Japanese government there were no loans on the London market for Japanese corporations. *The Times* noted on 26 June 1902: 'It is certainly regrettable that British capitalists cannot find investments in a country where the banks are paying 7 per cent on fixed deposits and where many profitable enterprises await the means to undertake them.' The author of this article then went on to give the loan made by an American bank to the Yokohama Water Authority earlier in 1902 for £91,875 at 6 per cent as an example of such business. Most such loans at this time came from the Americans, and British journalists claimed that their own banks were throwing away the advantages which were so open to them. The *Daily Mail* wrote to Baring Brothers on 14 August 1902, asking for an interview and stating: 'Our Kobe correspondent sends us some information tending to show that the Americans are making the most of their opportunities and are likely to supplant British capitalists altogether.'[27] Similar complaints about what Dr Geoffrey Jones and R. P. T. Davenport-Hines have referred to as the 'marginalization' of British enterprise have been heard from virtually every quarter of the globe in every year since then. In this case, those reproached advanced two main arguments in their own justification.

First, it was claimed that such transactions were beneficial neither to the creditor nor the recipient of the loan. Such small loans, it was said, did not require the assistance of foreign banks but were better raised locally. In Japan, also, this argument was used. Why was the country going abroad for such loans? It could only create an unjustified impression of penury and injure Japan's credit-rating. The *Japan Mail* for 15 October 1902 argued: 'They [the borrowers] get what they want for the moment, but they convey to the occidental mind an impression ... that the smallest mercies are thankfully received. It would be far better that the Treasury should become banker for these small enterprises.' British bankers certainly seemed to find it prudent to take this same view. They applied very tight criteria as to which business they would accept. Loans to the Japanese government were one thing, being backed by tax revenues and political power, but loans to corporations, whether public or private, were generally deemed unsafe. British banks expected the same rigorous standards as with domestic loans, but often did not even enquire into the standing of a would-be borrower. The full limitations on British lending were clearly described when the Tokyo Port Authority approached a group of British banks. The reply given was that it was an accepted policy to: 'Confine operations in Japan to mercantile business, in other words to credits for import and export, to finance to the business of the Government and first class private railways.' The banks 'doubted whether they would be prepared to extend operations outside this limit'.[28]

However, where they were genuinely interested, as in the case of railways, the London Banks did take very great care to look at the credentials of their clients. For instance, when considering credit to private railways, Barings dispatched Sir William Bisset, a British railway engineer, to Japan to make an exhaustive investigation. Although he was impressed by the efficient and professional way in which it was run, he could not recommend a loan to the Hokuetsu Railway on the grounds that it was too small. This was enough for Barings, who wrote to Sale Frazer in

Yokohama saying: 'This property [the railway] has so far been successful, but English experience of small railways in this country and in others has been uniformly unfortunate.'[29]

The Japanese government, on the other hand, indicated that they would do everything possible to facilitate the introduction of foreign capital. Mr Senjoku Mitsugu, President of the Kyushu Railway, wrote to Mr J. Stuart Horner at Barings on 28 June 1901, saying: 'There is no difficulty in obtaining the sanction of our government provided we go through these procedures, for they are always willing to help us introduce foreign capital.'[30] But the authorities were still thinking in terms of loans rather than equity. They were well aware of the strategic importance of the railways and were not willing to see the citizens of a foreign power exercising any degree of ownership or control over them. Even loans implied a possibly high degree of influence by the lender. They were quite determined to keep final control in their own hands. Sir William Bissett wrote to Mr Farrar at Barings on 2 September 1902: 'The susceptibilities of the Japanese are very great and I doubt if the railway party could influence the Ministry to propose a law which openly limited their present powers for the special advantage of foreigners.'[31] This reference to 'special advantage' covers the second major deterrent to British investment. What the banks required was special collateral, in the form of mortgages on the immovable property of the railways. The Japanese saw this as a threat to sovereignty in an area of vital national importance. In any case, the state of the law did not allow for such a procedure; it was expressly forbidden to mortgage property to a foreigner. On the other hand, it was legal for immovable property to be mortgaged to a 'judicial person' of Japanese nationality. It was therefore suggested that a foreign bank might establish a front company in Japan to take the mortgage, thus avoiding issues of both law and public interest. However, London banks were not willing to take such an easy step. They believed, with reasonable insight, that even in the event of a foreclosure their ability to dispose of sequestered assets would be very limited.[32]

The problem centred particularly on the attempts by Baring Brothers to negotiate loans to Japanese railways from 1902 onwards. It led to a total impasse. In a letter to their agents in

Japan, J. Birch and Co., dated 7 May 1903, Baring Brothers wrote: 'Until the law is altered, we are not prepared to entertain the business.'[33] This put the Japanese government in a dilemma. Preparations for the war against Russia had exhausted their own resources of governmental capital. The report of the British Foreign Office on 'Trade of Japan for the Year 1901' had contained the following passage: 'The scarcity of capital in Japan for government and private enterprises was perhaps more clearly recognized than ever before ... Private railway companies in particular stand in need of working capital.'[34] The government had really no choice but to give in.

Unfortunately, the problems of the railways and their prospective creditors were by no means over. There was considerable opposition of a nationalist kind in the Diet. Successive cabinets and administrative bureaux shunted the draft legislation to and fro. The *Japan Mail* complained in October 1902 that the Legislative Bureau had had over six months to draft the bill and that, if it delayed longer, the government must carry entire responsibility for blocking the inflow of foreign capital. But then it began to appear that there was more domestic capital available for such investment than had previously been believed. Between 1902 and 1903 the Hokuetsu Railway Company floated a par loan at 7.5 per cent which was 50 per cent over-subscribed. At the same time the Kyushu Railway Company was raising 6 million yen at 7 per cent at home, while the Tanko Railway Company was seeking 2 million yen at 6.5 per cent.[35] Considering that the government itself was borrowing heavily and that the economy was depressed, this state of affairs might seem paradoxical. But the money was coming from Japanese banks which were accumulating the assets of companies bankrupted by the current recession.

This state of affairs did not last. By 1905 the railways were obliged to return to the foreign markets. Extreme competition developed between British, American, and Canadian banks. Marcus Samuel and Co. offered terms so favourable to the client as to be held quite ridiculous, not to say unsportsmanlike, by their competitors. The bonds proved very unpopular on the London Market and the bank was criticized by its rivals as 'having rendered the business so nugatory as not to be worthy of

attention'.[36] The Japanese authorities stirred up this competition
by seeking to play off the rival banks against one another. In
December 1905 Mr Townsend of the Hong Kong and Shanghai
Bank discovered that he was being quoted by the Japanese as
willing to make a bid for a loan to the Sanyo Railway Company,
in order to stimulate Sir Malcolm Mac-Eachern of Marcus
Samuel to make a better one. There was a general feeling of
disillusionment. A letter from Baring Brothers to Mr Sale on 6
March 1906 summed up that bank's feelings: 'The [Japanese]
Government's attitude towards us has not been such as to induce
us to ask any favours of them, nor do we think from our own
experience . . . as to the Japanese character that we are likely to
get the forwarder by asking.'[37]

Finally, the government took a decision which no one had
expected. Just as the legal amendment required by Barings was
about to come into effect they decreed the nationalization of the
main railway system. In future, Japanese railway development
would be funded entirely by large government loans. Four years
of coaxing, pressure, and negotiation had been entirely wasted.

NOTES

1 Richard Storry, *A History of Modern Japan* (Penguin, Harmondsworth, 1983), pp. 134–41.
2 Barings Archives.
3 Ibid.
4 Takeshi Hamashita, 'A History of the Silver Yen', in F. H. H. King
   (ed.), *Eastern Banking* (Athlone Press, London, 1983), p. 337.
5 The *sen* was $\frac{1}{100}$ of the silver yen.
6 *Banking in Modern Japan* (The Fuji Bank Ltd., Tokyo, 1967),
   p. 37.
7 Equivalent to about 38 million sterling.
8 F. H. H. King, *History of the Hong Kong and Shanghai Banking
   Corporation*, (Draft MS kindly supplied by the author).
9 Richard Reed, *The National Westminster Bank: A Short History*
   (Nat West Bank, 1983), pp. 35–6.
10 Umekichi Yoneyama, 'A Banker's Reminiscences', Japan Times
   Pamphlet.
11 Nat West Archives.

12 Letter books of Barings' Archives.
13 Ibid.
14 Nat West Archives.
15 Barings Archives.
16 Ibid.
17 John Orbell, *The History of Baring Brothers to 1939* (Baring Brothers, 1985), pp. 68–9.
18 Barings Archives.
19 Rothschild Archives.
20 Ibid.
21 Barings Archives.
22 Ibid.
23 Ibid.
24 Ibid.
25 Ibid.
26 Ibid.
27 Ibid.
28 Ibid.
29 Ibid.
30 Ibid.
31 Ibid.
32 Ibid.
33 Ibid.
34 Foreign Office Archives.
35 Barings Archives.
36 Ibid.
37 Ibid.

6

JAPANESE FINANCIAL DEVELOPMENT
1895–1914

Japan's External Balances

In the last chapter (p. 49) it was noted that, at the end of the China War, Japan extracted an indemnity of 230 million *taels* from the vanquished enemy. The *tael* was a silver coinage and Matsukata did not want silver. The price of the metal had fallen in Europe and the continuing trade deficit arose chiefly from payments for ships, arms, and raw materials that had to be made in Europe. At the same time, Japan was on the eve of moving to the gold standard. The problem was solved in a most ingenious way. Matsukata requested that the indemnity be paid in English money which was, of course, backed by gold. The Chinese were required to raise the sum by the issue of bonds in Europe and to deposit £38 million (the equivalent of the indemnity) by instalments with the Bank of England in London.[1]

It is probable that this deposit was originally intended as a temporary measure while Japan established its new gold currency. This is suggested by the fact that the Japanese government tried to withdraw a considerable amount of the money immediately to Japan shortly after its deposit in London. The British authorities, however, out of regard for their own currency, would not permit such a large quantity of specie to be removed at one time. To get around this the Japanese government transferred 50 million yen *in situ* to its own Central Bank, receiving the same value of convertible notes at home in exchange. The Bank of Japan then left the money on deposit in London, denominating it as part of the reserve fund required to cover the convertible notes in issue. Thus, the foreign balance of the Central Bank in London was being used as legal cover for paper at home. However, it was not until some eight years later, at the end of the Russo-Japanese War, that the necessary legal provisions were enacted to allow the foreign balances to be counted as part of the mandatory backing for the national note issue and thus be used to stabilize the yen.[2]

The mechanism by which the London balances played this role worked as follows. The Bank of Japan was required by law to hold gold, silver, or other specie as a backing for the issue of notes. The servicing of the mounting foreign debt and the growing trade deficit caused by the wars led to a rising demand for foreign currency and a consequent outflow of specie, aggravated by the fact that Japan had not evolved an adequate rate-of-interest machinery for controlling the trend. This outflow had had an alarming and destabilizing effect. But now, by maintaining its balances abroad with the Bank of England, Japan could meet international obligations by drawing on these assets overseas, without the need to send any specie out of the country. However, in order to meet its legal obligations and maintain the stability of the yen, the Central Bank had to match any diminution in the size of the reserve by cancelling an equal proportion of the note issue. This it did regularly and, generally speaking, paper currency was not allowed to outstrip the total specie available to support it.[3]

The system worked sufficiently well to attract the major part of Japan's foreign earnings to the deposits with the Bank of England for the next twenty years. The initial payments reflected the manner in which the Chinese indemnity was collected. For instance, the accounts of the Deputy Governor of the Bank of England for 1898 record that on 25 July of the previous year an account was opened in the name of the Russian Finance Minister for the credit of which, over the next five months, remittances were received from Messrs Hottinguer et Cie of Paris amounting to £11.5 million. On 31 October 1896 a sum of £7,250,000 was transferred thence to an account in the name of the Chinese Minister, from which it was again transferred to yet another account in the name of the Japanese Minister in London. Similar procedures were followed until all of the indemnity had been deposited in the name of the Japanese Minister. No doubt these reserves would have been depleted and eventually used up had it not been for replenishment by the foreign State Loans. All the money raised by the issue of bonds in New York was remitted to London. In time, it became increasingly the practice to maintain the overseas reserve as the principal support for the yen. Whereas in 1904 the domestic specie reserves stood at 120 million yen and the overseas reserves at only 19 million, the distribution was soon reversed. By 1914 the total reserves overseas had risen to 213 million yen while the domestic reserves were only one-eighth of this amount, at 28 million yen.[4] The balances in London were by far the largest element in this system and at the outbreak of the First World War amounted to two-thirds of the whole Japanese national reserve. As a result of this it was possible to maintain the value of the yen over the twenty years during which the system continued, without once reaching the point where specie had to be exported from Japan. Junnosuke Inouye summed up the situation as follows: 'It would probably be most fit to say that Japan's exchange rates have been decided by the amount of the country's specie holdings abroad and the Government's attitude in using these holdings.'[5] The yen rate of exchange was, however, naturally fixed by the Bank of Japan and not in London.

Although the system achieved its main aim so successfully, it did have two disadvantages. First, the Bank of England deposit was not just a passive backing for the domestic currency; it was also the active source of payments for imports. As this masked the effects of periods of deficit in foreign trade, it led to a rather loose attitude on the part of the Japanese authorities towards the control of imports, which continued to flood into the country. Second, all trade payments abroad were made to the Yokohama Specie Bank, exercising its monopoly of credits for Japanese trade. Since the Bank of Japan immediately earmarked them for the overseas reserve and would not allow them to be remitted, the Central Bank was obliged to assist the Yokohama Specie Bank by purchasing these credits through the issue of notes at home. Thus, the need to issue paper against the foreign currency reserve tended to become mandatory rather than discretionary and had an inflationary effect.

These Japanese balances in London, as already mentioned, were held in the Bank of England. A large part was from time to time invested in British Government or Government of India bonds. Some part was also spread around London in deposits with commercial banks. The Japanese managers were sometimes suspicious about the practices of the London Money Market, as well as being highly aware of their own responsibility to get the best return. Writing one of his almost daily newsletters to his Paris cousins in July 1906, Lord Rothschild remarks drily:

> These gentlemen here try to get as high a rate of interest as possible on the money which they have got on deposit with the Bank of England and other institutions and they really think it is an honour to keep their accounts and that one ought to work *pour le Roi de Prusse* [*i.e. for no return*].[6]

On the other hand, the Bank of England also profited by the arrangement since the Japanese deposit represented such a large proportion of total funds. In 1896 a member of the Committee of Treasury, B. B. Greene, pointed out that its withdrawal would reduce the Bank's own reserves to a hypothetical level of only £20 million, at which point a rise in the bank rate would normally be required.[7] The Bank had developed the practice of borrowing and repaying moderate sums from the Council of India as a stabilizer for its own reserves. In 1905 they entered into an arrangement with the Bank of Japan to use the Japanese account in a similar manner. In the course of the next year there were at least five such transactions, ranging between £500,000 and £1,500,000. So important had this deposit become, that for many years the balance was shown in the Bank of England's Daily Account in red ink as a subdivision of its own. Thus the arrangement well suited both sides.[8]

Before leaving this subject it may be worth considering why the Japanese government chose London as the destination for the Chinese indemnity, rather than the Central Bank of any other Western Country linked to the Gold Standard. The first and most obvious reason is that London was the leading centre of world finance and offered services and expertise of a greater range than available elsewhere, a fact that the Japanese recognized when they set out to raise foreign loans. Second was the fact that London had the world's largest silver market, and, since Japan was in the process of going over to the Gold Standard, London provided the most advantageous place in which to exchange reserves of silver into gold. Third, Britain was the next most important country after the United States in Japan's overseas trade. But whereas Japan exported considerably more to America than she imported from there her trade with Britain was regularly in the red. To take a typical year, in 1910 the United Kingdom imported goods from the Japanese Empire worth only 25,781,364 yen but exported goods to it worth 94,700,911 yen. If all the dominions and colonies of the British Empire are included, the discrepancy becomes even more striking, with British imports rising to 85,318,103 yen but exports soaring to 214,804,847 yen. Thus, for 1910 Japan ran a surplus with the United States and a deficit of 129,486,744 yen with Great Britain.[9] There were also deficits with France and Germany in that year, but the total volume of the trade was considerably lower. As a result, by far the largest transfers of cash by Japan were made in London and this may also have added to the convenience of keeping the reserves in that city.

THE JAPANESE LONG-TERM CREDIT BANKS

In discussing the Japanese State Loans and the overseas balances, the emphasis has been very largely on events in London and on the activities of British banks. But the Japanese government and financial community were certainly not aiming to become more dependent on foreign banks; during these twenty years from 1895 to 1914 they continued to build up their own financial institutions at a steady pace. Most of the steps which were taken were in the field of purely domestic banking and are of no relevance here, but some would have a considerable effect on relations with the City of London. Of these, the most important was the founding of a Hypothec Bank of Japan and the Industrial Bank of Japan.

In Chapter 5 (pp. 57–8) we discussed the difficulties met by Japanese corporations attempting to raise money on the London market in face of the prohibition on direct foreign equity investment and the reluctance of British banks to make loans to small or untried companies (or, indeed, any industry other than the railways). Therefore, the very large numbers of smaller enterprises, whose importance to the future of the country's economy was plain enough, had to raise loans on the domestic market. Here also, as we have already seen, capital was desperately short, because the government was trying to raise funds for war expenditure from the same source and had drastically raised the discount rate to discourage private borrowing. What was clearly needed was a means of channelling foreign capital towards smaller businesses through some central institution which would appear to foreigners as an attractive borrower. This was the reasoning behind the founding of the Long-Term Credit Banks.

Proposals for a Hypothec Bank had been mooted by Matsukata as early as 1885, but it was not until the end of the century that they were given really serious consideration. Funds obtained from the bank had to be used for productive purposes and were normally secured by a first mortgage. The loans were to be repaid within 50 years in annual instalments. The bank was kept under very strict supervision by the Ministry of Finance, while its interests in the provinces were looked after by Banks of Agriculture and Industry, one of which was located in each prefecture.

This bank failed in many respects to live up to the government's initial expectations. Agriculture, which was meant to be its primary beneficiary, was not normally in the hands of people or concerns which would be interested in borrowing large sums of money to carry out improvements. In time the activities of the bank were redirected along more fruitful avenues such as forestry, property development, and retailing.[10]

The Hypothec Bank was barred from funding large industrial enterprises, such as shipbuilding or iron-smelting, so an Industrial Bank of Japan was created for this purpose. It was founded in 1900 and began operations in 1902 but, like the Hypothec

Bank, it experienced initial difficulties. At first it found that much of its potential business was being pre-empted by the Bank of Japan, which was directly making industrial loans against the security of stocks. In 1905 the law was changed so that the Bank of Japan was no longer empowered to act in this way and the Industrial Bank started to make some progress. It began to develop its role as an importer of foreign capital and was able to raise 7,500,000 yen in 1906 on the London Market.[11] However, it experienced other difficulties. The great industrial combines of Japan (later known as *zaibatsu*) were already forming and had developed their own ways of raising capital without the help of the Industrial Bank.

Another disappointment was the attitude of London banks which were not willing to rely on the Industrial Bank as a partner in Japan. Mr Soeda, the first President of the bank, wanted to secure for it some of the business attached to the proposed railway loans, but the British financiers were determined that it should not. In an interview given to the Tokyo press, Mr Soeda made plain his aspirations. He noted that foreign capitalists were not interested in small private companies in Japan but went on to say:

> The case would be very different if Foreign capitalists should find a thoroughly reliable establishment which would hold itself primarily responsible for any money advanced, besides saving them all these troublesome proceedings ... The Industrial Bank of Japan intends to make such a medium.[12]

This well-intentioned but perhaps naïve invitation was tartly rejected from London. In a letter to Sale Frazer, Baring Brothers wrote: 'Approval [for the loan] will be withheld unless it is made plain that we will not work through a juridical person like the Industrial Bank of Japan.'[13] At the root of this apparently ungracious attitude lay the fear that the Japanese government was trying to substitute the 'good will' of a State institution for the legal security of mortgages sought by the British. The government had so far been very slow in passing the law allowing foreigners to take mortgages on assets in Japan (see pp. 58–60) and it was likely that they were trying to interpose the IBJ as a substitute. They had, after all, founded the organization and it was natural that they should want to see it active in such business. In a memorandum of 6 June 1905 Takahashi wrote that the Japanese government believed it desirable that: 'there should be a special organ under official supervision for facilitating transactions between [Japanese companies and foreign banks]'.[14] The important point here is 'official supervision'. The Japanese authorities wished to keep everything under their own ultimate control; the British (and other foreigners too) expected to have direct relations between lender and borrower, based on legal contract. There was a clear cultural difference which impeded the smooth functioning of the Industrial Bank of Japan.

COMMERCIAL BANKING

During this period there were also developments in the field of commercial banking. Having established by now a fully functioning system at home, the Japanese wished to see their own commercial banks operating outside their national frontiers, like those of other major powers. It was not intended to leave the Yokohama Specie Bank as the sole Japanese presence overseas. The Bank of Taiwan, for instance, had barely consolidated its position in the newly acquired colony, whose finances it was meant to regulate, when it extended its operations to import and export finance in Singapore and South China, in direct competition with the British Banks which had always been paramount in the area.[15] In the next section of this chapter we shall see how the extension of the activities of Japanese banks to the mainland became an essential part of Japan's expansionary policy in Manchuria, China, and Korea. However, it is interesting by contrast to note the extreme caution of the Japanese commercial banks in their attitude to working in Western countries and the deliberately slow pace at which they were permitted to advance their operations there. The period has been shown as one of intense financial activity between Tokyo and London, and yet, by the outbreak of the First World War, not one of the major Japanese commercial banks (now referred to normally as 'city banks') had opened a branch or representative office in London. The big

Japanese trading companies were established there but they used
local facilities when they needed them. For example, to meet the
needs of their associated trading company, Mitsui Bussan, the
Mitsui Bank in 1906 entered into a credit arrangement with
Barclays Bank in London against the security of Japanese government bonds and a fixed deposit of £10,000.[16] They remained
satisfied with this arrangement for the next twenty years. In any
case, given the circumstances and the desperate shortage of capital in the country, it seems unlikely that the Japanese government
would have approved of the export of capital for operations of
this kind.

The authorities still reserved a monopoly in foreign exchange
for overseas trade to the Yokohama Specie Bank and it may be
wondered how the British banks in Japan were making a living.
As we have shown, by 1914 the British share of Japan's foreign
trade had fallen from its earlier high point to only 25 per cent.
But the volume of that trade had grown so greatly that the
business remained adequately rewarding. The local branches of
British banks were able to offer credit services to their compatriots and other foreigners, as well as offering facilities for
Japanese companies overseas from time to time.

This period also saw the first attempt to set up a joint venture
in banking. This was the Anglo-Japanese Bank, founded in 1906.
It had a nominal capital of £2 million. The Board of Directors
was to be manned on the British side by representatives of British
overseas banks, such as the Imperial Bank of Persia, while among
the Japanese directors was one of the most influential men in
Tokyo financial circles, Kihachiro Okura. It was hoped that this
bank would finance Anglo-Japanese trade, but little seems to
have come of the venture and it was dissolved in 1914.[17]

There was one further event at this time which, in other circumstances, might have led to fundamental changes in Japan's
financial relations with London and other centres. With the revision in 1899 of the Commercial Law, Japan ostensibly ceased to
be purely a loan economy as far as foreigners were concerned.
Direct equity investment was now legally permitted. Very few
British firms pursued the new opportunity opened to them. One
notable joint venture was set up between the Dunlop Rubber Co.

and Mitsui, which led to the construction of a factory in Kobe in 1909 to manufacture rubber products. Dunlop played a pioneering role in developing this sector of Japanese industry and, together with other foreign firms, dominated the rubber trade in Japan right up to the Second World War.[18] Another important venture was headed by Vickers and Armstrong Whitworth, which established a consortium with Japanese companies in 1907 to build a steel and armaments factory, Nihon Seikosho, at Muroran.[19]

Whatever the state of the law, most foreign entrepreneurs found the prospects discouraging. The permission of the government was necessary for such ventures and was only readily forthcoming in cases of serious technological or financial need. Nor were most Japanese businessmen willing to give any degree of control over their activities to foreigners. The barriers were traditional, cultural, psychological – and they are still familiar to would-be direct investors in Japanese industry today.

LOANS TO CHINA: ANGLO-JAPANESE RIVALRY

Even while Japan was raising loans on the London Market to pay for its war against Russia, she felt it incumbent to demonstrate her position as the leading economic and industrial power in the Far East by giving assistance to her former enemy, China. In 1910, the Yokohama Specie Bank extended considerable credits to the Government of China and acted as underwriter for some of its national bond issues. Ten million yen's worth of these were floated on the Tokyo Market. This was the first time in history that foreign bonds were offered there.[20]

Japan's colonial empire now extended to Taiwan, Korea, Southern Sakhalin, and Dairen – Port Arthur. In addition, and in acknowledgement of her military strength, the Western Powers had recognized her claim to a so-called 'sphere of influence' in Manchuria and in the Chinese province of Fukien. This carried the responsibility to supply financial support and development capital to the new colonies and areas of influence. A Japanese journalist, Yosaburo Takekoshi, summed up the country's new-found sense of big-brotherhood by writing:

> For many years now the countries of the West believed that they alone bore the responsibility to open up the uncivilized parts of the world. Now our nation too is to take part in this great and glorious task.[21]

International loans to China were at this time being organized under the directions of a multinational consortium including Britain, France, Germany, and the United States. The British element was for a long time represented by the Hong Kong and Shanghai Bank, but pressure from other houses ensured that participation was eventually extended to Barings, Rothschilds, Schroders, and the Chartered Bank of India, Australia, and China. Although still short of capital, Japan was understandably convinced that she too must join the consortium in order to reflect and support her dominant position in the area. She also expected such participation to increase her direct influence with the Chinese government. In 1911 when the China consortium proposed to advance a loan of £60 million for the stabilization of the Chinese currency and for the development of Manchuria, Japan and Russia joined in opposing the loan as planned on the grounds that they both had special interests in the region and should be included as members of any such project.[22] The British chose to oppose this for two reasons. First, they argued that Japan's own industrial development was as yet incomplete and that she would therefore do well not to waste her limited resources on China. Second, they held that the consortium was quite unwieldy enough already without letting in extra members. Addis of the Hong Kong and Shanghai Bank wrote to the Foreign Office in 1911 to report that representatives of the consortium and of the Chinese government had reached agreement on a more limited loan of £10 million for support of the Chinese currency only. R. M. Grey of the Foreign Office minuted the following on the matter:

> This is not the first time that we have heard of the possibility of Japan evincing a desire to participate in the currency loan, but it is

hoped that the arguments used by Mr Addis to deter them have convinced them of the undesirability of their participating.[23]

Clearly, such arguments can only have irritated the Japanese and events in China soon made it much easier for them to penetrate the market there. In the revolution of 1911–12, the Manchu Dynasty was overthrown and replaced by the republican regime of Sun Yat Sen. In January and February of 1912, much to the annoyance of the British, the government of Prime Minister Saionji in Tokyo allowed loan contracts to be negotiated between Japanese financiers (most notably the Okura concern) and the new Chinese revolutionary government. These loans were never paid up in full, but they showed the futility of excluding Japan from a cartel which she could circumvent. In February 1912, both Japan and Russia were admitted to the consortium.[24]

This financial rivalry was leading to a deterioration in Anglo-Japanese relations. Japan had now been able to gain complete control of financing in Manchuria and Inner Mongolia. When Mr R. M. Grey instructed Mr Macdonald of the British Embassy in Tokyo to invite the Japanese to join in a new reorganization loan to China for £60 million the latter successfully insisted that: 'the proceeds of the present loan should not in any way be employed in connection with Manchuria and Mongolia'.[25] Furthermore, the Japanese now had a guaranteed share in any loan to the Chinese government which went far beyond what they might have been able to secure in open competition with such financial heavyweights as Britain and the United States. Under the terms of the consortium, the British share was limited to one-sixth of the whole.

The system of 'spheres of influence' was meant to work as follows. In the late nineteenth century, as the Great Powers scrambled to obtain concessions in China, a tacit agreement was reached whereby each one accepted the others' dominant position in a particular area of the country. As already noted, Japan had been recognized as having a special sphere of influence in Manchuria and Fukien. Now the Japanese financiers were threatening to upset these arrangements by extending their operations to other areas. They had already shown a particular desire to establish themselves in the Yangtze valley and it was partly this that led them to finance an insurrection there in 1913. This greatly angered Britain which regarded the area as its own preserve. The Japanese now attempted to make their ambitions acceptable to the British by presenting them as a means of extending the Anglo-Japanese Alliance into the field of economic co-operation in the Far East. In 1913, the Japanese launched internal discussions between the Yokohama Specie Bank and the Britain and China Corporation for possible co-operation in building a railway line in the Yangtze Valley, a project that did not have the approval of the Foreign Office. Mr Koike, speaking to Mr E. F. Crowe, the Commercial Attaché at the British Embassy, said that the enhanced alliance should take the form of co-operation between various companies on either side, noting that an example of this already existed in the China Merchant Steamship Company, which had been formed by the union of the Japanese Nippon Yusen Kaisha and the British Japan China Line, together with the shipping interests of Jardine Matheson and Butterfield and Swire.[26] At the same time it was hinted to the Hong Kong and Shanghai Bank in the course of the Yangtze Railway discussions that the Japanese might be prepared to offer opportunities to British firms to enter Manchuria in return for co-operation in British spheres of influence. It is very unlikely that the Japanese government would ever have agreed to such an arrangement and the British government was equally opposed to its own companies entering Manchuria, as it felt it would weaken the case for keeping the Japanese out of the Yangtze Valley and Southern China. Between 1909 and 1910 it actively discouraged British investment in Manchuria.[27]

The pace of competition rose rapidly. Eiichi Shibusawa visited central China and launched plans for transforming the Japan and China Development Company into a huge industrial combine based on Kiangsi, a city provocatively close to the Yangtze. Mitsui Bussan was ambitious to force its way into the region and lent money to the Canton Provincial Railway Company. Mr Alston of the Foreign Office wrote that: 'It would be clearly injurious to Hong Kong that the southern sector of the Canton – Hangkow Railway should fall into Japanese hands.'[28] In a similar way the Finance Minister, Inouye, said that he hoped Japanese

Banks would finance the railway from Nanking to Hsiangt'an. In 1914 Takaaki Kato, on taking office as Foreign Minister, demanded that Japan be allowed to build the railway from Nanchang to Hangkow. Mr Jordan, a British representative in China, wrote:

> There can, in my opinion, be no doubt that Japan is challenging our position in the Yangtze Valley ... The unnecessary retention of a large Japanese Garrison at Hang Kow and reported negotiations for a further large loan to the Hanyeping Company are indications of this ...[29]

While the Japanese government was thus challenging the whole system of 'spheres of influence' in China it was strongly defending the same system in its own interest in Manchuria. Despite discouragement from their government, some British banks had opened branches in Manchuria, notably the Hong Kong and Shanghai Bank, which had taken up residence in Dairen. Its request in 1909 to issue notes backed by silver was perhaps unrealistic and was firmly turned down by the Japanese Finance Minister of the time, Taro Katsura. But other obstacles were also systematically put in their way. British banks fared little better in Korea, where they were not allowed by the Japanese government to join in funding the Seoul–Pusan railway.[30]

The events described in this section provide a classic case of two rival imperialist powers competing in an open area. They demonstrate clearly the role of banks in helping to build political power through investment in infrastructure and industry. They also show that Japan now generally considered Eastern Asia as its own sphere of influence and was therefore challenging the presence of other imperial powers in the area. This was already an indication of what was to come in the 1930s and it put a severe strain on the Anglo-Japanese Alliance.

ANGLO-AMERICAN RIVALRY

By the turn of the century British banks began to find themselves effectively challenged by their American rivals throughout the Far

East and especially in Japan. In chapter 2 we saw how during most of the nineteenth century the United States was so absorbed in developing its own new frontiers that it had little free capital to invest elsewhere. The country ran a current account deficit right up until 1873. The US government had conserved its domestic capital by means of the Federal Reserve Act, which forbade American banks from establishing branches overseas. Such factors prompted the author of a Barings Memorandum to say in 1903: 'I am not in the least afraid of American competition. Unless I am very much mistaken [they] will need all the money they possess to finance their own affairs for some considerable time to come.'[31]

This state of affairs was not to last. By 1898 the United States had won its war against Spain and seized the Philippines, thus establishing a territorial presence in the Far East. It was actively exploiting its concessions in China. In Japan enterprising Americans could find ways of getting round the restrictions of the Federal Reserve Act. Sale Frazer and Co. were engaged in banking activities by 1906, albeit as a sideline to their main trading activities. By 1911 the International Banking Corporation of New York had established two representative offices in Japan and was already handling 7 per cent of all import–export exchange transactions.[32] The Americans had also been more active than the British in taking advantage of the opening provided in 1899 to make direct investment in Japanese companies or joint ventures although, for the reasons given on page p. 71, these investments were not extensive. But in the field of corporate finance the Americans were much more active than their British counterparts. American financiers were usually willing to consider loans to Japanese individuals or companies who would have been quite unable to put up sufficient collateral to satisfy a British bank.[33]

In 1913 the Federal Reserve Law was repealed. The activities of American banks mushroomed throughout the East. By the outbreak of war in 1914, they were challenging their British and Continental rivals, although London remained the principal centre for Japanese financial activity in the West. But then, with the firing of the first shot in August, the financial supremacy of Europe was to vanish.

NOTES

1 G. C. Allen, *A Short Economic History of Modern Japan* (Macmillan, London, 1985), pp. 54–6.
2 Hiroshi Saito, The Origins of Japanese Specie Abroad (MS kindly provided by the author).
3 Ibid.
4 Junnosuke Inouye, *The Problems of the Japanese Exchange* (Macmillan, London, 1931), p. 237.
5 Ibid.
6 Rothschild's Archives.
7 E. J. Sayers, *History of the Bank of England* (Cambridge University Press, Cambridge, 1976), pp. 40–1.
8 Ibid.
9 Robert Porter, *Full Recognition of Japan* (Clarendon Press, Oxford, 1911), pp. 354–5.
10 This should not be confused with the later Hypothec Bank (Nippon Fudosan Ginko) founded in April 1957 with the assets of the former Bank of Korea and now named the Nippon Credit Bank. The original Hypothec Bank eventually became the Kangyo Bank, now merged into the Dai Ichi Kangyo Bank.
11 Barings Archives.
12 Ibid.
13 Ibid.
14 Nat West Archives.
15 Robert Lowe, *Great Britain and Japan 1911–1915: A Study of British Far Eastern Policy* (Macmillan, London, 1969), pp. 120–30.
16 *The Mitsui Bank: A History of the First 100 Years* (Mitsui Bank, 1976), pp. 79–80.
17 R. P. T. Davenport-Hines and Geoffrey Jones (Draft MS kindly provided by the authors).
18 But today Dunlop is owned by a Japanese firm, the Sumitomo Rubber Co.
19 Davenport-Hines and Jones.
20 Bank of England Archives.
21 R. H. Myers and M. R. Peattie, *The Japanese Colonial Empire 1895–1945* (Princeton University Press, Princeton, NJ, 1984), p. 83.
22 Lowe, *Great Britain and Japan*, pp. 123–4.
23 Ibid., p. 123.
24 Ibid., p. 127–8.
25 Ibid., pp. 160–81.

26 Lowe, *Great Britain and Japan*, pp. 165–75.
27 Ibid. pp. 170–1.
28 Ibid. p. 165.
29 Ibid.
30 Ibid.
31 Barings Archives.
32 Hikomatsu Kamikawa, *Japanese–American Cultural Relations in the Meiji-Taisho Era* (Pan-Pacific Press, Tokyo, 1958), p. 435.
33 Ibid., p. 438.

7

THE FIRST WORLD WAR
1914–1918

General Consequences for Japan

The alliance which Japan had signed with Britain in 1902 compelled her to enter the First World War on the side of the Allies. She took little part in the actual fighting and the direct cost of it to her economy was very low, yet at the end of it she was able to acquire the former German concessions in China and some of the island chains in the Pacific which had been German colonies. She had also taken advantage of the fact that the other Great Powers were desperately engaged elsewhere to exact a series of concessions of her own out of China, in the form of the so-called 'Twenty-one Demands' in 1915.

The war had caused a major shift in political power throughout the world. None of the European countries, individually or jointly, was ever able to match the power of the United States again. In East Asia, France almost vanished from the stage, both politically and economically, and so did Germany until the creation of the Berlin–Rome–Tokyo axis more than twenty years later. Though Britain continued to play a major role in East Asia, her power was quite clearly not so great as before. The consequence of these changes for Japan was that she was now herself unquestionably the strongest presence in the area. Also, she had come to look on her relationship with the United States as more important than that with Britain. This last consideration applied as much in the financial sphere as in the political.

Overall, the economy of Japan benefited enormously by the

war. From 1914 onwards, the industries of Britain, France, and Germany were increasingly engaged in the manufacture of munitions. German shipping was almost entirely confined to its harbours while that of Britain became desperately engaged in feeding and supplying the country in face of the growing menace of the U-boats. These countries were therefore less and less able to supply goods to their former customers. Japan stepped into the gap and the demand for her products grew rapidly. The government was not so foolish as to believe that this state of affairs would last for ever and that once the war was over European countries would not again dominate their own home and colonial markets and compete for exports. So they encouraged Japanese manufacturers to build up a dominant position during these years in selected areas, such as the Far East and South America. This policy proved successful and Japan was able to maintain a permanently increased share in those markets. The result was a massive growth in Japan's shipping tonnage, in her heavy industries, and in some consumption goods such as textiles. Moreover she had earned large sums by the supply of armaments and shipping services to her Allies.[1]

In many ways the Great War represented a watershed in the nation's economic history. Apart from the growth in volume of trade, the pattern changed also. In 1913 finished manufactures made up 29 per cent of all exports. By 1929 the figure had grown to 44 per cent, most of the growth being accounted for by exports to those underdeveloped countries which had been cultivated during the war years.[2] The pre-war situation had been adequately described by Mr Kentaro Kaneda:

> Japan has only one path to follow in her economic development. She must play the part of an underdeveloped country to the nations of the West to whom she must export those products which she alone produces. To the inferior countries of Asia she must export products she has made using the skills and machinery she has imported from the West.[3]

Post-war Japan began to play the part of a developed country to East and West alike. Exports of raw materials were overtaken by manufactured goods, although silk remained the single largest item.

Most importantly, Japan was transformed almost overnight from a debtor to a creditor country. In 1913 the total of foreign loans had stood at the huge figure of 1,941 million yen.[4] Many believed that the country was on the verge of bankruptcy and that more money would need to be borrowed to finance the annual interest payments of 130 million yen. The war completely off set this deficit and put Japan in a position where she could have redeemed both her domestic and her foreign loans and still have had 380 million yen in hand.[5] Moreover, the yen became the most stable currency among those of all the countries engaged in the war.

PROBLEMS OF TRADE FINANCE

The war also brought problems for Japan. Britain and France almost immediately placed an embargo on the export of specie, so that although Japan was earning huge trade surpluses in these countries she could not remit them home and the money piled up in London and Paris. The United States did not place an embargo on the export of gold until 1917 and the importance of New York to Japan as a centre for international transactions increased greatly. However, at the beginning of the war, between 80 and 90 per cent of Japan's foreign-exchange bills were still payable in London and all her export bills were dispatched thither. To complicate matters, bills of exchange could no longer be sent on the Trans-Siberian Railway. Accordingly, although Japan's export trade was booming, she was having the greatest difficulty in financing it. This problem weighed most heavily on the exchange banks which were unable to remit their earnings. Faced with consequent bankruptcy in their home accounts, they were forced to borrow. At the end of 1915 they had debts of 20 billion yen but by June 1918 440 billion yen had been advanced by the Bank of Japan to the Foreign exchange banks against their liabilities. To make matters worse, there were wide discrepancies in the rates of exchange obtainable in Japan and overseas which had the effect that the foreign exchange banks were paying higher interest than their customers. They had to resort to the loan-call market and invest in two- or four-month export bills at high interest rates, a business which was not always profitable.[6] Worse still, although Japan had been catapulted into the position of international creditor, neither her government nor her banks seemed able to invest their balances overseas in a sensible way. The Finance Minister, Junnosuke Inouye, ascribed this to their total inexperience in such matters. To use his own later words: 'old brandy was served in pint pots, beer in liqueur glasses'. Of the 1,000 million yen invested, very little went into long-term projects which would yield a permanent income. Indeed, a good deal of money went into further loans to China, more motivated by politics than sound financial sense.[7]

The government of Japan did little or nothing to curb or reconstruct this paradoxically unrewarding system of trade. Indeed, it continued to encourage it. The reason for this lay, no doubt, in the fact that Japan had for years been saddled with foreign debts and now saw a golden opportunity to pay them off. Inouye wrote that: 'She envisaged the dazzling prospect of a Japan which, after all these years of indigence, would be able to rank with the rest of the world as its financial equal.'[8] Consequently, the government was obliged for a long time to allow the blocked balances to accumulate in London and elsewhere and then took the step of taking over all the domestic debts of the exchange banks in return for payment in foreign currency abroad. By 1918 it had acquired 1,400 million yen's worth of foreign currency in this way.[9]

COUNCIL OF INDIA BILLS

Because, during the years before the war, Japan had become so dependent on London as the main centre for all its financial dealings, this sudden freezing of transactions was bound to cause the problems outlined above. But the state of affairs in London precipitated one further problem which was so acute for Japan that it deserves separate consideration. It concerned the export of cotton cloth to the markets of less developed countries. One of the main features of Japan's transformation had been the development of its cotton spinning and weaving, with India as the source of its raw material. From long before the outbreak of the war Japan had run a current account deficit with India owing to the scale of its imports of raw cotton from that country. Even the large increase in Japanese exports to India after 1914 could not reduce the figure to less than 100 million yen per annum. To cover this deficit Japan would purchase Council of India Bills on the London market. These bills were sold by the India Office to pay for such outlays as the interest on bond issues or the pensions of retired Indian Civil Service officials. Every Wednesday the required number of bills were auctioned off in London and the purchaser was allowed to cash them for rupees in Bombay, Calcutta, or Madras. Most of the bills were bought by exchange banks or trading companies who used them to pay for their imports from India.[10]

In December 1916 the British government placed severe restrictions on the sale of Council of India Bills, thus making it very difficult for Japan to finance the import of cotton, so vital to its industry. The Japanese appealed in vain to their British allies to relax these restrictions. It was therefore decided that the Yokohama Specie Bank should try to find other ways of financing this trade. However, it proved impossible to cover the costs of importing raw cotton by using the exchange facilities of third markets and the Yokohama Specie Bank was forced to divert gold to India from its transactions in Western Europe and the United States. The total value for January to September 1917 was 93,700,000 yen. Most of this gold was earned in the United States, and so, when that country itself imposed an embargo on the export of gold in 1917, Japan was once again in serious difficulties.[11]

Consideration was now given to buying the raw material itself from the United States, but the higher price of American cotton and the technical difficulties of adapting Japanese plant to using a different staple made such a solution undesirable. Nor could payment be made by floating bonds for the government of India in Tokyo, since the Indian market was already saturated with bonds. A proposal to ship silver from Shanghai also proved fruitless as India had already taken as much Chinese silver as she could absorb and the local value had fallen severely.

The solution finally adopted was one which reduced Japan's dependence on London while increasing her economic influence in East Asia. India had a considerable requirement for sugar and was suffering from a shortage of ships. It was therefore decided to purchase that part of the crop of Javanese sugar which was destined for India and to ship it in Japanese bottoms. At the same time the government instructed the Yokohama Specie Bank and the Bank of Taiwan to conduct a survey of the availability of export exchange for India in the Pacific Area. Eventually, these two banks were able to raise 80 million yen in this way with backing provided by the Bank of Japan. The initial remaining deficit was covered by the export of gold from Japan. After October 1917 the exchange proceeded in a balanced way without the need for further exports of specie.[12]

JAPANESE LOANS TO THE ALLIES

The rate at which the surpluses were piling up abroad accelerated steadily as the war went on. Since the European balances could not be moved, much thought was given by the government to alternative uses. Mr Eigo Fukai, the Chairman of the Bank of Japan, recalls in his memoirs that the authorities hit upon: 'A plan to issue bonds domestically and to use the money obtained thereby to purchase foreign capital from the exchange banks and to use that specie to redeem foreign loans.'[13] Such a plan had the additional merit of helping to solve the problem of the illiquidity of the exchange banks, as seen earlier in this chapter. The authorities announced on 1 April 1915 that it would be permissible to issue domestic bonds when necessary to redeem foreign bonds, choosing to raise the money for the exchange banks in this way. Railway bonds worth 40 million yen were then released in the home market. To ensure a satisfactory sale, a group of leading Japanese banks was called to the Bank of Japan and entrusted with the task.[14]

While Japan was addressing herself to the possibility of debt redemption, her European allies were going rapidly into the red. The tremendous costs of the war in Europe were already being felt and they were desperately short of capital. Now the tide had truly turned and Japan was to become not just a repayer of loans but a lender to her former creditors. Permission was given for certain allied governments to raise money by selling bonds in the

Japanese domestic market, the proceeds being made available from the overseas balances. The Russians were first into the field; in February 1916 they raised 50 million yen in Japanese currency bonds. Four more foreign issues followed, one of them for £10 million in July being the first loan ever made by the Japanese to the government of Great Britain. These first five issues raised 251 million yen for Russia, Britain, and France.[15]

These various ways of tapping the overseas balances could not keep up with the rate of accumulation, which accelerated again in the latter half of 1916. By the end of August holdings stood at 600 million yen but by the end of November the figure had risen to 1,700 million. This greatly aggravated the serious crisis because the government's practice of purchasing the specie from the exchange banks was releasing a flood of inflationary domestic paper. Since it was still legal to ship gold from America, attempts were made to repatriate the New York balances, but only 100 million yen could be moved before danger on the sea-lanes raised insuperable problems of security and insurance. The government now had no option but to rein in its purchases from the exchange banks. The Yokohama Specie Bank and the Bank of Japan were only able to pass less than half of the outstanding overseas balances to the Government.[16]

The Bank of Japan now made fresh proposals for a solution. The main feature was the suggestion that the rate of lending abroad should be greatly speeded up by increasing the sale of foreign bonds, both inside and outside Japan. One may wonder again why the Bank did not include a recommendation for loans to or direct investment in profitable foreign enterprises, but they judged this to be far too risky. Instead, Russia, Britain, and France, individually and together, were licensed to issue short-term yen bonds in Japan. At the same time, the law was changed to permit the government to issue its own short-term bonds and to use the proceeds to buy some of the new foreign bonds if the open market could not absorb them. These measures, and other internal reforms, soon brought the situation under control.

In December 1916 the British government sold bonds worth 1,000 million yen, denominated in Japanese currency. To handle this and other issues, the Bank of Japan encouraged the formation of a syndicate of Japanese banks around the Yokohama

Specie Bank – the mirror image, as it were, of the former London Group in the days when Japan was the borrower. What justified satisfaction this must have given to the Japanese banks. They were next approached by the French and the Russians, each with a request for 50 million yen. Between March 1917 and January 1918 there were five more issues of such bonds by the three governments, one for the Russian government (150 million yen) being covered by the sale of the Japanese government short-term bonds, while the British issue (80 million yen) was underwritten by the Ministry of Finance on the open market. By the end of the war, Japan had lent 626 million yen to its former creditors – 280 million yen to Britain, 126 million yen to France, and 222 million yen to Russia – much of which was to prove a poor return for the achievements of Japanese industry.[17]

Thus, a rather large part of Japan's wartime earnings were expended in loans to her allies. The original intention to devote them to redemption of the pre-war debt was never carried very far and only a small part was bought in. This may have been due to difficulty in matching the repayments with short-term domestic issues as originally planned. Instead, foreign borrowing from Japan transformed her into the second largest creditor nation after the United States and still left her with very sizeable foreign reserves of specie at the end of the war.

THE JAPANESE NATIONAL RESERVE

In accordance with the now long-established practice described at the beginning of chapter 6, all the foreign specie purchased by the Japanese government during the war went into the national reserve. As we have seen, at the outbreak of hostilities, two-thirds of this was still in London and the British government's refusal to allow these balances to be used for trade settlements with third countries, which led to the Japanese government's decision to allow as much of its foreign trade as possible to be invoiced in New York rather than London naturally had an enormous effect on Japan's subsequent relations with the City of London. Up to now the yen exchange rate had been based on sterling;

henceforth, it would be based on the US dollar. Its strength against sterling was now made dependent on the sterling–dollar rate.[18]

The embargo on the export of specie from London was further tightened up in 1916 but the United States only adopted similar regulations a year later. The situation naturally provoked a fundamental debate on whether, after the war, the national reserve should be held abroad at all. Of central concern was the inflationary effect that these balances had had on the money supply at home. Fukuda, one of the outstanding economists at this time, inveighed against the use of specie held outside the country to back the note issue and claimed that it contravened the Banknote Law. He used the analogy of a fish-paste salesman who treats the fish still swimming in the water as if they were already safely his own. Some others took a more favourable view. Kawatsu, a professor of economics at Tokyo University, argued that reserves held overseas were used for two purposes: not only to support the domestic currency but also to pay off debts incurred abroad. Therefore, they should be held in the most 'suitable' country. If Japan had a lot of debts to pay in London, then they should stay in London. However, later in 1919, he recognized the inflationary effects of the system and said that restrictions should be placed on the proportion of the reserves which could be used to secure the currency.[19]

The debate had to be resolved at the political level. The Minister of Finance, Junnosuke Inouye, shared the views of Kawatsu. In a lecture given to the Tokyo University of Commerce he declared that: 'Strictly speaking, the law says that all the specie should be held in the Bank of Japan, but there are instances when it might be placed in foreign markets.'[20] He went on to say, however, that the amount kept abroad in future should be only that required to meet international obligations. Prime Minister Hara, on the other hand, went far beyond this and noted in his diary for 15 October 1919 that specie abroad should not be used to secure the currency but should be reduced or abolished altogether.[21]

Quite apart from the problems which had been caused by the war, the underlying truth was that, with her favourable balance

of current account, Japan now no longer had to fear outflows of
gold and the problem of inflation had become much more important. The reasons which had led Matsukata to place the foreign
reserves in London in 1895 were therefore no longer valid and
the time had come for a change. This was initiated in May 1919
when it was announced that foreign and domestic long-term
bonds bought with specie held abroad could no longer be used to
secure the currency.[22] Later in that year the Bank of Japan put to
the Ministry of Finance a proposal to limit foreign backing for
the yen on the following grounds:

> During the War, for reasons of economic necessity, we did not
> apply a definite limit to the amount of specie held abroad, which
> could be used to secure the currency, but now that the War is
> over, not only have these reasons vanished [but] the indefinite
> increase in these holdings [has become undesirable].[23]

The Ministry of Finance accepted this conclusion and the suggestion that, henceforward, the amount of specie held in Britain and
the United States should not exceed 200,570,000 yen. The gold
in America should be deposited among the major banking houses
in such a way that it could be quickly withdrawn when necessary, while that in Britain should be deposited with the Anglo-
Dutch Bank, a recommendation that does not seem to have been
followed.

This is perhaps a convenient point at which to end the story of
Japan's reserves in London. The proportion of the nation's reserve held in America and Europe had already declined to only
36.5 per cent of the whole by the beginning of 1918, of which
London now accounted for a small part. After the decisions of
1919 this continued to fall steadily. Then in September 1922 the
Yokohama Specie Bank requested the Bank of England to invest
£9,700,000 of the reserve in long-term British government Securities, which meant that it no longer formed part of the currency
reserve. Until 1926 the average annual balance on the drawing
account with the Bank of England stood at £157,967. Thereafter
it declined annually until in 1938 it was only £5,674. Treasury
Bills followed a similar trend, falling from between £20 million
and £30 million in the years before 1926 to nil by 1937. A

special 'A' account, which had been opened in 1905 for undisclosed reasons, was unworked after 1937 and contained only £5,000 by the following year. On 26 July 1941, upon the occupation by Japan of bases in the southern part of French Indo-China, the remaining assets were frozen and were subsequently seized on the outbreak of war with Japan.[24]

Notes

1　G. C. Allen, *A Short Economic History of Modern Japan* (Macmillan, London, 1985), pp. 114–15.
2　Ibid.
3　Masanori Nakamura, Kiito to Gunkan in Rodosha to Nomin Vol 29 of Nippon no Rekishi (Shokakan, Tokyo, 1976), p. 88.
4　Junnosuke Inouye, *Problems of the Japanese Exchange 1914–1926* (Macmillan, London, 1931), p. 229.
5　Ibid., p.8.
6　Ibid., pp. 9–28.
7　Ibid.
8　Ibid., p. 26.
9　Ibid., p. 30.
10　*Nippon Ginko Hyakuneneshi*, Vol. II (Bank of Japan, Tokyo, 1984), p. 375.
11　Ibid., pp. 375–8.
12　Ibid., pp. 375–8.
13　Ibid., p. 364.
14　Ibid., p. 363.
15　Ibid., p. 364.
16　Ibid., p. 362.
17　Ibid., pp. 367–8.
18　Hikomatsu Kamikawa, *Japanese–American Cultural Relations in the Meiji-Taisho Era* (Pan-Pacific Press, Tokyo, 1958), pp. 464–78.
19　*Nippon Ginko Hyakuneneshi*, Vol. II, p. 548.
20　Ibid., p. 550.
21　Ibid., p. 553.
22　Ibid., pp. 550–3.
23　Ibid., p. 553.
24　Bank of England Archives.

8

BETWEEN TWO WARS
1918–1941

THE NEW BALANCE

As we saw in the preceding chapter, the 1914–18 War brought many changes, three of which were of importance to financial relations with Japan. First, international economic power had shifted away from Europe to the United States; second, the industrial capacity of Japan had greatly increased and enabled her to change from a debtor to a creditor country; third, Japan could no longer be successfully challenged as the dominant military and political power in Eastern Asia. All of these factors were reflected in the events of the post-war period.

One effect of the shift towards the United States had been that the exchange rate for the yen was tied to the dollar rather than to sterling (page 87). In 1919 the wartime agreement between the Allied governments on exchange controls expired. The British government ceased to control the sterling–dollar exchange rate through J. P. Morgan in New York. The London–New York exchange became free and was at first marked by a decline in the value of the pound. Japan responded by lowering the pound–yen rate in response to the dollar–sterling rate. London was not the only centre which had to take a back seat to New York; all the other European exchanges were affected in the same way. However, towards the end of 1924 the London Market began to recover and this tendency was reinforced by Britain's return to the Gold Standard on 28 April 1925. Thereafter there were two centres affecting the yen rather than one; exchange operations in

Tokyo looked to the New York–London cross-rate as the basis for all exchange transactions. Nevertheless, because of America's vast accumulation of capital and what the Japanese considered as it's sound monetary system, New York remained the principal influence on Japan's exchange policy.[1]

The effects of the second shift mentioned above were, from the Japanese point of view, disappointingly short-lived. Much of the wealth accumulated during the war had been dissipated by bad loans (in China and Russia in particular) and by lack of sensible overseas investment. In time the Europeans were able to compete successfully again for some of their former markets. In Japan weak financial policies, and the inflationary results of redeeming the wartime surpluses of the exchange banks, had their damaging effects. The great earthquake of 1923 added natural disaster to man-made burdens. Within five years Japan was once again seeking foreign loans.[2]

It was natural enough in the new circumstances that the main source of loans to Japan should now be New York. Between 1923 and 1931 twenty-seven foreign bond issues were made by the Japanese, of which eighteen were offered from New York and only nine from London. This same proportion was reflected in their total value: $535,580,000 in US dollars and £57,400,000 in sterling. In other words, more than twice as much was raised in New York as was raised in London, and this may be contrasted with the old days of the Russo-Japanese War Loans when every issue originated from London. It should also be noted that until 1924 Japan had never issued a single bond in US currency. These loans will be considered in detail in the next section of this chapter.[3]

The main effects of the shift in power in Eastern Asia are discussed in detail below (pp. 100–3). There was, however, one general political development which profoundly affected relations between Japan and Britain. The Peace Treaties at the end of the war had redistributed the German colonies under mandate and had accorded, to France and Britain, important mandates in the Middle East, but they also effectively marked the historic end of European colonial expansion. The new world was supposed to be that imagined by President Wilson – a world of the League of Nations and democratic brotherhood. The reality of Japan, with its expansionist ambitions in China, Manchuria, and throughout Eastern Asia, did not fit comfortably into this dream. When the Treaty of Washington was negotiated in 1922, Britain saw the new order which it envisaged as an excuse to abrogate the Anglo-Japanese Treaty. While some attempt was made to do this as politely as possible, the Japanese understandably found the bland excuses of the British very provoking. They began to see Britain as an officious, though impotent, obstacle to their plans in China and Manchuria, while Britain began to see their former 'plucky ally' as the 'bully of Asia'. Gone were the heady days of the Alliance in its prime. Financial dealings between the two countries had always been conducted on a strictly practical basis, but in the old days politics had helped at times to oil the wheels and iron out difficulties; now they would rather exacerbate any disagreement.

THE DECLINE OF THE LONDON MARKET AS LENDER TO JAPAN

Japan Government Loan of 1924

By 1919 the Allied Powers had started to return to their former export markets. In face of this competition Japan began to run a current account deficit again. In 1923 this rose to 5,269,263 yen and by 1925 the deficit was 22,131,254 yen.[4] At first the problem was addressed by exporting specie, but once holdings of foreign currency had slipped to 44 million yen, it was realized that other measures would be needed. Then on 1 September of that year a massive earthquake, followed by gigantic tidal waves and sweeping fires, struck the Kanto (Eastern) district of Honshu. Yokohama was totally destroyed and a large part of Tokyo also. The cost was estimated at 706 million yen, a bill which neither the government of Japan nor (even less) the City of Tokyo could hope to meet. Both authorities, therefore, went in search of foreign loans. The earthquake thus brought to a head a situation that had been developing for several years.

Given their conservatism and loyalty to old connections, the Japanese at first ignored the new financial pre-eminence of New

York, returned to the scene of their successful borrowings of twenty years earlier, and approached their former friends of the London Group. The composition was, however, changed. In 1918 Parr's Bank had merged with the London, County, and Westminster which, in 1923, was renamed as simply the Westminster Bank. This institution headed the new syndicate, which included all the old members, the Yokohama Specie Bank, the Hong Kong and Shanghai Banking Corporation, and Rothschilds. These were joined by Schroders, Morgan Grenfell, and Baring Brothers, this last now released by the Great October Revolution from their obligations to the former Tsarist government of Russia. Panmure Gordon were included as brokers to the renamed 'Enlarged London Group'.

The new group successfully raised the Japan government Loan, 1924 for £60 million. About £25 million (40 per cent) was placed in London and $150 million (60 per cent) in New York, though the whole amount was underwritten in London.[5] It was a dual-purpose loan. While some of it was used for financing reconstruction after the earthquake, a large part was used for redemption of earlier debt. *The Times Trade and Industry Supplement* for 16 February 1924 announced that about £36 million from this loan would be used for redemption of part of the two series of 4.5 per cent loans of 1905 which would fall due for payment in February and July of 1925.

The London tranche of this 1924 loan was sold at a discount of 13 per cent and an interest rate of 6 per cent, while the larger New York tranche was sold at a discount of only 7.5 per cent but at the enhanced interest rate of 6.5 per cent.[6] *The Times Supplement* concluded by saying: 'The American investor is not yet really anxious to invest his money abroad; hence the high yield offered to America and the American desire to have the European market open for the resale of holdings.'

There had indeed been a dispute about this question of resale and it had been made inadmissible for the dollar bonds to be sold on the London market. The best that the Americans were able to obtain was the right to resell some of their bonds in Switzerland and Holland. Yet, in spite of the obstacles, when the government of Japan proceeded to raise further loans in 1925 and 1926, the issues were made in New York. This is particularly surprising when one considers the popular success of the 1924 loan in London of which *The Times Supplement* had noted: 'Japanese currency policy had been sound and skilfully managed ... Japanese loans [were] popular with the British investor ... the response was immediate and the London lists were closed after only two hours.'

The reason for this switch to New York was the distinctly sour attitude which the British authorities had meanwhile adopted towards the attempts of the City of Tokyo to raise more money for earthquake reconstruction.

City of Tokyo Loan

The Municipality of Tokyo had in fact approached the London Group even before the government of Japan with a request for a loan of £10 million for reconstruction. Sensing that a municipal loan might receive less enthusiastic backing than a government loan, the Group had advised the Japanese Financial Commissioner, Mr Kengo Mori, to postpone his application until the full amount of the damage had been substantiated and costed.[7] By the time this had been done the Japan Government Loan, 1924 had already been placed and the Bank of England was implacably opposed to any further loan to Japan in the same year. There followed a saga in which the characters suffered much anxiety, frustration, and resentment.

The difficulties encountered by the lenders were described in a letter dated 7 May 1924 from Mr Alan Cameron, Senior Partner at Panmure Gordon, to Mr John Rae of the Westminster Bank:

> Our mutual friend saw the Governor today, and had an opportunity to sound him out on the question of a Tokyo loan ... It appears that the Governor expressed himself quite strongly on the subject and was quite opposed to it for a number of reasons.[8]

Indeed, the Governor, Sir Montagu Norman, who had grave doubts about the economic situation in Japan, used such sharp terms that Cameron was unwilling to put them in writing and preferred to give a toned-down version orally to Mr Mori, adding: 'I have left the more sensational details to Addis [*Charles Addis of the Hong Kong and Shanghai Banking Corporation*].' Commenting on these events in a letter to Cameron from Tokyo on 15 April the following year, Mori wrote that the city of Tokyo's motto had traditionally been 'London first, New York after', but that

> When you and your friends found the Governor of the Bank of England adamant last autumn in spite of your repeated efforts to promote our wishes, the Municipality and even some of my friends began to think of an American issue.[9]

He concluded that although it was unlikely that the Americans would secure the deal he feared that irreparable harm had been done to relations with the City of London.

Japanese feelings were also upset by a new feature arising from difficulties in the London capital markets. The practice had developed of insisting on 'special security' for all foreign loans. *The Times* noted complacently: 'Some governments are rather sensitive about giving special security; they apparently think that it is derogatory to their credit to do so. This is an illusion.' Mori took a very different view. In a confidential memorandum to Cameron on 26 January 1926 he declared that his government could not and would not negotiate any special security. He threatened to withdraw from the negotiations and expressed disgust at the reluctance of the British banks to underwrite more than £11 million.[10]

In the end the loan was sanctioned by the Bank of England and launched in June 1926, but for very much less than Mori had wanted. The terms were £6 million, offered at a discount of 16.5 per cent and at 5 per cent rate of interest. The *Morning Post* for 10 June noted:

> There can be little doubt that the [City of Tokyo] Loan will be well received by investors in view of the attractive terms on which it is offered and the high standing deservedly enjoyed by Japanese loans in this country.

The newspaper proved right and the issue was a popular success, showing once again the wide rift between the government's view and the public's view of Japan's credit.

Utility Loans

Apart from the City of Tokyo, the main Japanese entities other than the central government to raise money abroad during these years were the large electricity companies. Their installations had suffered great damage during the earthquake. At the same time, the demand for power was rising much faster than the supply of domestic capital for its generation. Between 1920 and 1929, the total generating capacity rose from 1,378 kilowatts to 4,194 kilowatts. Well over half of this was in hydroelectric power (69 per cent in 1925) requiring a huge infrastructural investment.[11] The industry was therefore obliged to have recourse to the foreign capital markets in New York and London. Nevertheless, all these transactions were carefully monitored by the Japanese government, and one may see here a clear case of the practice of administrative guidance whereby other utilities and agencies were (not forbidden but) dissuaded from following the example of the electricity industry. As reported by the Commercial Counsellor of the British Embassy: 'The Japanese Treasury will as a general rule discourage such transactions with substantially the same effect as a positive restriction.'[12]

There was now a spate of such loans over the next few years – for example: Daido Electric Co. ($15 million at 7 per cent in 1924), Toho Electric Power Co. ($15 million at 7 per cent in 1925), Ujikawa Electric Co. ($14 million at 7 per cent in 1925), Daido Electric Co. again ($13.5 million at 6.5 per cent in 1925), Toho Electric Co. again ($10 million at 6 per cent in 1926). Exceptionally, the Industrial Bank of Japan ($22 million at 6 per cent in 1924) and the City of Yokohama (1927) were allowed to join the stream of electrical undertakings. Most of the money was raised in New York but several of the issues were placed in both London and New York.[13] Schroders, conscious of its role as the first bank ever to raise money for the Japanese government (see chapter 3) was particularly active in this field. It arranged the Daido Electric Co. loan of 1924 and £1.5 million in 7 per cent

Gold Certificates for Nippon Electric Power in 1930.[14] British firms also joined in the creation of the Japanese Electric Bond and Share Company in New York in 1926 with the participation of Lazards, the Whitehall Trust Co. and Messrs Sale and Co. of London.

The End of Japanese Borrowing

The Japanese government continued to raise money abroad until the end of the decade. In 1929, Japan returned to the Gold Standard and $120 million was raised in New York to stabilize the yen. The only London bank to participate was Schroders, which subscribed for £5 million.[15] In April 1930 the Japanese government raised, in London, its last foreign loan of the inter-war period. This was to cover the 4 per cent sterling loans of 1905, which were due for repayment on 1 January 1931. Since the Paris market was now closed to such transactions, the whole amount, including that portion which had originally been raised in France, was placed in London and New York.[16]

For several years the Japanese government had been increasingly reluctant to sanction further foreign loans. As early as the end of 1925 the British Commercial Counsellor in Tokyo had reported: 'It is understood that there is very little likelihood of Tokyo or any other municipality being authorized to make further borrowings.'[17] As sometimes happens, the British Embassy was wrong (city of Tokyo, 1926; city of Yokohama, 1927) but it had recognized a genuine trend. By 1930, with the onset of the Great World Depression, the government had concluded that the service of such loans placed too great a strain on the economy. There was no further foreign borrowing by the government and the last loan to a Japanese corporation was for the South Manchurian Railway in 1933. Those agencies which continued to hanker for foreign capital were warned in November 1935 by the Minister of Finance, Mr Hamaguchi, that they should not: 'disturb the Government's efforts towards the consolidation of financial and economic conditions and the improvement of the trade balance'.[18] Thenceforward, the build-up to the Second World War was to be financed entirely by the local economy.

Banking and Investment

It was during the First World War that the term *zaibatsu* first came to be widely used to describe the conglomerate trading, manufacturing, and commercial concerns, usually based on family holdings and control, such as Mitsui, Mitsubishi, Yasuda, and Sumitomo. The term is made up of two characters: *zai*, connoting 'wealth', and *batsu*, connoting 'group' or 'estate'. Although these groupings often had their origins in the early years of the Meiji period or even, as in the case of Mitsui, from long before 1868, it was only during the 1914–18 war and after it that the term came into accepted general use and was applied to a recognized number of groupings.[19] During the wartime boom period the strength of these combines was obviously greatly increased and, since each group had its own banking component, the financial power of the *zaibatsu* banks was also enlarged.

This growth in size and confidence was particularly marked in the case of the Mitsui Bank. It was now in a position to transform its 'correspondent' status (see p. 69) into the establishment of overseas branches. It opened a branch in New York in 1924 and one in London in 1926, this sequence of choice naturally reflecting the comparative importance of New York and London in Japanese eyes. Its example was soon followed by Yasuda and other competitors and by the end of the inter-war period there were four such Japanese banks with branches in London. These ventures were of a totally different nature from the branches long-since established in colonial or semi-colonial territories such as Taiwan, Korea, or Manchuria, or in 'spheres of influence' in China. They marked the first appearance of Japanese private-sector banks as genuine international operators. Their principal source of revenue was the underwriting of Japanese foreign bond issues. For example, in 1928 the Mitsui Bank was sole underwriter for the debentures of the Tokyo Electric Power Co., at that time the largest bond issue ever yet floated by a foreign private corporation on the American market.

Other Japanese banks which notably extended their activity at this time were the Sumitomo Bank, with new branches in

London, New York, India, and China, and the Bank of Taiwan, which became an important vehicle for growing Japanese interest in South East Asia.[20] The development of Japanese banking in London, however, soon came to a stop. The end of Japanese overseas borrowing, recession, the increasingly autarchic nature of the Japanese economy, and the growing prospect of a world war all damped down the activities of the branches. Not long after the outbreak of the conflict, without waiting for their own country to become engaged, the Japanese banks all closed their branches in London, Mitsui claiming for example that this was due to the inconvenience of German bombing.

Meanwhile, throughout this period, the 'marginalization', of British banking activity in Japan continued. In view of the great increase in strength of their Japanese rivals this was hardly surprising and the pace of decline was accelerated. Whereas before 1914 the British banks had only been losing their proportional share of the market, they were now losing business in absolute terms. However, there were still useful pickings. The Hong Kong and Shanghai Banking Corporation, for example, continued to play an important role in the financing of the silk trade, particularly for exports to the United States. Whereas in the past it had always conducted its activities through branches in the former Treaty Ports, in 1924 it considered it worth its while to open a branch in Tokyo from which it was able to finance a profitable trade to some areas where the Yokohama Specie Bank had not yet established a presence. Some of the trading companies also managed to swim against the tide and the chemical firm of Brunner Mond conducted a large business for the import of chemicals in the early twenties.[21]

Although the end of the 1914–18 war offered foreigners the opportunity to invest in Japan, following on the pre-war relaxation of the rules about foreign investment described in chapter 6 (p. 70), few foreign companies availed themselves of the opportunities. As from earliest Meiji times, Japan remained for foreign investors a loan economy rather than an equity economy. This was particularly true for the British. Whereas the Americans, led by the Ford Motor Factory in Yokohama and the General Motors Factory at Osaka, had built up an investment of $40.3

million in the manufacturing sector by 1929, British ventures
were few and far between. Dunlop's rubber business continued
and in 1927 the British company, Columbia Gramophone, took
over a Japanese rival named Nippophone. But the British armaments manufacturers referred to in chapter 6 were now trying to
cut their losses, although circumstances compelled them to hold
on until 1941. An unhappy case was that of Babcock and Wil-
cox, whose efforts to sell their investment in Japan and remit the
proceeds back to Britain were frustrated by the Japanese authorities who repeatedly refused exchange control permission. Such
incidents tended to convince British entrepreneurs that Japan was
a bad place in which to invest.[22]

CHINA AND MANCHURIA

It was noted in the last chapter that some of the Japanese wartime profits were put into loans to China. These loans often had
a clearly political content and were designed to extend Japanese
influence in that country. A striking example were the so-called
'Nishihara Loans' to the Anfu warlords, the majority of which
could never have stood much chance of repayment. In December
1916 the Japanese government had encouraged the formation
of a consortium made up of the Bank of Taiwan, the Bank of
Korea, and the Industrial Bank of Japan for the purpose of
'seeking means to enhance diplomatic relations by advancing
loans on preferential terms and thereby to make a profit for
ourselves'.[23] The last few words sound like rather an after-
thought. Whereas the first loan (for the reorganization of China's
transport and communications systems) was reasonably successful, subsequent ones took on a more political character, so that
in 1918 the Japanese government was obliged to guarantee them
and draft more banks into the consortium. During the wartime
Cabinet of Marshal Terauchi (1916–18) loans from Japan to
China exceeded 200 million yen.

All of this had been quite at variance with the Wilsonian
world-view, which held the old 'Imperial System' to be outmoded
and unjust. In a letter to American bankers of 9 July 1918, the
State Department wrote:

This war has brought the countries of Great Britain, France, Japan, the United States and some others into a state of harmony and helpfulness and has supplemented an intense spirit of competition by a spirit of mutuality and cooperation.[24]

This sentiment may be seen more as one of aspiration than of reality, but it was translated into the Treaty of Washington which specifically set out, *inter alia*, to replace the network of bilateral treaties and spheres of influence in China by a single all-inclusive agreement.

The Japanese view was a very different one. They had expended a great deal of money and military effort in winning for themselves spheres of influence in China and particularly in Manchuria. The phrase 'blood of our fathers' was a favourite cliché used at this time, when discussing the matter. The Japanese government therefore demanded that regions of special importance to themselves, namely Manchuria and Eastern Mongolia, be excluded from the new system. The Americans were obliged to point out, in a memorandum dated 11 August 1920, that

> the admission of such a claim to a monopoly of commercial interests in a large geographical area of China would be a direct infringement of the fundamental idea [that] ... spheres of influence should be abolished ...[25]

To resolve this dispute the Americans now proposed to resurrect the China Consortium. The preface to the Bank of England report on the New China Consortium remarks that:

> The United States had withdrawn from the old consortium in March 1913 and the revival of its interest in 1918 is to be explained by the way in which Japan's new financial ascendancy was encouraging a reckless flow of capital to China to the detriment of the existing creditor nations.[26]

From the point of view of Britain the financial implications were marginal. Whereas the pre-war consortium had limited Britain's financial opportunities in China to the benefit of the Japanese, she was now hardly in a position to invest any further. Indeed, during the Washington Treaty negotiations, it was suggested that the United States and Japan might have to take sole financial responsibility for future development in China and it was only on American insistence that Britain and France were included.[27]

In any case, the New China Consortium was never destined to become effective. The Kuomintang government took the line that it represented an infringement of Chinese sovereignty and while they were prepared to negotiate loans from individual members, they would not treat with the Consortium as a whole. Furthermore, aggressive Japanese policies in China had brought about a dramatic political crisis. A Foreign Office memorandum of 17 April 1931 noted: 'In any event, Mr Chun [*the Chinese Minister responsible*] was quite clear that China would not submit to borrowing from a consortium which included Japan.'[28] From then on Japan pursued its own path towards war with China, while further British investment in the country became a relatively minor matter.

Japan's policies were hard on the British and other foreign companies operating in Manchuria. A particularly flagrant case was that of the local oil industry which had been developed by the Anglo-Dutch Asiatic Oil Company and the American Standard Vacuum Oil Company. By the Oil Monopoly Law of 14 November 1934 the industry was reserved to local organizations controlled by Japan. Other foreign companies obliged to leave were the Jardine Engineering Group and Siemens of Germany. The foreign banks found their activities consistently impeded and were almost solely reduced to lending to official Japanese enterprises. By 1940 only three of them remained—the National Bank of New York, the Chartered Bank of India, Australia, and China at Harbin and the Hong Kong and Shanghai Bank at Dairen. This last was a particular target for victimization. Bank of England records state that when Mr Foulds of the Foreign Office approached the Governor of the Kwantung Leased Territory on 5 July 1938: 'Mr Miura, while denying the existence of any discrimination against the Hong Kong and Shanghai Banking Corporation ... scarcely disguises the intentions of the local authorities to continue an obviously discriminatory policy.'

No co-operation was possible in the climate of hostility that had by now developed between Japan and Britain in China.

RECESSION AND ISOLATION IN JAPAN

The Great Depression which began in 1929 brought about profound changes in Japan. Hitherto, it had seemed to many foreigners that, for sixty years, Japan had been steadily acquiring the institutions and the attitudes of a modern democratic state. The recent war had even strengthened this aspect of Japanese life; the fact that the democracies had achieved a total victory while autocratic regimes in Germany and Russia had been defeated, had encouraged the belief of many Japanese in the virtues and strength of democracy. But underneath, old traditions, values, ambitions, and resentments had remained with a large part of the population and were to come rapidly to the surface under the strains of poverty and unemployment.

After the crash, Japanese production fell by 7 per cent and exports by no less than 47 per cent in value. Two million workers were laid off and the condition of the peasantry (still a majority of the population) was depressed.[29] There was deep resentment that such hardship could apparently be caused by events far away on Wall Street. The sense of isolation and indignation was increased by the tariffs which other countries began to impose on Japanese exports, particularly of textiles. There was unrest in the Army, where radical officers banded together to throw out foreign ideologies and return to Japan's sacred heritage. In 1930 they attempted to assassinate Prime Minister Hamaguchi, and a number of 'weak' politicians, including Viscount Takahashi, were murdered by them in the following years. At the same time the army in China and Manchuria began to pursue a more or less independent policy which led to the expulsion of Chinese forces from Manchuria in 1931, the formation of the puppet state of Manchukuo, and eventually full-scale war with China after the incident at the Marco Polo Bridge.

In the domestic field, successive Cabinets moved steadily towards the economic autarchy which Hitler was practising in

Europe. This state of economic isolation is well expressed in a statement by Mr Takauji of the Japanese Financial Commission on 23 January 1935:

> Now all the countries of the world are striving for the adjustment of their individual economy, fortifying the trading bulwarks more and more [and] we cannot expect international cooperation in the field of currency and exchange problems.[30]

The British Empire, the United States, France, Switzerland, and others entered into a series of separate, mutual currency agreements which left the Japanese even more isolated, and prompted them to form a 'yen block'. While this was effective in Taiwan, Korea, Manchuria, and Mongolia, it made no advance in China where the sterling-based currency (the *Fapi*) continued to hold sway.

A currency dispute between Japan and Britain was caused in 1939 by the Japanese practice of financing their imports of wool from Australia and cotton from India by the sale of dollars for sterling in London. The British considered that this was upsetting the sterling–dollar exchange rate. Fortunately, a reservoir of good will was still available and the matter was settled by persuading the Japanese to ship to the Bank of England the gold which had formerly been sent to New York for the purchase of dollars.[31]

Anxiety about the effect of yen movements on the dollar–sterling rate continued to plague the British authorities. On 23 November 1939 the Westminster Bank reported to the Bank of England that Japanese sterling resources held in London had declined by £3,750,000 while in the same period their credit balances and holdings of British government securities had dropped by £4 million. However, the remaining balances were now so small that the problem could not arise again. On the other hand, the Japanese were still earning regular trade surpluses with the sterling block and spending them in the dollar block, thus hampering the efforts of the British government to stabilize the pound. The ill feeling which this aroused was expressed in a Bank of England report of 20 March 1940 which stated: If Japan refuses to come to terms regarding the use of sterling or to negotiate a sterling area payment [agreement], all those credit facilities can be cancelled and Japan declared a hard-currency area.'

Against this general trend of deteriorating official relations, many British banks and trading houses managed to maintain good working relations in the City with their Japanese contacts. The short-term credit rating of Japan on the London Market remained high for most of this period. This was still the result of the good experience which many London houses had enjoyed in dealing with Japan over the decades. Many merchant banks were most unwilling to distance themselves from Japan. The British government had to reprimand the Mercantile Bank of India severely for conducting foreign exchange transactions on behalf of the Japanese in a manner directly contrary to stated official policy.[32]

The fact was that by the end of the 1930s the protection of British interests in China from Japanese aggression and the granting and withholding of exchange and credit facilities for Japan had become inextricably linked in the dealings of the authorities. While the British were not as emotive as the Americans in wishing to 'punish' the Japanese for their action in China, they tended to waver between putting pressure on them and keeping the door open for them, according to the relative urgency of political, commercial, or financial events. Somewhat surprisingly, in the early stages of friction, one finds the Foreign Office taking the more commercial line in the debate. Thus, in a Memorandum of 25 November 1934, we read:

> Accordingly it seems desirable to seek such other means of relieving tension as would lie altogether outside the scope of the Sino-Japanese dispute ... The least uncompromising we have at present lie in the commercial and economic field.[33]

By contrast, a Labour MP, Mr Price, demanded on 1 August 1934 that London houses be stopped from importing Japanese woollen goods by the restriction of credit for Japan.[34] The intensification of the war in China strengthened such demands and political considerations became uppermost. By the outbreak of the Second World War the Treasury was taking a thoroughly political line. A Mr Hopkins, writing from Treasury Chambers on 10 January 1940, says:

> There is very little reason to hope that such financial facilities would produce any real improvement in Japanese treatment of our interests in China, while the grant of these additional facilities would be strongly resented by the Chinese Government and, what is even more important, by the United States.[35]

Only the Board of Trade had questioned the logic of the debate by pointing out, in a Memorandum of 12 July 1939, that Japanese acceptances in the City of London amounted to only some £500,000: 'Interference with this relatively small sum would have quite disproportionate repercussions on Japan's purchasing power.'[36] This process provides a foretaste of the difficulty of protecting British interests overseas in the face of waning political and military power in the area concerned, a problem which would become world-wide for Britain in the decades after the Second World War. That war had already started and Japan would soon be involved. In the last months before this happened, commercial and financial exchanges shrivelled away. As we have already seen (p. 99), the four private Japanese banks had closed their London branches before the end of 1940, leaving their affairs in the hands of the Yokohama Specie Bank. In Tokyo the British banks were finding it increasingly difficult to operate, not perhaps so much because of official discrimination as because of an unwillingness on the part of Japanese companies to do business with them. Japan was committed to its Tripartite Pact with Germany and Italy and there was a growing sense of hostility. By April 1941 the annual turnover in Japan of the Hong Kong and Shanghai Banking Corporation had fallen from 30 to 40 million yen to a rate of less than 500,000 yen. The manager, a Mr Grayburn, wrote: 'I only speak for the Hong Kong and Shanghai Banking Corporation of course, but considering all we have done for Japan in the past, their treatment of us now is nothing short of insulting.'[37]

One of the last recorded exchanges between British and Japanese before Pearl Harbour illustrates all too well the angry frustration of the former and the reluctance to help of the latter.

Mr Hancock of the Hong Kong and Shanghai Bank had been instructed to complain to a Japanese official about being forced to give up yen funds in return for Japanese government loans. He asked, 'Do you wish us to help finance Japan's imports and exports or do you not?' and received the following reply from Ito (through an interpreter): 'Yes, we would like you to carry on, but if you do not comply with our regulations we will have to take you to court.'[38]

Notes

1 Hikomatsu Kamikawa, *Japanese–American Relations in the Meiji-Taisho Era* (Pan-Pacific Press, Tokyo, 1958), pp. 464–78.
2 G. C. Allen, *A Short Economic History of Modern Japan* (Macmillan, London, 1985), pp. 100–6.
3 Thomas Adams and Iwao Hoshii, *A Financial History of Modern Japan* (Research Japan Ltd., Tokyo, 1964), p. 81.
4 Junnosuke Inouye, *The Problems of the Japanese Exchange* (Macmillan, London, 1931), p. 223.
5 Nat West Achives.
6 Ibid.
7 Ibid.
8 Ibid.
9 Ibid.
10 Ibid.
11 Allen, *A Short Economic History of Modern Japan*, p. 117.
12 Bank of England Archives.
13 Schroders Archives.
14 *The Times* (21 Dec. 1926).
15 Schroders Archives.
16 Nat West Archives.
17 Bank of England Archives.
18 Ibid.
19 *The Japan Encyclopaedia*, Vol. 8 (Kodansha, Tokyo, 1988), p. 361.
20 *Banking in Modern Japan* (Fuji Bank Ltd., Tokyo, 1967), pp. 95–103.
21 R. P. T. Davenport-Hines and Geoffrey Jones (Draft MS kindly provided by the authors).
22 Ibid.
23 Bank of England Archives.

24 Bank of England Archives.
25 Ibid.
26 Ibid.
27 Ibid.
28 Ibid.
29 G. C. Allen, *Japan, the Hungry Guest* (Allen and Unwin, London, 1938), p. 134.
30 Bank of England Archives.
31 Ibid.
32 Ibid.
33 Ibid.
34 Ibid.
35 Ibid.
36 Ibid.
37 Ibid.
38 Ibid.

PART II

1946–1988

GENERAL COMMENT

This book is about the financial relationship between Britain and Japan. For eighty years, from 1859 until 1939, this can be seen as 'a special relationship'. After 1945, however, it becomes very much more difficult to confine the subject-matter to just Britain and Japan. This is not simply due to the severe shrinkage of British economic power, since this was eventually offset by the regrowth of the City of London as a financial centre. It is due, in the first place, to the gradual 'globalization' of markets and their increasing integration into twenty-four-hour world-wide processes. In the second place, much of the interest consists in the creation or invention of new financial institutions, instruments, communications, or practices and, though many of these may have originated in London or Tokyo, it does not make sense to consider them in isolation. Nevertheless, in the belief that British people engaged in financial dealings with Japan, and Japanese people in a similar relationship with Britain, have a special interest in knowing about their mutual links and problems, we shall embark on this narrow path which sometimes skirts around the edge of events and sometimes plunges through the middle of them.

9

OUT OF THE ASHES
1945–1953

JAPAN IN 1945

When the Emperor Hirohito took it upon himself to declare the surrender of Japan on 15 August 1945, his capital lay largely in ashes. Two cities, Hiroshima and Nagasaki had been virtually obliterated by atom bombs and the nation's resources of food, materials, and energy were exhausted. The population was on the edge of starvation and inflation was raging. Although a fair part of the country's industrial plant was still intact, much of it had been geared to war production and the creation of a new peace-time economy would be a tremendously difficult task.

Alongside these physical difficulties, Japan found itself economically and politically in a quite new situation. The immediate concern of its leaders in the Meiji period and the inter-war years had been to establish Japan's total political independence and then its domination of Eastern Asia. The creation of a powerful, modern economy had been chiefly a means to those objectives. But in 1945 political independence had been replaced by foreign occupation and the United States and the Soviet Union had emerged as two world super powers which Japan could not possibly have envisaged equalling. As for the dominance of Eastern Asia, all the gains of earlier fighting – Taiwan, Korea, Manchukuo, China, the 'Asian Co-prosperity Sphere' – had been swept away and with them the hundreds of millions of yen invested there. It followed that the future would have to be along quite new lines. Certainly, the nation must be rebuilt as an economic rather than a military society. Quite soon a consensus began to emerge that effort should no longer, as in the past, be devoted to the production of cheap goods but to the creation of an advanced industrial society, respected by the outside world. As early as October 1945, still in the year of defeat, Mr Noda, President of the Japan Cotton and Silk Trading Company, was quoted as saying: 'When we participate in world trade again, it will not be on a recklessly competitive basis. We shall try to make better quality goods and to remain within the bounds of international cooperation.'[1] Noda was not alone in putting forward such views. A remarkable group of industrial leaders quickly emerged to pursue this policy. Many of them belonged to a generation of men who had been in their thirties when Japan began to develop its policy of isolation after the 1929 crash and had little experience of foreign contacts or languages. Nevertheless, it would be their lot to put Japan back on the international map. In their discussions within their own groupings, in the Keidanren and in the Nikkeiron, and in their contacts with their successive governments, they planned and achieved the new Japan. The country was extraordinarily fortunate to have produced such people. It was with them that British businessmen and bankers would have to deal in the coming years.

THE AMERICAN OCCUPATION

When the Americans entered Japan in 1945, their plans for its future were not altogether different from those for the future of Germany. Japan was to become 'an Asian Switzerland', bereft of both the means and the inclination to wage war. In both countries these plans were quite soon dropped. The development of the Cold War called for a prosperous Germany and a prosperous Japan. Hungry and disorientated populations would be an easy target for Communism and it was vital to give them a sense of purpose and optimism as a prophylactic against the red measles. In the case of Japan this became particularly urgent as Mao Tse-tung proceeded to overwhelm America's ally, Chiang Kaishek. Equally cogently, the US Treasury was not willing for long to meet the cost of feeding these populations; they must be enabled to earn their own living. For Japan, with its chronic deficits of food, raw-materials, and energy, this would require a strong exporting economy.

Before the country was yet firmly set on this path the American occupation authorities (collectively referred to as Supreme Commander Allied Powers or SCAP) had exacted retribution through war-crimes trials and had carried out fundamental reforms of politics and society. These included a change in the status of the Emperor, reconstruction of the parliamentary system and the civil service, and reform of education and agricultural landholding. Two of them were of special importance to the future development of financial institutions.

The first such reform was the intended break-up of the *zaibatsu*. 'Trust-busting' was, of course, an essential part of twentieth-century American history and equally part of their policy for the Free World. Just as they insisted on a programme of Deconcentration and Decartelization in Western Germany, so they proceeded to dismantle the concentrations of economic power in Japan. Family control was removed, the constituent elements in the groupings were made independent, and safeguards were set up to prevent one company from re-acquiring others. In particular, the banks were removed from identity with the industrial groups.

This reform was satisfactory on paper but it overlooked deeply ingrained Japanese characteristics of loyalty to associates, and the need for strong and enduring bonds in business relationships and for common decision-making. It also ignored the fundamental role of Japanese banking as the nation's main supplier of enterprise capital. Little by little, and more overtly after the termination of the occupation, the old elements of the former *zaibatsu* began to drift together again, in each case around the related bank. The new associations came to be known as *Keiretsu*. The word is made up of *Kei*, connoting 'group' or 'faction', and *retsu*, connoting 'ranking' or 'order'. These *Keiretsu* differ from the old groups in several important ways. First, family control has been largely eliminated, though it is still of importance in certain individual companies. Second, cohesion is ensured by a multiplicity of cross-holdings in the shares of the companies, today usually of 5 per cent or less[2] in each case but sufficient within the group as a whole to secure control against outsiders; such a structure resembles a net rather than a pyramid. Third, group policy results from regular meetings of the nominally equal Presidents of the member companies, rather than from a hierarchy. As far as the associated banks are concerned, they are able to retain a great part of the autonomy which came to them from the dismemberment of the *zaibatsu*.

A second important change introduced by SCAP was designed to separate banking and investment on the lines of American law. Based on the Glass Steagall Act of 1933, the reform was carried out by Article 65 of Japan's Securities and Exchange Law of 1948. Under this legislation banks are forbidden to take part in the Japanese securities industry and may not hold more than 5 per cent of a securities company. They may not sell equity nor underwrite equity issues in Japan. Conversely, the securities companies are forbidden to lend or take deposits within Japan. Further, the insurance industry was separated from the securities industry. However, it can be no surprise that each major *Keiretsu* today will include one major 'city bank' and one of the major security houses, still legally separated by Article 65 but loosely linked by the practice of the group, as well as an insurance company. It will be seen later how this structure was to become reflected in Japanese activity in the City of London.

The decision of the US government to rebuild the Japanese economy began to take effect in 1949. In that year Joseph M. Dodge, a Detroit banker, took over the Finance Division of SCAP. He severely reduced spending, thereby bringing inflation under control and providing stable conditions for development. This was slow at first, but in 1950 the Korean War broke out and Japan's position as the forward base for the United Nations forces attracted to it heavy military expenditure by the United States and the placing there of large orders for supplies. At SCAP the strengthening of Japan's industrial, commercial, and financial condition was relentlessly pursued, taking care only that no harm should be done to the United States itself. The interests in Japan of the allies in the recent war were ignored or swept aside. This would cause problems for the British, both in banking and trade, which will be discussed below. On 8 September 1951 the Treaty of San Francisco was signed. Its ratification by the signatories put an end to the state of war with Japan and terminated the Occupation in the following year. SCAP gave up its powers, but Japan was now able to look after itself as well or better than most of the victors of the war.

THE REPAYMENT OF JAPAN'S PRE-WAR LOANS

The first question to be raised in the City of London as soon as the war was ended was whether or not Japan could be made to honour its pre-war obligations. Even before the fighting was over, but when the outcome was clear enough, the banks were considering the matter. A Baring Brothers memo of 18 August 1945 put the question: 'If it has not already been done, would it not be desirable to remind H. M. Treasury of the Japanese Loans outstanding in London and the arrears thereon?'[3] The memorandum went on to point out that the Yokohama Specie Bank was no longer functioning. With the old London Group in mind, it suggested that its two leading members, the Westminster Bank and the Hong Kong and Shanghai Banking Corporation, might handle the arrangements for repayment.

When the state of these loans could be looked into at the end of the war it was found that the Japanese financial authorities had acted with meticulous probity. Interest payments had been made promptly right up to Japan's declaration of war in 1941, leaving the amount now outstanding for the ensuing period at £4,943,000. As for the capital, in 1943 the Japanese had passed a 'Law Pertaining to the Treatment of Japanese Bonds'. That part of the loans which was in the name of domestic or 'Axis-country' investors was exchanged for yen-denominated bonds. The remainder was presumed to belong to enemy creditors. The value of these bonds was paid in yen to a Special Property Administration Account with the Yokohama Specie Bank. The British element amounted to £90 million.[4] The Japanese government acknowledged its responsibility for paying the interest thereon. There was no challenge to the claims of the bond-holders by SCAP or by anyone else in Japan. Repayment should have provided no problem once Japan was again in a position to pay.

Nevertheless, when the London banks approached the Chancellor of the Exchequer on behalf of the British creditors to whom they were responsible, Dr Hugh Dalton was almost abusive. He told them: 'If there is anything to be screwed out of the Japanese, there is a long list of stronger claimants than the pre-war owners of Japanese bonds.'[5] The government was, in fact, considering suggestions (never realized) to exact large-scale reparations from the former Axis powers and to oblige the Japanese to pay one dollar to every allied prisoner for each day of his captivity. Some Labour MPs condemned the 'greedy capitalists' who had purchased bonds and suggested that it was unpatriotic for any British subject to have held Japanese bonds, the implication being that the proceeds might ultimately have gone to finance Japan's recent war effort. The press, however, strongly criticized the Chancellor for his comments.[6] They reminded their readers that the original holders of these bonds had purchased them at a time when Japan was a close ally of Britain. To reject the obligation to present holders was against the national interest. The war had stripped Britain of most of her overseas assets and foreign bonds were an important part of the few that remained. By refusing to champion the bond-holders, the Chancellor was almost inviting the Japanese to default. As if to prove the validity of this argument, the London bond market immediately wiped £5 million off the value of all foreign paper.[7] Hugh Dalton, however, refused to withdraw his remarks and when questioned in Parliament, stated that the bond-holders had been unwise.[8] He did not explain how they should have foreseen their error.

The Conservative MP, Mr William Teeling, took up the cause of the bond-holders. He suggested that Japan's current trade surplus with the Sterling Area should be used to make the repayments. Under pressure from the Americans, the Commonwealth countries had increased their imports from Japan, which was now earning enough to be in a position to pay every penny she owed. In a letter to the *Financial Times*, Teeling wrote:

> It is monstrous that ... we should this year have to sell £10 million worth of goods over and above the equivalent of what we import from them [the Japanese], because our overseas trade

officials would not claim the money owed to us by Japan, even though the Japanese asked us to do so. The Foreign Office would not let us do it. It would be unfair.'[9]

Teeling's claim that the Japanese had asked to pay their debts has not been substantiated. It was not until 1948 that the Industrial Bank of Japan wrote to the English banks that had constituted the enlarged London Group. The letter gave an account of the state of the City of Tokyo Loan of 1926 and expressed the hope that any difficulties 'could be settled in an amicable way'.[10] On 25 July 1950 the *Financial Times* reported that several Japanese business leaders, including the Governor of the Bank of Osaka and the President of Shibaura Electric Co., were visiting Britain. They agreed publicly that Japan had a duty to pay all outstanding debts but surprisingly claimed that she was waiting to be approached by her creditors. In fact negotiations were already in progress in New York.[11] Repayment of the pre-war loans was finally begun on Christmas Eve 1952, the choice of date being an engaging act of Japanese fantasy.

BRITAIN RESUMES BUSINESS WITH JAPAN

In July 1947, the US Occupation authorities announced that measures would shortly be published to allow the resumption of private trade with Japan. It so happened that Mr Norbert Bogden of the New York bank, J. Henry Schroder, was a senior member of the finance division of SCAP. He saw no reason why his bank should not profit by this and proposed that the New York and London associates should offer to the Japanese government credits of $25 million and £6 million respectively.[12] Schroders in London immediately proposed to form a syndicate of their own for this purpose. This provoked a sharp reaction among those who felt that the London Group should be revived. One of those concerned recorded that Schroders representatives had expressed the view: 'that this Japanese group was such an old one that they regarded it as having come to an end'.[13]

A somewhat acrimonious debate followed and only the Hong Kong and Shanghai Bank was willing to join with Schroders. In any case, the governor of the Bank of England questioned the legality of providing finance to a country with which a state of war still existed. It was not until responsibility for foreign exchange operations was handed back by SCAP to the Japanese government's own control board in 1950 that this scheme came to fruition and Schroders and the Hong Kong and Shanghai Bank became the first firms, since the war, to open a line of credit for Japanese firms on the London Market.

Trade between the two countries now began to develop rapidly, but not on a basis that was very satisfactory to the United Kingdom. The American policy of putting Japan in a position to earn its own keep required a current account surplus with other manufacturing nations. A Bank of England memorandum of 2 July 1949 runs: 'In effect, therefore, the Sterling Area, instead of balancing its trade with Japan, has incurred a deficit in the neighbourhood of £18 million, partly because SCAP has not bought anything like the amount he promised to.' Already one can see the pattern that would increasingly mark Anglo-Japanese trade for the coming forty years. It caused immediate concern that it would bring about a run-down of Britain's reserves of dollars.

There was also strong objection to the way in which the United States was permitting the use of Japanese sterling in settlements with third countries such as France, Norway and Finland. Sterling was being paid into 'fixed' bilateral accounts, so that it could not be transferred out of one into another. HM Treasury feared that fluctuations in these accounts would cause local distortions bearing little relation to the movement of sterling as a whole. On 14 October 1949 Mr S. J. Portsmore, an Assistant Under-Secretary at the Treasury, wrote: 'We must maintain that the pound, as an international currency, must be as homogenous and uniform as circumstances allow ... It would be intolerable to have Japan-Norway sterling and so on ad infinitum'.[14] The British began to object to financing the recovery of their recent enemy through an imposed trade deficit and threatened to make Japan a hard currency area, thereby making it difficult for British importers to obtain foreign exchange for the purchase of goods from Japan. This threat was not carried out, however.

BRITISH BANKS RETURN TO TOKYO

The first British bank to return to Japan was the Hong Kong and Shanghai Banking Corporation in 1947, followed soon by the Chartered Bank of India, Australia, and China. Both firms reopened offices in Tokyo, Yokohama, and Kobe. In the same year, the Mercantile Bank, destined to be swallowed some time later by the Hong Kong and Shanghai Bank, opened up in Osaka. These were the hardy adventurers who had been the last to leave Japan and Manchukuo before war broke out. Their initial activity was to engage in trade finance and in this they were much helped by the presence of a Hong Kong government trade office which steered business in their direction. There were also accounts to be run for the ANZAC element of the Occupation Force.[15] But when the banks tried to adventure into wider activity they were dismayed to discover that the US authorities on the scene were so concerned to build up the Japanese banks that they would discriminate against their British allies. Mr Mason, the head of the Hong Kong Bank's office in Tokyo, was particularly sharp in his complaints about the attitude of SCAP. The British Trade Mission which visited Japan in 1949 thought his remarks 'jaundiced' but were nevertheless concerned at the American attitude. They singled out one official of SCAP in particular, a Mr Janow. Their report contained the following passage:

> I do not believe that people such as Lecount [of the Finance Division] go nearly as far in their intentions as to seek to preclude foreign banks from performing any banking function that the Japanese considered that they might be able to perform as well, but the possibility that the Bank of Tokyo may have Janow in their pocket is disquieting. Janow has always been solicitous about the welfare of Japanese enterprises and hard-boiled as regards the foreign trader.[16]

The Mission also singled out a Mr McDiarmid of SCAP who was reported to have said that: 'he considered it unwise to [let] foreign banks compete on an equal basis with Japanese banks in the period immediately following the War.'[17] Some Americans, evidently, had a clear and consistent idea of their mission in

Japan. It should also be remembered that some Democrats, who had served with the Roosevelt administration, viewed the British as outdated imperialists of limited relevance.

The Bank of Tokyo, referred to above, was the new entity designed to replace the Yokohama Specie Bank. At the beginning of the occupation SCAP had wound up the latter and taken over its functions, considering it to have been an undesirable feature of the old centralized state economy. In 1949 they perceived the need for such an element in the reconstituted Japanese banking system. It was therefore revived, as a private bank under the name Bank of Tokyo, to lead the foreign exchange business of Japan and the financing of its foreign trade. The 1949 Trade Mission found that the bank had already been open for some time and they heard rumours that its foreign currency reserve in New York had been supplied by the Japanese government. They reported:

> The Bank of Tokyo, adequately housed and over-staffed with the Specie Banks' executive officers, has completed its campaign of post-war expansion. The Bank of Tokyo has press-ganged the Japanese manufacturers and industrialists and boasts of having 80 per cent of the foreign trade reserved to themselves at the instant the flood-gates are opened.[18]

The British banks were clearly nervous of being driven out, or at least of having their activities seriously 'marginalized', as in pre-war Japan. The Bank of Tokyo was eager to give assurances that this would not be so. In fact the authorities now gave licences to twenty-one banks to engage in foreign exchange dealing, of which ten were foreign banks. Nevertheless, the Trade Mission felt that: 'It seems ultimately that foreign banks holding Japanese Government deposits would find that a substantial part of their deposits had been withdrawn.'[19] The Mission were correct in their assessment but added, as an expression of their sense of fair play: 'The fact that over half the foreign exchange transactions until now have been done by foreign banks is resented and preferential treatment by the Japanese Government in favour of the Bank of Tokyo is only to be expected.'[20]

This state of affairs was codified in an Exchange Control Law, passed on 1 December 1949. This provided that foreign financial houses could set up branches in Japan to engage in general banking business on receipt of permission from the Ministry of Finance. Such authorized banks could buy and sell foreign currencies, open letters of credit, and accept and pay collections accepted between Japan and foreign countries. Directly related activities were also permitted. Since all other spheres were excluded, and the permitted areas were those already largely monopolized by the Bank of Tokyo, the outlook was severely restricted. Not surprisingly, the small British banking community did not increase in numbers for some time.

The Treaty of San Francisco and the ending of the occupation did not affect these matters. The United Kingdom concluded a commercial treaty with the new fully independent government of Japan. This covered banking activities and recognized the legitimacy of the 1949 Exchange Control Law. The British government, consciously or unconsciously, had accepted that, as before the war, the Japanese would dominate, and indeed largely monopolize, all financial activity within their own country. The Japanese certainly interpreted things in this way and there was a certain amount of friction. A retrospective letter of 25 December 1956, from Mr Patterson of the Bank of England to his colleague, Mr Hogg, ran: 'From time to time we have [had] to take up with the Japanese various matters brought to our notice by the British banks in Japan and which were claimed to discriminate against their operations in that country.'[21] Two examples of such problems will suffice. In 1951, the Hong Kong and Shanghai Bank complained of difficulty in obtaining local currency, owing to restrictions placed upon them by the Bank of Japan in re-discounting promissory notes. This problem was overcome when the complaining bank was given a privilege already enjoyed by the Chartered Bank and was allowed to effect sterling exchanges. In 1953 there were complaints of the unprofitable rates at which export bills had to be purchased, of preferential treatment for Japanese banks in obtaining sterling deposits, and of British banks being excluded from providing Japanese firms with yen finance. The first complaint was satisfactorily settled but the others were not pressed. As sometimes would happen, the British companies were not fully agreed amongst themselves and the

Chartered Bank said that it had not suffered any discrimination in re-discounting Japanese notes, while the Bank of Japan denied that it was behaving partially. These issues of discrimination were largely held over for discussion at the Anglo-Japanese Trade and Payments Review two years later.[22]

JAPANESE BANKS RETURN TO LONDON

The return of the Japanese banks and trading houses to London after 1945 was a painful and slow process. Memories in Britain, as shown by the debate over loan repayment and Chancellor Dalton's outbursts, were extremely hostile to Japan. The companies which had previous connections with the Far East had often lost members of their staff, who had died in Japanese prisoner-of-war camps. Nevertheless, old links were not disregarded. The first operating bank to return was the Yokohama Specie Bank, in its new guise as the Bank of Tokyo. This was a natural decision in view of the bank's position as the main agent of Japanese overseas finance. In the summer of 1952 they arrived in the City and appealed to their old connection with the Westminster, now absorbed into the National Westminster Bank. They were given a room in the National Westminster Bank office and were able to recruit an English assistant. Three months later they obtained permission to open a Representative Office in Birchin Lane. One or two of the Japanese trading companies had also reopened and the small and still apprehensive Japanese business community would meet regularly at the Palmerston Restaurant in Bishopsgate to compare notes. They very much wanted to be accepted again and behaved with the discretion and modesty characteristic of Japanese people in those circumstances.[23]

As already noted, the Japanese authorities had assigned to the Bank of Tokyo the task of handling the nation's obligation to pay off the outstanding foreign loans. The bank chose to channel the repayment moneys through the Hong Kong and Shanghai Bank, enabling the latter to make a quick return on the deposits. Earlier in the same year, a small Japanese delegation had gone to Hong Kong, where staff of the bank had agreed to look after them and to entertain them at the races.[24] Also, the Hong Kong and Shanghai had been the first British bank to return to Tokyo in 1947 (see p. 120). This nibble at the loan funds was perhaps their reward. The Bank of Tokyo was soon delighted to find that with the economies of Europe developing rapidly under the stimulus of the Marshall Plan there were excellent opportunities for the development of trade finance from London.

In the same year of 1952, representative offices were also opened in London by the Sanwa, Mitsubishi, and Sumitomo Banks. The first of these was assisted by Schroders, while the National Westminster acted as clearing agents for the Mitsubishi Bank. Sumitomo opened arrangements with the Hong Kong and Shanghai, Schroders, and Rothschilds Banks.[25] In 1953 the Bank of Japan itself opened an office in London; Schroders helped them to find premises. When Schroders' office manager, Laurence Mackie, retired two years later, he was taken on by the Bank of Japan as an adviser.[26]

The Japanese banks in London were authorized by their own Ministry of Finance to carry on trade finance with foreign exchange. They now received permission from the Bank of England to open sterling accounts and sought advances from their correspondents to fund these. The British banks were doubtful at this time about Japanese credit and insisted that half of any such account should be funded by the Ministry of Finance from its own foreign exchange holdings in London. The provision of this special 50 per cent requirement very much irked the Japanese authorities, who had been insisting for 100 years that Japanese companies should be treated on an equal footing with others. As this requirement diminished and fell into disuse, the Japanese in London found that they enjoyed the same freedom and equality as the domestic and other foreign banks in all respects, subject to the general application of the regulations governing financial activities and the use of sterling.[27]

The activities of these banks were somewhat limited by opportunity and their main interest was in trade finance. As we have seen, trade between Britain and Japan was beginning to pick up. It had been helped by the institution in 1951 by the British authorities of a method of sterling payment called the 'pound usance system'. Under this arrangement, British banks could extend sterling credits to the Foreign Exchange Control Board in

Tokyo to enable Japan to import twelve vital commodities, such as petroleum, raw cotton, and wool. The term was 120 days and the transactions took the form of acceptances in London. Since Japanese imports of raw materials from the Sterling Area were large, the credit line was soon exhausted and transactions suspended. In 1953 the Japanese government found itself running out of sterling and asked for the system to be revived. This time, however, the London banks involved were to extend their credits, not to the Foreign Exchange Control Board but to individual Japanese banks. For the importer, the system remained more expensive than obtaining a simple foreign exchange loan and the balance of usances never exceeded the permitted level of 400 million yen. However, their popularity increased as the interest rate on them eventually fell to 3 per cent or at such times as the Japanese government introduced credit restrictions at home to reduce imports. The system introduced at this time continued to run for many years as a minor but significant element in the field of Japanese overseas trade financing.[28]

NOTES

1 Barings Archives.
2 Japanese Banks are not permitted to hold more than 5 per cent of any domestic company.
3 Barings Archives.
4 Bank of England Archives.
5 *The Times* (27 Feb. 1946).
6 Ibid.
7 *Financial Times* (28 Feb. 1946).
8 Ibid. (14 Mar. 1946).
9 Ibid. quoted in *North China Daily* (11 Feb. 1950).
10 Bank of England Archives.
11 Ibid.
12 Courtesy of Dr Roberts of Schroders.
13 Barings Archives.
14 Bank of England Archives.
15 Information provided by Sir Michael Sandberg.
16 Bank of England Archives.
17 Ibid.

18 Bank of England Archives.
19 Ibid.
20 Ibid.
21 Ibid.
22 Ibid.
23 Information kindly provided by Mr Shin'ichi Yoda formerly of the Bank of Tokyo.
24 Information kindly provided by Prof. F. H. H. King.
25 Bank of England Archives.
26 Mr Mackie only resigned from this position in 1985 when, having reached the age of 97, he felt that commuting from the South Coast was becoming a little difficult.
27 Bank of England Archives.
28 Ibid.

10
THE RISE OF INDUSTRIAL JAPAN
1953–1972

Japan's Economic Miracle

By 1953 one hundred years had elapsed since the arrival of Commodore Perry's ships in Yedo Bay. During that time the Japanese had seen their country opened up to foreigners, the creation at great speed of a modern industrial state, imperial military conquest of East Asia, the dropping of atom bombs on their cities, and foreign occupation. In the next thirty-five years they would see their country emerge as the leading industrial power after the United States and then as the largest exporter of capital in the world. The intensity and speed of change in Japanese history have not always been kept in view by those who have to deal with Japan.

By 1953 the world was well on the way to recovery from the recent war. The United States, despite the heavy burden imposed upon it by its assessment of the needs of the Cold War, was increasing its economic strength and providing a large share of the capital requirements of the Free World. Europe was responding very successfully to the stimulus of the Marshall Plan. The need for development aid for the Third World had been recognized and large programmes undertaken. Japan, through the policies of SCAP and the inflow of money as a result of its situation during the Korean War, had been fairly launched on the path of economic recovery, regaining her ability to pay her own way and seeing rapid industrial expansion.

The end of the occupation period in 1952 did not represent a significant break economically, since American forces and bases remained. From 1952 to 1956 receipts on account of the US military presence amounted to nearly $3.5 billion, enough to pay for 25 per cent of all commodity imports. Even in 1959 this source of finance still covered 14 per cent of such imports.[1]

During the twenty years from the signature of the San Francisco Treaty to the 'Nixon Shock', 1952–72, the Japanese economy grew at an extraordinary rate. As in other countries, the process sometimes overheated. Successive Cabinets formed from the Liberal Democratic Party, which had now started its course as seemingly the permanent government of Japan, were obliged to keep a tight rein on the pace of advance and even to engineer temporary recessions, notably in 1952–4 and 1964–6. Nevertheless, Japan was following a 'go-go' policy rather than a 'stop-go' policy. By 1957, Japanese industrial production had reached two and a half times its pre-war level in real terms and growth was at around 7 per cent a year. From 1961 to 1963 it was 10.7 per cent and then, after the temporary check of 1964–6, averaged 12.7 per cent from 1967 to 1971. Between 1960 and 1970, the GNP had grown by five times from 15 trillion yen to 73 trillion yen. Japan had now far outstripped Britain in industrial production and GNP and was beginning the long task of catching up with other leading industrial countries on total earnings per head of population, wage levels, and other indicators of a prosperous society.[2]

By 1972 the outside world was aware of Japan's extraordinary achievement and anxious to study how it had come about. A surprisingly large section of British industry still chose to talk as if Japanese industry was just a matter of copying other people's goods, cheap (even shoddy) manufacture by underpaid labour, and sale by dumping. Serious businessmen, however, now acknowledged the high quality and careful adaptation to market needs of Japanese goods and the painstaking sales campaigns by which they circulated abroad. Foreigners became aware of such concepts as the Japanese work-ethic, the country's high rate of saving (30 per cent for part of the period), long-term projection and research, consensus decision-taking, market-determined design, indicative planning (as opposed to 'socialist' planning), the role of Japan's Ministry of Trade and Industry (MITI), and the unfamiliar concept of 'administrative guidance' as opposed to the legal regulations and administrative orders used in the West. But the main concern of foreigners was whether the conduct of the Japanese had been 'fair' or whether it was a compound of protectionism, discrimination, and dumping. This debate, of course, still continues.

The critics had a number of points to make. It was said that Japanese industry was 'subsidized' in the sense that government had been responsible for 30 per cent of the capital formation over this period through grants and low-interest loans.[3] It was said that the Japanese had used outright protectionism. There were many allegations of dumping, although Europeans and Americans had adequate legal means for dealing with this if they could justify their charges.

There were indeed some grounds for complaint. It had been the practice of MITI to select successively a number of favoured industries (for example: steel, shipbuilding, chemicals, motor cars, electronics) and to tilt all the needed national resources in their direction. The chosen industry would then be nurtured behind a protective tariff wall. Only when the industry had grown to great strength in a captive internal market of 120 million citizens were the barriers removed. By this time the Japanese companies in question were ready to unleash a 'cascade' of exports on foreign markets, while their own domestic markets had become invulnerable.

By 1972 this process was almost complete and Japanese tariffs were as low as any in the world, and sometimes lower, except in a very few (but important) special areas such as computers, footwear and leather goods, tobacco, confectionery, and whisky. The debate shifted to Japan's supposed non-tariff barriers, such as licensing, health and safety regulations, labelling requirements, customs procedures, and so on. Unfortunately, such matters were sometimes very difficult to prove. Talk began to be heard of 'psychological barriers', such as Japan's inter-company loyalty, the *Keiretsu* effect, outmoded distribution systems, Japanese distrust of foreign goods and preference for their own, resistance to change of habit. But the one complaint on which most foreigners were agreed was that the old, traditional administrative guidance could be used, and was used, to favour Japanese interests and to

discriminate against those of foreigners. This suggestion was
made in particular about Japan's financial markets.

The Experience of British Banks in Tokyo

During the twenty years dealt with in this chapter the number of
British banks operating in Japan remained almost static. Profitable activity was at first largely limited to the foreign exchange
market. In spite of the problem, already discussed, of the overwhelming predominance of the Bank of Tokyo some foreign
banks were able to build up a complementary trade in discounting export bills and certifying letters of credit. But the difficulties
which they were experiencing were well known and discouraged
the rest of the banking community from following the road to
Japan. The outstanding exception was Barclays Bank which, with
the increasing difficulty of carrying on its traditional business in
Africa, undertook a careful review of overseas opportunities in
1969 and decided to open a representative office in Tokyo in the
same year.[4] A second British joint-stock bank, the National
Westminster, followed suit in 1972. Towards the very end of the
period, a number of London merchant banks were either scout-
ing in Tokyo or had opened representative offices there, as we
will see in a later chapter.

Meanwhile, however, a completely new factor had appeared at
the beginning of the 1960s. The rapid growth of the Japanese
economy was generating a huge demand for investment and
working capital which could not always be met from domestic
resources, in spite of the very high rate of saving. There was a
particular shortage also of foreign exchange. It became necessary
to have recourse to foreign capital, though its admission was
carefully controlled by the Ministry of Finance. In October 1962
a delegation of British bankers, under the leadership of Mr Alexander Hood (now Viscount Hood) of Schroders was invited to
visit Tokyo by Mr Okamura, President of Nomura Securities.
They met with a group of leading Japanese bankers and called on
the Governor of the Bank of Japan. It was suggested to them that
British banks should play a more active role in lending to the

Japanese economy. However, the mission was not reassured by the condition of financial markets in Tokyo. In particular, they were put off by the huge discrepancy between the external interest rate of 4 per cent and the very high rates commanded by Japanese lenders in the internal market, sometimes even rising (they understood) to 40 per cent. They felt that the ground was too unsure and the idea was not pursued.[5]

For those British banks willing to take advantage of Japan's capital needs, the field of commercial lending became for a time a very attractive one. Administrative guidance was by no means one-sided. During the two tight-money periods in the 1960s, the loan activities of foreign banks were less severely restricted than those of domestic ones and Japanese banks steered their client companies to them for much needed capital, usually in foreign currency. These foreign currency transactions were known as 'impact loans'. Usually, borrower and lender had some previous connection which was often of long standing. Barclays, for example, found many opportunities because they had been able to arrange payments for Japanese firms dealing with China.[6] By 1971 foreign banks had 1.5 per cent of the loan market, a small proportion but representing quite a large turnover in a large market. This had already led to complaints by Japanese Banks to the Ministry of Finance and the foreigners detected a more restrictive attitude. The Ministry was particularly sensitive to the growth of impact loans because of their effect on the foreign exchange reserves.

Some British bankers who were active in Tokyo at that time say that 1968 marked an important turning-point. That year also marked the first appearance of a current account surplus and it is possible that it was this factor which gave the Japanese authorities the confidence to consider greater latitude in their capital markets. Then, in 1970, banking activities were included in the third round of the government's trade liberalization measures in response to pressure from foreign governments, particularly that of the United States. The most important concession of principle was that foreign banks should be allowed to establish new offices, but the Ministry of Finance took the view that the country was already over-banked and licences were obtained only with delay and difficulty.

In July 1970 foreign banks were allowed to borrow in the call market and in June 1971 the Bank of Japan permitted them to enter the newly established bill discount market. Once again, little business resulted, because foreign banks had only limited amounts of paper. Another continuing difficulty was the inability of British banks to obtain yen. In principle, they could either accept yen deposits or could convert foreign currency, but Japanese depositors were few in these early days, while conversion was prohibited after the onset of the monetary crisis in 1971. It was more than clear that foreign finance houses were not taking any significant part in the astonishing explosion of Japan's national wealth.

FIRST STEPS TO LIBERALIZATION

It is now necessary to go back some years so as to see how the particular events just described have to be judged against the whole background of the liberalization of capital markets and the deregulation of banking. Whereas by 1972, as already seen, Japanese tariffs had generally been reduced to a very satisfactory level by GATT standards and the attack on Non-Tariff Barriers had begun, plainly very much less had been achieved in the financial field. This was partly due to Japan's vulnerability to exchange movements and to its lack of experience in post-war international banking, and partly to the rigidities of the banking system. The differentiation within this system came not only from the separation of functions under Article 65, it reflected also the multiple classifications of foreign exchange bank, city banks, long-term credit banks, regional banks, trust banks, co-operative banks, etc., each with its own defined functions, regulations, and prohibitions. This complex web often made it difficult for foreign houses to operate in the way in which they would have wished. Progress towards liberalization was extremely slow.

Some Japanese officials and bankers had been aware of the need for change from an early stage. Mr Masao Fujioka of the Ministry of Finance wrote: 'It is important to recognise that Japan should liberalise not because of external pressures, but because it is an inevitable process that the nation must go through for the sake of the future development of the national economy.'[7] As ever, Japan had to be seen to be adopting the best modern practices such as were necessary to give her appropriate status as a financial 'great power' with the International Monetary Fund. Again, Masao Fujioka: 'It was the wish of all concerned that Japan should join the group of advanced nations by becoming an [IMF] Article 8 country.'[8] In any case, it was felt by other IMF members that Japan's development had now reached such a high stage that she was no longer justified in retaining so many restrictive practices. The same message had been given to Germany in 1958 and to Italy in 1959.

In the early 1960s the Japanese government announced a new basic policy. It committed itself to bringing its practices into line with those of the other leading countries by gradual, incremental steps. The first of these measures included removal of some of the controls over the induction of capital into the country, a relaxation of discrimination in favour of the dollar, revision of the import usance system, and the abolition of some of the licensing requirements which still applied to certain imports. Another jolt to this step-by-step process was given when Japan joined the OECD in 1963 and was put under considerable pressure to meet the highest requirements of membership.[9]

An important field for liberalization was that of Japan's overseas investment. As already noted, the enormous requirements for capital for Japan's own industrial development mopped up nearly all the available resources throughout the fifties and sixties, in spite of the tremendously high rate of saving. The authorities were determined that it should do so and kept tight control of the situation. It was forbidden to lend to foreign persons and companies, other than within Japan, and there were severe restrictions on investing overseas. Licences to export capital were only given if it could be proved that the investment would bring a quick return to Japan's overseas earnings. In 1956 an Overseas Investment Programme was started to encourage such 'beneficial' investments. This helped to speed things up and by March 1966 there had been some 1,300 applications, since the end of the war, for licences to set up subsidiaries overseas. The amounts of money involved, however, were tiny. The figure for the United Kingdom, which saw well over half the total investment in

Europe, was only $1.29 million, mostly for Japanese companies to open offices in the City of London. Portfolio investment by Japanese in foreign securities was still completely forbidden, the only exceptions being authorized banks, which sometimes invested their overseas working balances on a short-term basis, and insurance companies, which invested those funds which they were obliged to hold abroad. However, in February 1970, investment trusts were allowed to acquire up to $100 million each of overseas securities. After April 1971 such trusts could hold up to 50 per cent of their assets abroad. Encouraged by this, the Big Four securities houses: Nomura, Daiwa, Yamaichi, and Nikko set up international investment trusts. In October 1971 the right to buy foreign bonds and shares was extended to individual citizens.

FOREIGN CAPITAL IN JAPAN: DIRECT INVESTMENT

In part I, we saw how limited foreign investment was in Japan up to the outbreak of the Second World War. Now, with their country building one of the world's most vigorous economies, there was a growing demand from foreigners for better opportunities to invest there. Quite a number of obstacles had first to be removed. Foreign investment was first permitted again only in 1960. An incentive for foreign investors, introduced on American insistence, was contained in the National Insurance Nationalization Law. It provided a three-year remission of tax on the manufacture of any product which was 'new to Japan' and 'important to the national economy'. This was the only time that the Japanese attempted any fiscal privileges for foreigners and this alien scheme was not taken very seriously, for only two items (computers and synthetic rubber) ever qualified under it. It was discontinued in 1966. Apart from this insignificant 'blip' in the proceedings, progress was very slow for the foreign investor. At first no funds at all could be remitted home but in April 1960 permission was given to remit profits from a limited category of investments and in 1963 from all foreign investments of any kind, direct or portfolio.

The Japanese government took an even more restrictive attitude to movements of capital than to movements of goods. The Ministry of Trade and Industry (MITI) conceived its role to be the promotion of Japanese industry, not foreign industry in Japan which, in any case, would be more difficult to control. Equally, the Ministry of Finance required absolute control over the supply of capital in order to regulate inflationary and foreign exchange effects. Business opinion was also hesitant. A rather mystifying article supplied by the Keidanren to the journal *Nihon Kogyo* on 21 September 1963 reported: 'The attitude of Japanese Business circles towards the liberalization of capital is divided into positive (iron and steel, securities and monetary bills) and the negative argument (automobiles, petrochemicals, etc).' This presumably meant that the Japanese considered their steel industry to be safe against all foreign competition which might, on the other hand, take over or set up enterprises of a highly competitive kind in the automobile and chemicals sectors. This was looking a long way ahead; hitherto, only 5 per cent of any one Japanese firm could be held by foreigners and at the time the article was written this had just been raised to 15 per cent.

When Japan joined OECD in 1963, most of these restrictions should have been swept away. She was able, instead, to negotiate a total exemption for herself from the obligations accepted by the other leading members to liberalize capital movements. Only additional reporting requirements were imposed. This unwelcoming climate certainly discouraged the British from direct investment. By 1968 155 British firms had put down their money to open in Japan, but little of this could be classified as directly productive investment; most of it went into obtaining premises and staff for British banks, trading houses, or sales offices. Only a few companies, such as ICI, Unilever, BP, Shell, and Dunlop, were engaged in industrial activity within Japan. Nevertheless, the obligations of membership of the IMF and of the OECD, together with intermittent pressure from the American, British, and other foreign governments, kept the Japanese authorities on the move. In 1967 a Japanese quango, the Foreign Investment Council, recommended a policy of step-by-step capital liberalization, to be completed in 1971.[10] In that latter year the Ministry of Finance did indeed announce a number of reforms which included the right for foreigners to own up to 50 per cent of the equity in any commercial or industrial company, except in seven reserved sectors. By 1988 there were 228 classified industries in which 100 per cent foreign ownership was permitted.

As it is not intended to return to this subject, it may be brought up to date here. The concessions described were real ones and made in good faith by the Japanese authorities, but they have produced very modest results. Few foreign firms have been willing to provide the management resources and the huge sums of money needed to set up manufacturing facilities in Japan and open the local markets to the products. There is a tendency among foreigners to translate the fact that it is a 'difficult' country into believing that it is an 'impossible' country. The Americans have been by far the most willing to come forward and some British, German, Swiss, and other European companies have done well, but there is still marked reluctance. Perhaps the Koreans and Chinese will do better? At the same time there has been a reluctance on the part of Japanese boards of management to sell going concerns to foreigners. Traditional attitudes portray such sales as acts of disloyalty. The foreign sector of Japanese industry is still a very minor one, in glaring contrast to Japan's own industrial expansion overseas. At the end of 1988, Japanese direct investment abroad (excluding portfolio investment and real estate) amounted to $186 billion of which $10.6 billion or 5.7 per cent was in Britain. During the same year, Britain held about $1.6 billion or 1.1 per cent of its overseas assets in Japan. During 1988 Britain invested $180 million in Japan while Japan invested $4 billion in Britain or over 20 times as much.[11]

Foreign Portfolio Investment in Japan

In the Securities and Exchange Law of 1948 conditions were laid down for the future functioning of stock exchanges in Japan. The Tokyo exchange, together with those in Osaka and Nagoya, reopened on 16 May 1949. As in the case of direct investment, foreign ownership of Japanese securities was not permitted until 1960, and then only under severe restrictions which made it unattractive, since the proceeds of sales could not leave Japan.

This problem was resolved in 1961 when 'depository receipts' were introduced in Britain and the United States. Foreign purchasers of Japanese shares lodged them with a Japanese bank and received in exchange depository receipts which could be traded abroad. Another great advantage of this system was that whereas foreigners had been obliged to pay rather large commissions to Japanese agents to effect direct purchases, the depository receipts carried no such charge. In 1963 the proportion of the equity in any Japanese company that could be held by foreigners was raised from 8 per cent to 15 per cent. By contrast, in 1963, an important event occurred when the London Stock Exchange formally approved the application for a listing by Honda, making it the first Japanese company to be officially traded in Europe. Others soon followed.[12]

In spite of these developments, foreign ownership of Japanese shares grew slowly and erratically during the 1960s. It reached a temporary high in 1963 and then dropped to less than half in the following year. In 1968 it had regained its previous level and then leapt to 3.7 times that amount in 1969. The most popular stock among foreigners by the end of 1971 was Sony. Nevertheless, total amounts of all stock held were still modest. In November 1971 they were estimated at between $2.5 million and $3 million or 4 per cent of total market capitalization. At this date it was estimated that 39.5 per cent of all foreign investment in Japan since the war was represented by portfolio investment while only marginally more, 41 per cent, was in the form of loans, although the Japanese authorities had always preferred the latter form of capital induction. As an OECD report had noted in 1968, 'The attitude of the [Japanese] authorities toward inward portfolio investment is basically positive but characterised by a certain precautionary reluctance and by preoccupation with disguised direct investment.'[13]

An increasingly important, and eventually predominant, part in the growth of foreign portfolio investment was played by investment trusts, specializing in Japanese securities. The first of these was the Anglo-Nippon, a closed trust with 20 million shares, launched in 1951 by Vickers da Costa, in association with Yamaichi, for the sole purpose of investing in Japanese shares. The original idea for this venture appears to have come from the late Lord Kaldor in 1959. He had been engaged in a study of economic growth and, based on his analysis, had helped Vickers da Costa to create the British 'Investing in Success' Fund. He was one of the earliest British economists to recognize the extraordinary nature of Japanese growth. The Anglo-Nippon Trust almost came unstuck during the Japanese liquidity crisis of 1965, when the value of its shares suddenly halved but it was steadied by the advice of another outstanding economist on its board, Professor G. C. Allen, who believed that Japanese progress was unlikely to be held up for long.[14] This trust served as a prototype for the hundreds which were to follow. Within a few years, many had sprung up in Britain, the United States, France, Switzerland, Hong Kong, etc. Today there are over 250 managed Japan funds of different kinds traded on the London Stock Exchange, as well as an equal number of Pacific and Far Eastern funds with a Japanese equity content. With few exceptions, the returns which they have brought to long-term investors have been outstanding.

THE JAPANESE PRESENCE IN LONDON

At the end of chapter 9 we saw the first Japanese banks which returned to London after the war opening their representative offices in the City. The numbers grew slowly and in 1956 there were only the Bank of Japan, the Bank of Tokyo, and six of the City Banks present. In the same year, the Japanese authorities approached their British counterparts to find out whether the Japanese private banks could now open full branches. A Mr Oda of the Bank of Japan was sent to London to conduct these negotiations, in which he was successful. As a result, applications were made and granted within weeks, the Sumitomo Bank opening its full branch on 2 July and the Mitsubishi Bank on 16 July. The Japanese government, as it had been from Meiji times onwards, was most insistent that its companies be accorded absolute equality of treatment with all other banks and, in accordance with the traditional practice of the City of London, such requests were invariably granted. This was better than the experience of British banks in Japan. It may be noted here that the formal legal position on 'most favoured nation' treatment was not regularized until 1962 when, after years of negotiation, an agreement was reached which gave to Japan this right in Britain.[15]

In the course of the discussions with Oda the responsible official in the Bank of England wrote the following minute: 'I suggested to Mr Oda that they [the Bank of Japan] might well follow the example of [other] Japanese banks, who had obtained the services of officials lent by London correspondents.[16] Oda agreed and asked that a retired member of the Bank of England staff might be recruited to advise on exchange control questions. In Tokyo the Ministry of Finance and Bank of Japan had been, and have continued to be, most helpful in finding retired Japanese bankers to work for foreign firms there. Indeed, they have always insisted on such an arrangement. Many British banks and brokerage houses have testified to the outstanding services which they received from such employees.

There were two principal reasons why the number of Japanese houses in the City of London rose so slowly in the ten years after 1956. The first was owing to their own domestic legislation: under the terms of Article 65 of the 1948 Law (see p. 115) they could not take part in bond issues. The second was that they were forbidden to lend to foreigners. This was the natural result of the insistence of the government that all capital generated in Japan should be conserved to develop the country's industry. Indeed, the Ministry of Finance did not like to see even the small outflow of funds needed for Japanese banks to set up offices overseas. Each bank was therefore only allowed to set up one representative office abroad in any year and one branch every two years. This state of affairs changed sharply in the mid-sixties, largely due to the great importance which the London Euro-dollar market had suddenly acquired for the financing of Japanese industry. Even though the banks could not yet under-write such issues it was important for them to be on the scene. They also seem to have sensed that with the growing wealth and economic power of Japan restrictions on lending and other activities overseas would soon be released or removed. It was therefore desirable to establish a presence, make contacts, and train staff to work overseas. By the end of 1971 there were fourteen banks, five securities houses, and nine insurance companies, as well as thirty-five trading houses established in the City of London, giving the Japanese already the largest foreign presence after the Americans.

At about the same time Japanese banks began to enter into joint ventures to acquire holdings in local companies in the City of London. Previously such participations had been mostly in the United States and Brazil and further important joint ventures with American banks were being formed at this time, but attention also turned to London. In December 1970 two large banking consortia, the Japanese Bank International and the Associated Japanese Bank (International) were formed, solely with the participation of Japanese banks and securities houses. Their declared purpose was to raise medium- and long-term finance for Japanese companies and their formation marked the first attempt to take advantage of relaxation by the Tokyo authorities of the application of Article 65 abroad. They were followed by a spate of joint ventures with British banks to form Japanese merchant banking subsidiaries (discussed in chapter 11.) A different sort of participation was that of the Mitsubishi Bank which was invited by the Orion Bank in 1971 to join the existing British, American, German, and Canadian members.[17] The Sanwa Bank similarly acquired a 14.66 per cent stake in the international Commercial Continental Bank, with British, Australian, American, and French interests.[18]

THE 'NIXON SHOCK'

Events in August of the year 1971 were to bring Japan face to face with its new situation as a major trading power. The country suddenly found itself deeply involved as an active participant in a world economic storm, no longer able to play a passive spectator role under the protection of the United States.

Hitherto, Japanese politicians, civil servants, and businessmen, while deeply satisfied with the progress that their country had made, still viewed it as a poor country, totally without resources and potentially at the mercy of the outside world. No Japanese thought of his country as 'rich', but rather as a 'striving' one, dependent on the hard work and skills of the population. Memories of hunger and destitution after the war were still unpleasantly fresh. This uneffaced siege mentality, allied to natural caution, had contributed to make the process of liberalization so slow. While some of these considerations were valid ones the reality of the situation was very different. Japan was now earning a regular and growing surplus with the rest of the world on current account and was beginning to create capital at a faster rate than could be put to internal use.

The Americans, on the other hand, seemed to have outrun their course as the principal supplier of capital to other countries. The United States was also beginning to show a comparative decline in industrial competitiveness, marketing ability, and financial judgement. At any rate, she was now running a persistent and increasingly serious current account deficit, of which Japan's own surplus was a significant part. On 15 August 1971 President Nixon declared that the convertibility of the dollar was suspended and that an import surcharge of 10 per cent would be placed on goods arriving in America. These measures went well beyond what the world had been expecting and caused such consternation that they came to be known as the 'Nixon Shock'.

Great dismay was aroused in Tokyo. While the Japanese may have been relieved that no unilateral measures had been taken against them, they were likely to be the most seriously affected of all the trading partners of the United States. Their difficulties were increased when the Canadian dollar and most of the European currencies were floated off to find new levels with the dollar. For several days Japan was isolated. The Ministry of Finance, as always preferring regulation to free market forces and unwilling to believe that Japan was about to be thrown into the world on its own, declined to follow the Europeans. Instead, they announced they would retain yen parity within margins of 1 per cent in accordance with their IMF obligations. Meanwhile, they debated what to do. The foreign exchange banks in Tokyo were reluctant to cover their own and their customers' dollar positions by recourse to overseas credit facilities and were permitted to use interest-bearing dollars, supplied by the Ministry of Finance from a special reserve, to sell to the Bank of Japan for yen. It is thought that by 27 August the Central Bank had purchased nearly $4 billion. The government then announced that the yen would be floated within 6 per cent to 7 per cent of parity. Like other currencies, the yen continued to fight a kind of rearguard action against revaluation until international agreement was recorded some months later under the Smithsonian arrangements and it settled at a value about 10 per cent above its original parity.[19]

The reactions of the Japanese authorities to the 'Nixon Shock' appear all the more surprisingly delayed when it is seen that the yen had been under attack for several months before the event. Some foreign banks, including British ones, had spotted that the currency was seriously undervalued and had attempted to increase their holdings of yen, as a currency speculation, by exploiting any loopholes in the Japanese regulations. These attempts had been actively resisted by the authorities.

The first such foray had been made in March 1971 into the market for short-term government securities. These could be purchased from Japanese dealers with a maturity of only sixty days and the proceeds remitted immediately. This represented an attractively short position for rapid turnover, whereas other government securities carried longer maturities and a six-months' delay on the remittal of proceeds. Moreover, this paper earned an attractive yield of 5.625 per cent as compared with US Treasury bills offering only 3.3 per cent after 90 days. In the first two weeks of March foreign firms bought nearly $30 million of these yen-denominated, short-term bills. The Ministry of Finance reacted by decreeing, on 15 March, that specific permission would be required for any further such purchases. The market immediately disappeared.[20]

At much the same time there was a rapid rise in the number of free-yen accounts held by foreigners. Foreign currency would be submitted to a Japanese exchange bank, which would convert the deposit into yen with the right to remit interest and principal at any time. The government countered this in late 1971 by giving the exchange banks the power to fix their own interest rates for such deposits. Not wishing to build up large stocks of foreign currency the banks lowered their rates to the point where they became unattractive.

In May there was a shortage of funds in the Tokyo market and the rate offered on new bonds and debentures went up to 8 per cent. These attractive securities had the added advantage that all of them, with the exception of convertible bonds and telegraph and telephone bonds, were eligible for collateral loans from the Bank of Japan and therefore highly liquid. By 17 May foreigners had purchased $300 million of such securities and the Ministry of Finance announced that, henceforward, their approval would be needed for each individual purchase. The trade immediately died in the same way as had that in short-term securities.[21]

These manœuvres illustrate very well the ability and the readiness of the Ministry of Finance and the Bank of Japan to prevent any activities which they considered to be speculative. At the same time, such actions by the authorities ran counter to real progress towards liberalization.

Japan now entered 1972 with a currency which was generally held by the rest of the world to be undervalued. This naturally became a major factor in Japan's rapidly growing trade surplus. As the years went by there were more and more complaints that this parity was maintained by a 'dirty float'. By the 1980s the 'undervalued yen' and 'non-tariff barriers' had become continuous and increasingly bitter matters of complaint. It must be said that by no means all experts in Britain or the United States agreed that the Japanese were maintaining a dirty float and they themselves again and again denied it. Nor were the proponents of the accusation able to offer fully satisfactory evidence as to how the low rate of exchange was maintained. It cannot have been an entirely artificial arrangement as it lasted for more than twelve years under severe pressure. Suffice it to say here that throughout this period careful management by the Japanese authorities and a new and growing export of capital served to keep the yen at a rate which was severely damaging to Japan's trading partners.

NOTES

1 G. C. Allen, *A Short Economic History of Modern Japan* (Macmillan, London, 1985), pp. 189–92.
2 Ibid., pp. 192–5.

3 G. C. Allen, *A Short Economic History of Modern Japan* (Macmillan, London, 1985), p. 226.
4 Information kindly supplied by Mr Collin Stevens formerly of Barclays Bank.
5 Information kindly supplied by Viscount Hood.
6 Information kindly supplied by Mr Collin Stevens.
7 Masao Fujioka, *Japan's International Finance Today and Tomorrow* (The Japan Times, 1979), p. 7.
8 Ibid., p. 4.
9 Ibid., pp. 7–10.
10 Thomas Adams and Iwao Hoshii, *A Financial History of Modern Japan* (Research Japan Limited, 1964), pp. 254–62.
11 Information supplied courtesy of the Central Statistical Office and from the Japanese Ministry of Finance.
12 Information supplied courtesy of the London Stock Exchange.
13 *OECD Annual Country Report 1968.*
14 Information kindly supplied by Mr Ralph Vickers.
15 Bank of England Archives.
16 Ibid.
17 Information kindly supplied by Mr Ronald Grierson.
18 Thomas Adams and Iwao Hoshii, *A Financial History of the New Japan* (Kodansha International Ltd., Tokyo, 1972), pp. 468–74.
19 Wilbur F. Monroe, *Japan: Financial Markets and the World Economy* (Praeger Publishers, New York, 1973), pp. 7–11.
20 Ibid., pp. 20–1.
21 Ibid., pp. 22–3.

11

INTERNATIONAL BOND MARKETS
1945–1988

LONDON AS A SOURCE OF CAPITAL
1945–1963

Before the war Japan had, from time to time, invited infusions of capital from abroad to develop her industry. The utility loans of the 1920s, discussed in chapter 8, provided outstanding examples. After the war the requirements for development capital were so great that, despite the tremendously high rate of saving and capital formation at home, Japan eventually had again to go abroad to raise money. Because the United States was the occupying power and because it possessed the world's leading economy it was to New York that the Japanese first turned for funds. Bond issues for Japanese industry were made at an early date. Important sums of money were raised by the Japan Development Bank, which was set up in 1951 as one of a number of new institutions to take over the former responsibility of the Industrial Bank of Japan for raising capital abroad for Japanese industry (see pp. 67–9). This new entity was forbidden to raise money within Japan and contracted loans, first from the World Bank and then by a number of bond issues in various countries including Britain. The borrower passed on the proceeds on very favourable terms to the coal, shipping, and electrical industries.[1]

For a long time after the war London was in no position to provide Japan with funds. Indeed, within a few years the economic outlook in London was bleaker than in Tokyo. Poor management, bad industrial relations, uncertain government policies, and extreme vulnerability to outside events were the features of British economic life for three decades and underlay the wearisome succession of 'stop-go' policies. In the wake of the Suez Crisis, for example, it was decided to limit the amount of credits available to non-residents and the use of sterling-acceptances in trade between non-sterling area countries was forbidden. These were the days when some people seriously doubted whether London would continue to be a major centre of world finance.

The City was kept going as an international centre by the experience and skills of its members, but the modest limits of its ability to raise money were plain for all to see. In 1961 the time had come to repay the Japan government Sterling Loan of 1907, a sum of only £23 million. It was not possible, however, to find that amount by a new bond issue in London, and the Japanese government decided to go to Switzerland instead. *The Times* of 21 November 1961 reported: 'Yesterday's report from Tokyo that the Ministry of Finance is planning to fund at least part of ... the issue ... in Switzerland shows how far the London Market has to go to regain its leading role as a world financial centre.' There were far too many British and Commonwealth borrowers chasing the limited funds in the market to give a Japanese issue much of a chance. Besides, interest rates in London were much higher at this time than in other comparable centres.

There was, however, one exception which needs to be noted. In 1963 the British government of the day had imposed a temporary embargo on foreign loans. In spite of this the Japanese government wished to raise a small sterling loan. It is nice to record that the old London Group was able to ride into action on behalf of Japan for the last time. Seven London banks, led by the National Westminster, as tradition required, raised £5 million in sterling bonds at 5 per cent, a very modest sum but representing a remarkable achievement in the circumstances. Thus ended a happy and successful financial relationship which had lasted for sixty-four years.[2]

At just this time an event took place which would not only fundamentally alter the pattern of Japanese borrowing but would restore, and make greater than ever before, the importance of the City of London. This was the explosion of the London

Euromarkets. It came only just in time. The large Japanese borrowings in the pipeline were certainly not on their way to the
United Kingdom. In February of 1964, Swiss Fr. 50 million was
raised in Switzerland to finance road construction and the
electric-power industry. This was exactly the sort of loan which,
before the war, would have been raised in London. The Federal
German Republic was also by now a thriving capital market and,
at much the same time in 1964, the Deutsche Bank concluded an
issue for the Japanese in Frankfurt for DM 100 million.[3]

JAPAN ENTERS THE EURODOLLAR MARKET 1963

Euromoney is money deposited in Europe with banks uncon-
nected with the country of issue. As may be seen from this
definition, it is therefore money which is out of the control of the
issuing government. Since the end of the war American money
had been spent in Europe on relief, on reconstruction through the
Marshall Plan, in support of American forces overseas, and in
other ways. These dollars found their way into offshore deposits, principally in Paris, Rome, and Canada. An early use was
for trade finance and they became of particular interest to London banks in 1956 when, in face of the British government's
prohibition on the use of sterling to finance trade between third
countries, British merchant banks began to finance trade in Eurodollars. Throughout the 1950s the active use of these funds
continued to become more popular, partly as a reflection of their
carrying more attractive interest rates than United States sources,
their lesser regulatory requirements, and their availability for
settling balance of payments accounts. In 1958 the introduction
of general convertibility of foreign exchange in most European
countries greatly increased their flexibility and gave impetus
to their previous rather limited use for wholesale banking.
They rapidly became a major source of finance for industrial
expansion.[4] Hitherto, London had lagged behind Paris and Rome
as a centre for dealing in Eurodollars but it now took a firm lead.
A significant part in this sudden expansion in 1959 was played
by the Moscow Narodny Bank. Presumably for political reasons

during this active phase of the Cold War the socialist banks had
preferred to keep their foreign deposits in Europe rather than the
United States, and the Soviet Banque Commerciale de l'Europe
du Nord had been the first to initiate onward lending to French,
German, and Italian bankers for corporate financing. Now the
Moscow Narodny Bank began to attract large-scale deposits in
London from all the socialist banks.[5]

In July 1963 President Kennedy's administration imposed the
Exchange Equalization Tax which was designed to prevent capital outflows and protect the structure of US domestic interest
rates by insulating them from external influences. But this measure in no way diminished the appetite for dollar funds which
would now largely be met in the Eurodollar Markets, American
banks overseas themselves supplying a large contribution of
offshore dollars. As *The Times* commented: 'If this move was
primarily designed to protect the American balance of payments,
it has already thrown up desirable side-effects in the revitaliza-
tion of European capital markets – particularly London.'[6] The
American regulations, although further reinforced in 1965, were
full of loopholes, and dollars continued to flow into Europe from
the United States, creating a symbiosis of markets in the two
areas. Although Eurodollar markets were available all over
Europe, London reinforced its lead. The required manpower,
experience, and resourcefulness were plentifully available and the
Bank of England took an encouraging and relaxed attitude. By
contrast, the German authorities gave no encouragement to the
growth of an offshore market in Frankfurt.

The Japanese quickly saw the advantages of these facilities.
The first Japanese Eurobond issue was made in December 1963
for the Canon Corporation. In the four months between then and
April 1964 there were eleven Eurobond issues for Japanese
applicants, comprising seven industrial companies, one trading
company, one bank, the government of Japan and the City of
Tokyo.[7] The Eurobond market became the standard way of
raising overseas finance for Japanese companies and London the
principal centre for doing so. In fact, all of these initial twelve
issues were made in London, the first being arranged by Vickers
da Costa.

The Japanese government, cities, and state institutions quickly became major borrowers. In April 1964 the government announced plans to issue a total of $125 million of such government or government-guaranteed bonds abroad, of which $70 million would be placed in the Euromarkets, made up of $20 million for Tokyo City, $25 million for Osaka City and Prefecture, and $25 million for its own industrial development programme. Other planned issues were $20 million each for the state-owned Nippon Telephone and Telegraph Company and the Japan Development Bank. While the government favoured this method of raising money for private companies they kept a traditionally strict watch on the situation to ensure no risk of default should damage Japanese credit. Licences demanding stringent criteria were required for all issues which were not officially guaranteed.[8]

The lead managers for all these issues were usually a UK–Japanese pair or a UK–US–Japanese trio. Since both the Japanese and the American banks were debarred by their domestic legislation from participation, their places were taken by Tokyo or New York securities houses. Daiwa, Nomura, Nikko, and Yamaichi were already operating in the City of London, endeavouring to retail Japanese securities to foreign buyers, and they were able to join as co-managers for such issues, to be followed later by smaller colleagues. In time, the banks inevitably came to regret their exclusion from this profitable business. Pressure was put on the Ministry of Finance to relax the regulations. Needless to say, this was opposed by the Securities companies, but eventually the banks obtained a measure of participation, though only indirectly. The approved solution was to rule that subsidiary banking companies, incorporated in the UK or elsewhere in Europe and not carrying out the parallel functions of the parent bank, could be classed as lying outside the provisions of Article 65. This led to the formation of a large number of Japanese 'merchant banks' in London, often with the word 'International' incorporated into the name. Initially they were usually joint ventures with British merchant banks, but as time went by they mastered their trade and preferred to become wholly Japanese owned. Virtually all Japanese banks in London now have such subsidiaries. At the time of their original creation they were almost solely engaged in the Eurobond market, introducing clients and trading in the bonds.

From its inception to the present day the Eurobond market has continued as a major source of capital for Japanese industry. Despite the constant supervision of the Japanese authorities, many loans were raised in the Euromarkets which could have been placed inside Japan. The main attractions were usually the favourable interest rates available and the simpler and swifter conditions for issue, but it is sometimes hard to see why Japanese corporations raised Eurodollar loans and swapped them immediately into yen rather than resorting to the domestic market. Speculation on the future strength of the yen has played its part. An element of 'fashion' perhaps also crept in, causing companies to vie in showing their international credit-worthiness. The development of Euroyen bonds from 1977 onwards will be discussed below. For 1988 the Eurobond market as a whole, for all types of instruments, totalled US $174 billion, of which 22.1 per cent or $38.5 billion was for Japan. She was then by far the largest borrower in the market. Japanese securities houses continued to be extremely active in these issues, the Big Four accounting for 26.6 per cent of the total business as book runners, with Nomura as the largest participant. Moreover, Nomura appeared as a lead-manager in 19.3 per cent of all issues and Daiwa in 11.1 per cent.[9]

JAPAN BECOMES A LENDER: SAMURAI BONDS 1970

By 1970 Japan was becoming conscious of its own tremendous financial power and there was a general feeling that she must now begin to play her part accordingly. Not since the end of the First World War, more than sixty years earlier, had any foreign borrower been allowed to float yen dominated bonds in Japan. So when the first Samurai bond, as these instruments were to be known, was announced in 1972, there was a most understandable wave of pleasure and satisfaction that the country could now be seen, as one Tokyo newspaper put it, as 'a financial power of the first order'.

Official pronouncements also suggested that the bonds would enable Japan to help developing countries by transferring to them part of the country's rapidly accumulating national wealth.

This decision was not reached without an intense struggle during the long process of consensus-forming, known in Japan as *nemawashi*. James Horne has pointed out that if the internationalist lobby won the day they nevertheless had to overcome much opposition from those who clung to the restrictive practices which had served so well up until then. It is natural that the two proponents of the Samurai bonds, Mr Takeo Fukuda (the Minister of Finance) and Mr Satoshi Sumita (his Administrative Vice-Minister) should both have been formed in the Ministry of Finance, which has always had a more accepting view of the outside world than MITI. There was serious resistance too from the Securities Bureau, which saw that the separation of banking and securities business would be eroded if banks were allowed to underwrite bond issues. The securities houses were obviously opposed for the same reason. A compromise was reached; the securities houses would underwrite bonds but would pay part of the fees to the banks.

The first organization permitted to float yen bonds was the Asian Development Bank (ADB) because it justified the point that lending would aid Third World development, because Japan was a founding member of the ADB, and because its governor, Mr Takeshi Watanabe, was an ex-official of the Ministry of Finance. He visited Tokyo in March 1970 and the matter was arranged. The problem of collateral was solved by treating the ADB as if it were a sovereign entity and therefore required no such security under the Ministry of Finances current regulations.[10]

The original position of the Japanese government was that Samurai bonds might only be issued by these 'sovereign entities' such as governments or international organizations of which Japan was a member. Many of those concerned may have suspected that this state of affairs would not last for ever, but it enabled the authorities to control the situation carefully while they waited to see if the country's trade surpluses had really come to stay. They therefore only permitted one issue every quarter and there were only thirteen issues between December 1970 and

December 1973, nine by international financial institutions, three by governments, and one by the Provincial government of Quebec.[11]

Japanese corporations felt increasingly frustrated at their exclusion from this market where such large sums could be raised without collateral. In the Japanese domestic bond market all issues had to be secured by collateral and the arrangement of this was a major source of income for the banks. Mitsui and Komatsu both tried to break through the barrier in 1972 but were unsuccessful in face of the pressure brought by the banks on the Ministry of Finance. The issue lay dormant.

By the end of the decade foreign corporations also had become attracted by the low interest rates and lack of collateral required for Samurai issues and several applied to join the queue. The initial reaction of the Japanese was extremely hostile. Apart from anything else, as just noted, they had refused even their own most powerful corporations the right to raise unsecured loans. If foreigners were given the right, domestic rules would have to be changed too and the whole standard of domestic credit-backing for industry would be lowered. Furthermore, a vast amount of traditional business would be transferred from the banks to the securities houses which alone, under Article 65, would be allowed to underwrite such issues. Nevertheless, under intense foreign pressure the Ministry of Finance gave way. In March 1979, Sears Roebuck of the United States, with a triple-A rating, was permitted to sell a five-year issue without security. It was ruled that any company that had issued such private placements (*shibosai* in Japanese) might not return to the market for a second issue. This in no way detracted from the appeal of the bonds. The walls had now been breached and the Ministry of Finance announced that any other corporations with similar triple-A rating might apply to sell bonds. This immediately qualified forty European and American companies, while Toyota and Matsushita Denki (National Panasonic) also won the right to issue unsecured bonds on the domestic market.[12]

This was the heyday of the Samurai bond. By the end of 1976 there had been 273 issues. During 1979 and 1980, 10 per cent of all foreign bond issues world-wide took place in Tokyo. British banks took a leading role in finding clients and arranging issues. S. G. Warburg took part, between April 1978 and December 1984, in no fewer than forty-seven Samurai issues, totalling 943 billion yen, of which the bank underwrote, or guaranteed, 4.5 billion yen. This activity continued right up to the end of the period covered by this book, a recent Warburg client being the Halifax Building Society, selling 20 billion yen of 5 per cent notes in June 1988. Many other UK houses have been active in such issues, particularly Barclays de Zoete Wedd (BZW) and Baring Brothers.[13]

The authorities found it difficult to take their hands off a process of internationalization which was radically altering the whole credit system. Takeshi Hosomi points out how different the practice in the Japanese Market had been from that overseas up until then: 'It had been standard practice for foreign bonds denominated in yen issued by corporations overseas to be sold unsecured, whereas, in Japan, it was now a tradition that they should carry security.'[14] All of this was now rapidly going by the board and the authorities were trying to slow down the rate of change by such regulations as the 'no-return rule', triple-A rating, and temporary restrictions. As James Horne so clearly puts it

> the involvement of the Ministry of Finance indicated a continued daily interest in the management of the market and of capital controls more generally. The fact that the level of direct investment abroad was not subject to regulatory control, no matter how temporary, showed the discriminatory character of the regulations which were applied to the yen bond market.[15]

Such controls were clearly seen when the issue of Samurai Bonds was suspended for several months after the first 'oil shock' of 1973. After the second 'oil shock' of 1979 it was no longer considered right to take such an arbitrary step but issues were rationed to 30 billion yen a month.

The big change in the Tokyo yen bond market did not come until the Samurai bonds were challenged by Euroyen bonds (see below). Euroyen bonds were first introduced in 1977 in London. With no security, no regulation, and the minimum of requirements and formalities, they were fast displacing Samurai bonds by the early 1980s. The Japanese authorities eventually reacted to maintain their own market and prevent the extinction of the Samurai bond. In 1984 there was a programme of deregulation, in 1986 the 'no return' rule was abolished, credit rating requirements were gradually lowered, and the securities houses began to sponsor quite small companies as applicants. Life Insurance companies were also given the right to arrange private placements. In 1987 balance sheet requirements for capital–equity ratios were lowered. By now licences were being granted to corporations with only a single-A rating and comparatively modest assets.[16]

Under the impact of deregulation the pace of Samurai issues has fluctuated. In fiscal 1985, issues rose to 1,115 billion yen. In the first six months of 1986 they ran at much the same rate with a total of 500 billion, but this was only one-sixth of issues on the Euroyen market. In fact, that year saw very large redemptions of Samurai bonds which were replaced by Euroyen. 1987 brought an upsurge again and the number of foreign companies planning issues rose from ten to three hundred. However, this enthusiasm was not maintained and business at the end of 1988 was said to be very slack.

Other Japanese Bonds

A Shogun bond is one which is issued in Tokyo in a non-Japanese currency. They were introduced in 1972 for private placements. Foreign companies were the issuers and Japanese banks the primary purchasers. Like Samurai bonds, they were susceptible to the reactions of the authorities to outside events and did not really take off until the 'oil shocks' had been finally surmounted. There were then four dollar-denominated issues for European entities, underwritten by both foreign and Japanese banks. Tokyo's share was some 80 per cent while the rest of each issue was placed in European markets by a syndicate of foreign banks.[17]

In 1985 this modest market reached its height with eight issues. (It is interesting that one of these was denominated in Ecu; another European link is that Shogun bonds are listed on the Luxemburg Stock Exchange.) In 1986 the total amount of capital raised was only 240 billion yen and, in spite of steps to deregulate, these bonds seem to be at present as much on the wane as Samurai bonds.

Japanese financial institutions have tried to be receptive to the particular needs of their clients and to tailor special issues for them. These have resulted in a number of hybrid instruments, such as the Daimyo bonds, first issued by the World Bank in 1987 in both the Euromarket and Japan. Sometimes special bonds have exotic names, such as the *Sushi* bond, designed to be held by Japanese trust banks and insurance companies.

JAPANESE WARRANTS

In 1981 the Japanese Commercial Code was amended to permit the issue for corporations of Eurobonds carrying equity warrants. These are detachable portions of the bonds which entitle the holder to purchase equity in the issuing company at any time during the life of the bond. This may be from four to seven years but is generally five years. The purchasing power of the warrant is the same as the face value of the bond, that is, a $100 bond carries a warrant for $100. The equity purchase price and the currency rate are usually fixed at the time of issue.

The first such issue was made for Mitsubishi Chemicals in 1982 on the London Market. It attracted little attention, but within eighteen months the practice started to increase rapidly. For the issuer the low interest rates attaching to all Eurobonds compared with raising money in Japan was accompanied by two further advantages. First, as five-year bonds, a yen swap could be made immediately; this was not possible with earlier Eurobonds, which were usually fifteen-year convertibles. Second, they provided for a future flow of equity capital at a time when Japanese industry was set on increasing securitization.

For the purchaser the advantages became clear when a secondary market was started mid-1983. The issue would be made at a face-value of $100. On separation the bond itself would take up a value at a level with a small premium to US Treasury rates, say $80, leaving a warrant for $100 obtained at the residue of the purchase price, that is $20. There was little risk attached and the equity options were very favourably priced. The benefits of such a cheap way into the stocks of Japanese companies proved irresistible. When the strength of the Tokyo bull market became clear in 1984 there was a flood of such issues. In the year to December 1988 they exceeded $28 billion.

Because the transactions were in Eurobonds, they were originally placed in the London market. The issues have been almost solely for Japanese corporations, perhaps because they were less concerned than others about the effects of dilution. In 1988 only 7 issues out of 216 (less than 2.5 per cent in value) were for non-Japanese companies. Most of the bonds are denominated in US dollars or Swiss Francs. The Swiss were heavy buyers from the start and now a considerable proportion of the issues are made in Switzerland.[18]

The original dealers in London were Robert Fleming, Daiwa, and Nomura. In 1985 there was a frisson in the market when a large part of the senior team at Flemings departed for Barings, which has been an important operator ever since. Until the end of 1985 Japanese were not allowed to deal in warrants and they were held by British, American, and Middle East investors. As soon as this obstacle was removed Japanese brokers began to recommend the warrants to their private clients. By October 1987 70 per cent were still held abroad and 30 per cent in Japan. During the week following Black Monday many foreigners sold precipitately and the proportions were reversed in a few days, Japanese investors obtaining them at remarkably low prices. The rate of issue has increased rapidly as demand became insatiable in Japan, not only from the original private investors, but from Japanese institutions and *tokkin* (see p. 174). Many American and Swiss banks have joined the Japanese securities houses to manage these issues. Although the total face value of all equity warrants in 1988 was only 16.3 per cent of the total Eurobond issues for that year, the proportion looked set to rise.[19]

The trade in Japanese warrants has been of enormous interest to the City of London, to the British operators in the secondary market, and to investors. In early 1989 a secondary market opened in Japan in which Flemings, Barings, and others planned to become active participants.

THE EUROYEN BOND MARKET 1977

Euroyen are deposits of free yen in European banks. In 1980 the sum of offshore deposits of yen was roughly 8 billion, of which 50 per cent were in Europe, thus becoming Euroyen. Most of this sum was held by the London branches of Japanese banks.[20]

By 1977 there was mounting pressure from the governments of Japan's trading partners, and particularly from that of the United States, to ensure the greater use of Japanese currency as a means of international settlement. It was believed that this would help to secure a more realistic valuation of the yen. The proportion of Japanese trade invoiced in yen was extremely small and not in keeping with the country's position as having the second largest economy after the United States. Hitherto, the Japanese government had resisted the use of yen as an offshore currency, precisely because of the effect this might be expected to have on the exchange rate. Now, for a number of reasons, they were reaching the conclusion that the expected 'yen-shift' towards an increased international use of the currency could not be resisted indefinitely. A secret mission was dispatched to study the operation of offshore markets and reported that such a market for the yen need not necessarily lead to a loss of control over the currency. Thus, the chief objection to the creation of a Euroyen bond market was removed and the first issue was made in April 1977. The May 1977 edition of *Euromoney* contained the following interesting account of the views of the Japanese authorities:

> According to the Japanese themselves, the issue and its successors represent the first time since the Russians created the Eurodollar market that a national government has proposed to use the market as a deliberate instrument of national financial policy and to control its currency's sector of the international financial sea.

The use of the word 'control' was significant.

This first issue was made by the European Investment Bank (EIB) for 10 billion yen at 7.25 per cent. The idea had been hatched during talks in Manila, sponsored for the purpose the previous year, between Monsieur André George of the European

Investment Bank, Mr Yukio Hosoi of Daiwa Securities, and Mr Masao Fujioka of the Japanese Ministry of Finance. The EIB enjoyed great international prestige and it was not easy for the Japanese to ignore the Bank's desire to diversify their holdings by acquiring yen. As Monsieur George said after the issue had been made: 'All we could find were dollars, Deutschemarks and sometimes a few florins. So another currency was very welcome.'[21] Originally, the Ministry of Finance wished the bonds to have a maturity of five years. The EIB, however, insisted successfully on a seven-year life, making the new facility more attractive for future issues.

It was natural for Daiwa to have been involved in the initiation of the new market. They had taken a leading part in a joint venture with the development bank of the government of Singapore and in reorganizing the market in Asia-dollars – the Far Eastern equivalent of Eurodollars. In the course of this they had co-managed two Asia-dollar issues for the EIB. Daiwa also seems to have been the first Japanese securities house to sense that the attitude of the authorities in Tokyo was changing, and this insight emboldened it to take the lead in pressing for a Euroyen market.

The other essential participant in these events was S. G. Warburg and Co. This bank had particularly close ties with Japan, originating perhaps from the relationship which had been formed by M. M. Warburg in the days of Russo-Japanese War Loans and now sustained by a close friendship between Sir Sigmund Warburg and Mr Jiro Shirasu[22]. Although Warburgs had grown up in London totally independently of the German bank, its chairman-founder, Sir Sigmund Warburg, had maintained his family's warm friendship with the family of the late Prime Minister Takahashi. S. G. Warburg had played a leading part in introducing Japanese clients to the Eurodollar market and had been very active with Samurai bonds. The May 1977 edition of *Euromoney* quoted Mr Martin Gordon of S. G. Warburg as saying: '[Warburg people] have been regular visitors to Japan in fair and foul weather for fifteen years ... selling the yen to Euroinvestors ... When we rubbed shoulders at cocktail parties, one of the things we talked about was what would happen if the euroyen got going.' Thus Warburgs had been anticipating the development of the market for some time and it identified a pool of likely customers. It was therefore a natural choice as joint lead manager with Daiwa for the EIB and for the next two issues for the International Bank of Reconstruction and Development and the Asian Development Bank. By the end of 1983 it had been lead manager of twelve Euroyen issues and co-manager of a further nine, thus securing second place in the league for lead managers and seventh place in the two functions taken together.[23]

Between 1977 and 1983 the demand for Euroyen developed slowly and most of the large issuers were either governments or international organizations. Total issues amounted to only about 420 billion yen. The reason for this was not so much the novel and relatively undeveloped state of the market as the fact that Japanese corporations were barred from raising capital by this means. The only small exceptions made to this rule were placements by the supermarket chain Ito Yokado for 5 billion yen of bonds with the Kuwaiti government in 1980 and four other private placements with OPEC countries. When much greater freedom was given to Japanese entities to raise money in this way, by the relaxation of the rules of the Ministry of Finance in 1985, the figures started to rocket. In that year there were some eighty issues worth over 2,000 billion yen and, for the first time, Japanese corporations borrowed more in Euroyen than in the domestic market. In 1988, borrowings in the Euroyen market in dollar terms reached $21.7 billion, with a very high proportion going to Japanese corporations.[24] Eurodollar bonds with warrants attached proved outstandingly popular in Japan. The lower interest rates and the great ease and speed with which these issues could be made rendered them very attractive.

An extremely important feature of this market was the way in which the Japanese securities houses and merchant banks were able to take over the book running. By 1986 Warburgs, which had played such a pre-eminent part in its inception, had fallen to sixteenth place and the only other British firm playing a significant role, Kleinwort Benson, was not even in the top twenty. By 1988, of the other major foreign players, only Bankers Trust and Salomon Brothers had managed to maintain their position in the top ten. Of the eighty issues in 1985, seventy-three were managed by Japanese firms, and in 1986 one Japanese company alone, Nomura, led half of the Euroyen issues for North American corporations.[25] In so far as issues for Japanese corporations were concerned, the Big Four securities houses had managed to monopolize all issues, of whatever currency, in the Euromarkets while with the two leading Japanese long-term credit banks they serviced over 20 per cent of all issues. An analysis of the reasons for this is given by Aaron Viner in his book 'Inside Japan's Financial Markets'. While the prevalence of Japanese borrowers in the market and their loyalty to their own banks and securities houses is understandable, the practice described by Viner as 'systematic predatory pricing of issues' is clearly injurious.[26] The implications will be discussed in Part III of this book. The market has been described as being really a Japanese domestic market with Jalpak tour attached.

While this trend towards Japanese domination of the Euromarkets is due to the preponderant size of their corporations, both as borrowers and operators in the market-place, and is certainly not due to lack of skills on the part of the British, European, or American houses, it should not be thought that the Japanese themselves are in any way lacking in similar skills or powers of innovation. Although they arrived on the scene in force comparatively late and not very well equipped for the task, they quickly took to the water and have been responsible for a number of startling innovations. Examples of their ingenuity include the introduction of the $100 million 'Heaven and Hell' bond issue for the IBM Credit Corporation. This deal involved three interest rate swaps and five currency swaps. It was designed to ensure that the investor would be covered regardless of whether the dollar had risen or fallen at the time of maturity. In 1986 the first reverse dual currency bond was floated by Kawasaki Steel. This is a yen bond with interest paid in dollars, intended to allow the investor to take a foreign exchange position without incurring a foreign exchange risk. Other hybrid bonds have been developed by Japanese firms such as the Performance Exchange Listed bond. Whether these prove to be inspirational or levitational must perhaps await the moment of maturity.[27]

NOTES

1 Thomas Adams and Iwao Hoshii, *A Financial History of Modern Japan* (Research Japan Ltd., Tokyo, 1964), pp. 120–1.
2 Nat West Archives.
3 *The Times* (25 Feb. 1964).
4 Takeshi Hosomi, *Tokyo Ofushoa Shijo: Sekai Sandaikoku Kokusai Kinyu Senta no Tembo* (Toyo Keizai, Tokyo, 1985).
5 K. J. Robbie, *Moscow Narodny Bank Quarterly Review*, 16/4, (1975–6), p. 21.
6 *The Times* (25 Feb. 1964).
7 Information supplied courtesy of S. G. Warburgs.
8 *The Times* (7 Apr. 1964).
9 *IFR Global Financing Directory* (Jan–Sept. 1988), pp. 5–15.
10 James Horne, *Japan's Financial Markets: Conflict and Consensus in Policy-Making* (George Allen & Unwin in association with the Australia–Japan Research Institute, Australian National University, Sydney, 1985), pp. 173–5.
11 Aron Viner, 'Inside Japan's Financial Markets', *The Economist* (1988), p. 119. Cf. also information supplied courtesy of Warburgs.
12 Horne, *Japan's Financial Markets*, pp. 173–92.
13 Information supplied courtesy of S. G. Warburgs.
14 Hosomi, *Tokyo Ofushoa Shijo*.
15 Horne, *Japan's Financial Markets*, p. 182.
16 Viner, 'Inside Japan's Financial Markets', pp. 122–3.
17 Ibid., pp. 122–3.
18 Information kindly supplied by Mr Allen Gibbs of Jardine Fleming.
19 *IFR Global Financing Directory*.
20 Andreas Prindl, *Japanese Finance* (John Wiley & Sons, New York, 1981), p. 46.
21 *Euromoney* (May 1987).
22 Mr Jiro Shirasu had been the principal liaison officer between the early post-war government of Mr Yoshida and SCAP. He introduced Sir Sigmund Warburg to many influential Japanese such as Mr Kiichi Miyazawa, later Minister of Finance, and Governor Morinaga of the Bank of Japan.
23 Information supplied courtesy of S. G. Warburgs.
24 Viner, 'Inside Japan's Financial Markets', p. 131.
25 *IFR Global Financing Directory* (Jan.–Sept. 1988).
26 Viner, 'Inside Japan's Financial Markets', pp. 137–9.
27 Ibid.

12

FOREIGN FINANCIAL DEALINGS IN
TOKYO
1972–1988

After the brief general survey in the preceding chapter of capital markets and of some of the instruments devised to raise money from them in the post-war period, we will now return to the point reached at the end of chapter 10 and continue to trace the history of foreign banks and securities houses established in Tokyo from 1972 onwards.

THE BRITISH PRESENCE

By 1972 important changes in the Japanese economy were becoming apparent. Although the 'oil shock' of the following year would cause enormous problems and temporarily mask the underlying trend, the basis had been laid for the massive and permanent trade surpluses of the coming decade. Second, although saving was no longer at its highest level, the rate of capital formation was outstripping the requirements of domestic investment. This had permitted the recent opening of the market in Samurai bonds and would now lead the Ministry of Finance to lift the prohibition on Japanese banks from lending to foreigners. As soon as the period of dislocation caused by the first oil shock was over, the world would experience the beginning of a steadily growing export of Japanese capital. The new position of Japan as a highly important factor in world financial affairs (hastened by the events of the 'Nixon Shock') increased both the justification and the outside pressures for liberalization of Japan's financial markets.

Various considerations of this kind tempted foreign merchant banks and stockbrokers to enter the Tokyo markets. In chapters 9 and 10 we discussed the presence and activities in Tokyo of British commercial banks but the first British merchant bank to open a representative office was Kleinwort Benson in 1970. Its early start and energetic conduct under the management of Mr John Cousins, gave it a leading position which it has managed to maintain in various activities ever since. Kleinwort Benson was followed by Jardine Fleming in 1971, Hambros in 1972, and Schroders and Barings in 1974. Two British stockbroking houses, Grieveson Grant and Vickers da Costa, also established themselves in Tokyo. The most active American player in these fields at the time was the investment banking house of Salomon Brothers. Considering their high activity in the Eurodollar and Samurai bond markets, it is surprising that S. G. Warburg did not open a representative office until 1979; the explanation lay in the Chairman's philosophy of avoiding a multiplication of costly local offices and preferring to use a squad of plane-hoppers. It is interesting that they were eventually strongly pressed to open a representative office by the Japanese Ministry of Finance itself.[1]

The foreign arrivals were courteously received by the Bank of Japan and the Ministry of Finance. Both were invariably helpful with advice and in finding local staff. All of the British bankers who have worked in Tokyo have, not surprisingly, stressed the great importance of having experienced and competent local staff and advisers. Some difficulties were encountered in dealing with the banking unions, which proved to be extremely tough. Relations with the Japanese banks were courteous and co-operative, though competition would soon develop and the Japanese would periodically complain to the Ministry and seek to be shielded if they felt that the foreign banks were building up a commanding position in any area.

This raises the whole question of administrative guidance and how this has been used to affect the position of foreign banks. None of the British banks approached has been willing to complain of deliberately unfair discrimination by the authorities. They claim that their complaints were always heard and often acted upon and that although procedures are maddeningly cumbersome and licences and permits slow in coming, persistence is more often rewarded than not. Japanese companies work under the same restraints. It was said that head-offices at home were more likely to grumble than those on the spot. There seemed to be a consensus that it was the defensive nature of the system as a whole that tended to frustrate foreign enterprise rather than specific determination to prevent it.

This response may reflect the natural caution of bankers and an understandable desire not to make trouble for oneself. It does also imply acceptance of the inevitability of foreigners taking a small minority role as their fate. It is a glaring fact that, whereas Japanese banks and securities houses have built up a dominant, indeed almost monopolistic position in some sectors of the London and New York markets, the British banks in Tokyo have increasingly been confined to niche banking or boutique banking. This may appear to be inescapable in a situation where the Japanese houses dispose of much greater financial resources and domestic corporate connections than their British counterparts and where advantages of skill, experience, and innovation often cannot be deployed in competition because they are frustrated by regulation. These facts of life have been of more fundamental importance than the day-to-day nudgings or restraints of administrative guidance. Fortunately, in spite of all these difficulties, the fields open to the British banks for profitable pursuit have been wide enough for most of them to remain in Tokyo and to grow there, sometimes to a remarkable extent.

Before going on to examine these fields, a rather curious point may first be made. The offices of the British and American merchant banks and brokerage houses, as opposed to those of the commercial banks, were usually staffed by men in their twenties or early thirties. In Tokyo it was unknown for any Japanese to enjoy a position of comparable authority at such an early age and the newcomers had to deal with much older men. At first the Japanese, even with some experience of life abroad, must have wondered if the foreign houses were really serious in wanting to do business. Personal contact gradually removed any such misunderstandings and the Japanese came to appreciate the ability, intelligence, and originality of this small and youthful foreign community in their midst. Today, some fifteen years later, there are the first signs that Japanese companies themselves are beginning to break the old age-hierarchy and give rather greater responsibility to younger persons, at least in their overseas subsidiaries.

IMPACT LOANS

The merchant banks, unlike the commercial banks, were not permitted to accept deposits. They had to find some business quickly which would meet the high costs of their presence in Tokyo. This was provided by 'impact loans', the foreign currency loans to Japanese corporations on a short-term basis already mentioned (see p. 131). Since Japanese banks were prohibited from acquiring foreign exchange for such purposes, they were obliged to steer their customers to the foreign banks, who enjoyed a monopoly of this market. At first the number of such banks was still relatively small, so that each enjoyed a reasonable share of the proceeds. The onset of the 'oil shock' sent the demand for foreign exchange rocketing overnight. In 1974 Japan would have to find between $30 billion and $35 billion to meet its foreign exchange requirements. The foreign banks were besieged by requests for impact loans from corporations which much preferred this method of raising money to the issue of bonds, since problems of credit rating and security were less demanding. The margins on these loans at this time were quite exceptional; one British merchant bank claims to have placed such a loan with a margin of 4 per cent. However, 2 per cent to 2.5 per cent was quite common. Some banks were earning 40 per cent of their income in Japan from such transactions.[2] The maximum level permitted to be carried on the balance sheet of the Tokyo branch of a lending bank at any one time was $650 million. Some Japanese companies would at times borrow beyond their requirements and deposit the surplus with the lending bank, a practice agreeable to both parties but which would no doubt have been unwelcome to the authorities if reported. Swaps into yen were permitted up to a maximum of $10 million and were used by corporations to cover foreign exchange risks.

The demand continued after the effects of the first 'oil shock' had been absorbed and was a useful way of recycling part of the now enormous OPEC surpluses. From 1975 onwards the Japanese government ran a series of deficit budgets financed by trillions of yens' worth of domestic bonds. These mopped up a great deal of the liquidity in the capital market and maintained the need for foreign funding. But by now so many foreign banks had been attracted to Tokyo that individual shares of the cake were falling steadily. This state of affairs continued until 1980 when the revised Foreign Exchange Law removed the restriction on Japanese banks making impact loans and gave them free access to the purchase of foreign currency for yen. The monopoly of the foreign banks disappeared and their share of the market fell to 60 per cent in 1982 and 18.6 per cent in 1984.[3] The fact was that Japanese banks could offer cheaper rates with their greater accessibility to funds, and also call on the loyalties of their clients. Not only did this represent a serious loss of revenue to the British and other foreign banks but it also diminished their usefulness and standing in the market. The August 1986 edition of *Euromoney* reported that the Fuji Bank had formerly had relations with ten foreign banks on the Tokyo market but had now cut its links with all of them except the Deutsche Bank, on which it relied for intelligence on overseas markets.

This disappointing shrinkage of business led some American banks to withdraw from Tokyo, or just to move out of the corporate loan sector. A few European banks, on the other hand, such as Credit Suisse and the National Westminster, stepped up their efforts to increase their exposure. The *Far Eastern Economic Review* for 9 April 1987 reported the view that only by maintaining such links with Japanese corporations could they hope to maintain their business in offering advisory services.

YEN LOANS

Many foreign banks have carried on a small but comfortable business in advancing yen loans. This has always been limited by the difficulty of obtaining yen, other than by interbank deposits and such purchases of free yen as were not discouraged by the authorities. Nevertheless, as early as 31 March 1976 the Tokyo balance sheet of the National Westminster Bank showed outstanding loans of around $180 million, of which two-thirds were impact loans and one-third yen loans.[4] The total of yen loans made by foreign banks outstanding at the end of 1986 was somewhat less than $20 billion. This looks like a lot of money, but the amount was falling steadily. Not much of it was attributable to British banks: Marine Midland pulled out and closed its Tokyo office in 1985.

FOREIGN EXCHANGE BUSINESS

Foreign banks were able to a considerable extent to offset the demise of impact loans by stepping up their foreign exchange operations. According to the *Far Eastern Economic Review* for 9 April 1987 the Bank of America estimated that 40 per cent of the profits of its Tokyo Branch in 1986 came from foreign exchange dealing. Lloyds Bank expected to quadruple the number of its staff in this sector between 1985 and 1990.

The Tokyo foreign exchange market became active after the floating of the yen in 1971. The chief reason for its rapid growth thereafter was the fluctuating behaviour of the yen–dollar exchange rate. In 1984 the 'real demand rule', which had stipulated that transactions should be linked to trade contracts, was removed. Thereafter, participants began to engage in the arbitrage business and Tokyo became the principal centre for yen–dollar transactions. In 1987 these were averaging nearly $10 billion a day. The market has the advantage, because of its position in an eastern time zone, of being the first to open every day, and by 1988 was open for twenty-four hours. Though continuing to grow rapidly, it was still third in volume after New York and London. A foreign exchange dealing room is held by some to be the present essential requirement for any banking operation in Tokyo.

The Government Bond Market

The Japanese government bond market has grown very rapidly since the recession which followed the first oil crisis. The subsequent practice of Japanese governments of financing budget deficits by Revenue bonds released a flood of paper. The market is now approaching the US bond market in size. More than four-fifths of the Japanese bonds traded are government issues. Corporate bonds include convertibles and bonds with warrants attached. Trading in futures is now permitted. The market has one unique feature – the provisions of Article 65 of the Securities and Exchange Law do not apply to government securities and the banks are therefore able to participate. This has led to the formation of syndicates or *Kisaikai*,[5] dominated by the domestic banks, which determine the conditions of issue and the allocation of the bonds.

The system has created great difficulties for British and foreign companies trying to get into the market. For example, all medium-term (ten-year) bonds used to be allotted to members of a special syndicate only, who were also required to have accounts with the Bank of Japan. No British company met these requirements. Now, however, these bond sales are open to auctions in which foreign members compete. The long-term bond issues were not by 1988 open to auction and in spite of pressure the authorities were unlikely to agree to them becoming so because of the effect on interest rates. Instead, sales were allocated by the syndicate, of which there were 775 members in 1987, the forty-two foreign members then securing 1 per cent of the long-term bonds between them.[6]

There is considerable dispute about the profitability of operations in this market. In March 1987 Mr Shogi Oshima of Citicorp Vickers da Costa was quoted as saying that his company would not join the pressure to open the market further; other things were more important.[7] At the same time Mr Eugene Atkinson of Goldman Sachs expressed the belief that his firm could extend their clientele for these bonds from overseas purchasers to Japanese investors.[8] The *Far Eastern Economic Review* on 9 April 1987 quoted the Bank of America as saying that it had increased its returns by three or four times since 1984 and now considered trading in Japanese government bonds was its second highest source of profit after foreign exchange dealings. The major British contender in this market has been the National Westminster Bank, through its merchant banking arm, County NatWest.

SHORT-TERM MONEY MARKETS

The two interbank markets, the call market and the discount bill market, which had been opened to foreigners in 1970 and 1971 (chapter 10, p. 132) are supplemented by a third market for trading in bonds called *gensaki*. These instruments are nominally long-term but they carry attachments saying that they will be redeemed on a specified date and they are invariably completed with short maturities. The market is open to corporations as well as financial houses.

There is foreign participation in all the short-term markets. In the interbank call market, it has fluctuated sharply, rising to a peak in 1984 when foreigners became active borrowers in over 10 per cent of the transactions.[9]

MERGERS AND ACQUISITIONS

Mergers have never been a favoured method of Japanese growth, although there are important exceptions. The banking field, for instance, has been the scene of many mergers in the last 100 years, some of them induced by government pressure, particularly between 1930 and 1944. The most notable such merger in the post-war period was that of the Dai Ichi and Kangyo Banks to form the largest bank in the world in terms of capital assets. In August of 1989 the Mitsui and Taiyo Kobe Banks also joined together to form the second largest bank. Shinnitetsu, the largest steel company in Japan (Nippon Steel) was the result of the massive merger of Fuji Steel and Yataka Steel. But manufacturing industry has always tended to develop by growth of individual

companies, steadily increasing market share and assets by internal growth with the weaker companies going to the wall or being
revitalized by the shareholders under a new name. Another feature has been that there is little impulsion to vertical integration.
Many large companies traditionally relied on a host of small
suppliers and subcontractors who could be picked up or dropped
according to the business cycle. This too has discouraged
building-block growth.

While mergers seem to be becoming more accepted, take-
overs are still a comparative novelty. They have, in the past,
sometimes been used for rescue operations – the take-over in
October 1977 of Ataka by C. Itoh being a case in point. Of
course, it can be no surprise that in a society founded on the
practice of consensus, a hostile take-over bid should be seen as
shocking and unacceptable, particularly when coming from
overseas. Mr Terry Ramsden's bid for the Minebea Corporation, for example, was considered as thoroughly opportunistic.
It is not only that the management teams are intensely loyal
to the existing company structure, the unions also may wish to
guard it from outsiders. Mr Toyo Gyoten, formerly Vice-Minister of Finance, cited a proposed merger between a mutual bank
and a large city bank which fell through because of union opposition. An article in *Euromoney* in February 1986 summed up the
situation as follows: 'The Japanese distaste for merger and acquisition activity is so strong that even the new friendly mergers
that have been created result in notably fragile alliances. The
constituent parts may remain at arm's-length for years if not
decades.' On the other hand, many years of foreign pressure for a
reform of Japanese distribution may be leading to a more modern
retail system which will come about in this way. Mr Takeshi
Uemoto, of the retail chain Ito Yokado, told *Euromoney*: 'Our
company's policy is that we will go with merger and acquisition
activity if it becomes more acceptable ... We are already talking
to foreign banks about how to make acquisitions.'[10] Because
merger and acquisition has not been acceptable, Japanese banks
have been slow to move into the field and businessmen like Mr
Uemoto have turned to foreign banks, particularly when making
acquisitions abroad. British banks have actively pursued merger
and acquisition business in Tokyo and some claim to have found

it rewarding. More recently, Japanese banks began to build up their own in-house teams. At the beginning of 1990 the Long-Term Credit Bank of Japan had built up its merger and acquisition staff to fifteen, the Sanwa Bank to thirty in Tokyo and twenty in the United States, and the Sumitomo Bank to forty-four. In the securities industry Nomura Wasserstein Perella were employing thirty-five.[11] There can be no doubt that the Japanese will soon be able to meet much of their own requirement in this field.

VENTURE CAPITAL

At first glance it is surprising that a number of British banks (Kleinworts, Schroders, and Hambros in particular) should have staffed departments to manage venture capital business in Tokyo. Traditionally in Japan, small or new companies would go for financial support to the *sogo* (mutual loan and savings) banks or to the credit associations. Today, when much of venture capital is either in the field of high technology or of special and new situations which require skilful detection, these rather pedestrian and old-fashioned providers of capital are not always suitable. Nor do the large Japanese banks have the practice of dealing with untried small fry. Foreign banks have therefore been able to occupy quite successful niches in this field.

FUND AND PORTFOLIO MANAGEMENT

In chapter 10 (p. 137) the creation of the first foreign investment trusts to invest in Japanese equities was discussed. Although the majority of such trusts run by British houses are London-based and run from head offices, most of them depend on their branches or representatives in Tokyo to provide them with investment information and in some cases to deal on their behalf. The level of foreign investment in the Tokyo market continues to fluctuate, having fallen sharply after Black Monday in 1987, for example, but in recent years has tended to move between 3 per cent and 15 per cent, with a tendency towards the 7 per cent level. At any rate, Barings, which is the leading British house in this field, claims that in 1988 no less than two-thirds of all the investment funds which they raised in the United States was placed in the Japanese market.

Since 1972 foreign firms have also been allowed to run investment trusts for Japanese investors wanting to put their money into foreign securities. These have often given better returns than Japanese trusts, investing in their own home market. This can only reflect a difference in management policies and skills. More recently, foreign banks and brokers in Tokyo, acting under the provisions of the Investment Advisers Act of 1986, have been searching for direct Japanese clients and have been not unsuccessful. There is little point in a British firm pursuing the private Japanese client, unless he were to be a very big fish indeed; the picture of the young British broker chatting up the loquacious Japanese housewife-investor on the state of her portfolio is not a convincing one. But corporate clients are a different matter and have provided an increasing amount of business.

Japanese entities wishing to invest abroad can either use the services of the Japanese securities houses, many of which (like the Big Four) have been operating in American and European markets for decades, or they can turn to foreign investment advisers. Originally, national loyalty, long-standing connections, *Keiretsu* links, and other such factors would tend to favour the Japanese adviser, but performance has become increasingly important. As Japanese investment overseas has expanded rapidly, so has the role of the foreign investment manager.

British firms have, therefore, also been looking for corporate business on the domestic Japanese market. It would seem unlikely to a Japanese client that a foreign company would be able to offer advice on the Japanese market which could not be much better given by a Japanese securities company. However, when a British broker in Tokyo was asked by a Japanese rival what his firm had to offer, he replied: 'We give sell recommendations.' He was referring to the supposed fact that, whereas Japanese advisers will give plenty of advice on what to buy, they are inclined to leave the investor with his purchase for an indefinite period, regardless of performance. This may reflect the ingrained

Japanese attitudes of loyalty of shareholder to company and that wise investment is a long-term business. But it also has been suggested that the close involvement of securities houses in the affairs of client corporations makes it difficult for them to give selling advice.

This whole question of relative performance as investment manager has been opened up by the decision of the Ministry of Finance to license nine foreign companies (of which six were American and Barclays was the sole British bank) to undertake the management of trust funds, a field hitherto reserved to Japanese Trust Banks, insurance companies, and securities houses with special licence. The performance of such funds has often been indifferent and pension funds have shown little growth, owing to stodginess of management. There is a feeling that foreign management may be able to work revolutionary change. In 1986 the first Japanese business seminar on investment performance was held. *Euromoney* described this event in the following exuberant terms: 'The seminar is an oblique but powerful tribute to the swathe that nine newly licensed foreign-owned trusts have been cutting through Tokyo's financial community.'[12] Mr Chris Nowakowski of the performance management firm Connecticut Intersect, commented: 'Pension Fund sponsors in Japan want more meaningful performance figures. The foreign banks are very eager to give more detailed information and that is bound to force Japanese fund managers to improve their reporting.'[13] However, even at the end of 1988, these were still serious obstacles in this field. The Japanese government did not seem disposed to give to foreign entities any share at all in the investment of State Pension Funds. As far as Corporate and Life Insurance pension funds are concerned, those foreign companies which have been licensed as trust banks are permitted to operate but negotiations still continue for the admission of foreign securities houses into the field on terms which would permit them to work effectively. There are still also many restrictions on the operation of Japanese investment trusts and mutual funds and the industry remains almost entirely in the hands of Japanese securities houses and trust banks. It was hoped in London that a satisfactory solution would be reached in time for foreign securities houses to begin operation in 1990 in such new fields. Even then, marketing of British services would not be easy; Japanese clients need a high degree of servicing.

A special kind of investment vehicle which has appeared in recent years is the *tokkin* (special money). This is a temporary discretionary trust fund for the liquid funds of corporations and financial companies which offers attractive tax advantages by treating profits as income rather than capital gains. Management of *tokkin* can be very lucrative. There has been a growing tendency for the assets to be invested outside Japan and British banks have been particularly successful in attracting advisory or management business.

OPERATIONS ON THE STOCK EXCHANGE

The representative offices of the British banks and stockbroking firms opening in Tokyo in the early seventies could not, of course, deal on the Japanese Stock Exchange. When purchasing or selling securities for their managed trusts or clients they had to use a Japanese broker to carry out the transaction and pay an appropriate fee. In this way close links were formed with the securities houses which could be useful in bringing Japanese business in London to the British firm involved.

The process of acquiring membership of the Tokyo stock exchange was to be a long and difficult one. The first step was to upgrade the representative office to Branch status – a slow business usually requiring two years or more before Ministry of Finance permission could be obtained. Having achieved this, foreign banks were still debarred from carrying out securities business by Article 65 of the Securities and Exchange Law, while the brokerage-houses were excluded from membership of the Stock Exchange by Article 8 of its regulations which forbade foreign membership. It was forbidden by the Japanese authorities for banks and securities companies to merge and so new joint companies had to be set up in Hong Kong, London, or elsewhere, for instance, Grieveson Grant and Kleinworts. These companies then applied for securities licences. The first such licence obtained by a foreign company was by Merrill Lynch in 1973. This process again would take a long time and although the licence conferred certain rights to practise investment management and advice, and entitled the holder to join in underwriting domestic Japanese bond issues, the company could still not operate on the exchange. In 1982 membership of the Tokyo stock exchange was opened to foreign companies, but it was claimed that there was no physical room for further members. The building was indeed small and crowded, even with only eighty-four seats, and no Japanese firm seemed willing to retire. Then, in 1984, there was a merger between Japanese companies which created one vacancy, and there was a general expectation that it would be filled by a foreign firm. But when the auction took place, although Merrill Lynch put in a hefty bid, it was found that a Japanese firm had won. This brought matters to a head and the United States and British governments protested strongly to the Japanese government. There was great resentment in London where Japanese securities houses had already been admitted to the Stock Exchange for some years. In 1985, under pressure from the Ministry of Finance, the Council of the Tokyo Stock Exchange announced the creation of ten new seats. Six of these went to foreign firms, of which three, Vickers da Costa, Jardine Fleming, and Warburgs, were British (although Citicorp had acquired control of Vickers da Costa). It must be said that the cost of such seats was extremely high and there was no immediate rush to pursue those further applications which were in the pipeline. It was felt, nevertheless, that the situation was unsatisfactory and there was criticism in the British parliament. In April 1987 a Minister from the Department of Trade and Industry, Mr Michael Howard, visited Tokyo and pressed for early and visible concessions, not only on the question of seats on the stock exchange but for the grant of banking licences also. He suggested that unless such facilities were quickly given, retaliatory action might be taken against Japanese companies in London, particularly against the securities houses. The Japanese authorities felt that they were being unduly pressured and spoke of the need for evolutionary rather than revolutionary change, claiming that each financial centre must express its own culture and traditions. They pleaded that the difficulties arose from the separation of banking and securities dealing and made play with the fact that foreigners now occupied 6.5 per cent of the seats on the Tokyo exchange (although, of course, enjoying a very much smaller proportion of the business). The press was inspired to hint that the British were foolhardy to put at risk the presence in London of great Japanese institutions with their inexhaustible funds. Nevertheless, three more licences were eventually forthcoming and British membership rose to six with the admission of Kleinwort Benson, County NatWest and Barings. Barclays de Zoete Wedd and James Capel remained in the queue. In January 1989 Mr Francis Maude, the Minister responsible for Corporate affairs at the Department of Trade and Industry, visited Tokyo and again urged the grant of these licences, as well as discussing some of the outstanding problems of fund management. When their seats are finally granted, these two companies will no doubt have to pay the going price for an entrance fee of £6 million or £7 million. This may be enough to discourage further applicants, even though the new Tokyo Stock Exchange building opened in 1988.

The six British houses now able to operate on the market appear to be reasonably active. One broker described the business as 'the crumbs which fall from Nomura's table', but another has pointed out that if British firms could get even only 1 per cent of total market business, they would increase present earnings by four or five times and earn a fair margin over the undoubtedly heavy costs. Relations with Japanese houses are good and several of those involved have said that the authorities have been extremely helpful. In 1986 Lord Trenchard of Kleinworts became the first foreign member ever appointed to the General Affairs Committee of the Japan Securities Dealers Association, the regulatory body of the securities industry. But the situation is hardly satisfactory. In 1988 it proved very difficult to make reasonable profits.

There has been considerable interest in the listing of British shares on the Tokyo market. Again, costs are high and dealings very limited, but there are possible advantages. Membership may help to keep the company's local activities in Japan in the public eye, it may encourage purchases of the stock in London and New York by Japanese corporations and trusts with overseas portfolios, and there may be advantage in having a twenty-four-hour time-spread for a share listed in Tokyo, London, and New York. Among those listed are such Tokyo operators as Barclays and the Standard Chartered Bank.

INFORMATION AND ADVISORY SERVICES

In all of the fields of activity in Tokyo discussed in this chapter there is also an opening for foreign banks to assist Japanese financial and industrial corporations with information and advice on parallel situations, opportunities, or operations overseas. Japanese banks and corporations at first needed guidance in the Euromarkets. Direct investment has been another important field where the acquisition or establishment of overseas industries is involved. Japan's direct foreign investment was at the rate of $22 billion in 1986, $33 billion in 1987, and $47 billion in 1988.[14] Japanese companies have also become big buyers of real estate overseas. When such activities are carried out in Britain, the services of British banks and specialist advisers are often needed. Japanese businessmen are quite willing to pay tribute to such services. For example, Mr Nobuyuki Hariuchi, of Toshiba, in an interview with *Euromoney*, stated that foreign banks were: 'a valuable source of information regarding financial and general economic conditions abroad'.[15] On the same occasion, Mr Kiichiro Aiwa, President of the shipping company Mitsui Osk, said: 'They can give us more and better service than the Japanese banks. We have old friends among the Japanese city banks, of course ... but foreigners give us more detailed information.'[16]

In spite of such encouraging remarks, foreign banks only receive a limited amount of this business and much in the future will depend on the extent to which Japanese businesses become truly assimilated to international practice.

NOTES

1 Information kindly supplied by Mr Martin Gordon.
2 Thomas Adams and Iwao Hoshii, *A Financial History of the New Japan* (Kodansha International Ltd., Tokyo, 1972), pp. 480–2.
3 Ibid.

4 Copy of balance sheet supplied to Japanese Ministry of Finance by the National Westminster Bank.
5 Kisaikai indicates 'syndicate' from Ki (to raise), sai (bond), kai (group).
6 *Euromoney* (Mar. 1987).
7 Ibid.
8 Ibid.
9 Robert Alan Feldman, *Japanese Financial Markets: Deficits Dilemmas and Deregulation* (Cambridge, 1986), p. 151.
10 *Euromoney* (Feb. 1987).
11 *Financial Times* (4 Jan. 1990).
12 *Euromoney* (Feb. 1986).
13 Ibid.
14 Source: Heisei Gannendo ni okeru Taigai oyobi Tainai Chokusetsu Toshi Todokede Jisseki, June 1990, Ministry of Finance.
15 *Euromoney* (Feb. 1986).
16 Ibid.

13

TOKYO AS A WORLD FINANCIAL CENTRE
1972–1988

THE BACKGROUND TO LIBERALIZATION

Just how far foreigners have become active in all the financial fields described in chapter 12 reveals the extent to which Japan has acquired or has failed to acquire the characteristics of an international financial centre. The great changes which have been seen since the end of the American occupation have been the result of the extraordinary growth of Japan's economy and the emergence of the country, first with the largest regular trade surplus in the world and then with the largest reserve of surplus capital. It might be thought that as these goals were reached the internationalization of Japan's physical and financial markets would have developed smoothly; but that is not what happened. Certainly, in the financial field regulatory barriers and prohibitions were removed far more slowly than tariffs in the commercial field.

There were two reasons for this. First, by no means the majority of people in politics, administration, and business were necessarily in favour of Japan becoming an international financial forum – quite the contrary. After all, this had never been the Japanese tradition. Furthermore, from 1930 onwards, for more than twenty years, Japan had lived in a state of economic isolation so that politicians and civil servants had no experience at all of international dealings, and businessmen rather little. There was also the conviction of Japan's differentness and special vulnerability, because of lack of natural resources and past experiences, which has already been discussed. Second, events themselves from time to time seemed to the Japanese to warn against becoming too involved with the outside world. The two recessionary crises of 1965 and 1975, the 'Nixon Shock', the two 'oil shocks' of 1973 and 1979, the problems of *endaka* (see p. 189) all produced situations (even though sometimes self-induced) where fears of Japan's special vulnerability to outside influences seemed justified. Such happenings naturally tended to check the process of liberalization.

It is not surprising that some British bankers interviewed in the preparation of this book should have said that they found themselves dealing with officials in the Ministry of Finance and MITI who were very strongly opposed to internationalization of the Tokyo financial market. The surprise is perhaps that so many Japanese leaders should have seen the necessity for it. In this process, foreigners played an important part. First, the activities of foreign banks and securities houses in Japan and in the Euromarkets, often helpful to Japan's own interests, produced situations with which the Japanese authorities were obliged to deal and gave opportunity for constructive advance. Second, by opening their own financial markets to Japanese penetration, the Americans and Europeans greatly speeded up the development of Japan's own banks and securities houses, thus building up internal pressure for deregulation. Although the Japanese have never been partisans of reciprocity for others, the enormous advantages enjoyed by Japanese firms in London and New York clearly made it more difficult for the authorities to keep Tokyo as a national preserve. Third, foreign governments became increasingly exasperated as the gap between Japan's industrial and financial power and its willingness to import foreign manufactures and financial services grew wider and wider. The direct pressure put on successive Japanese governments by foreign governments, and particularly that of the United States, was conclusive in bringing about change. But the debate within the Japanese administration never let up. It is interesting that in 1977 officials in the Ministry of Finance, representing the opposing points of view, invited

Barclays, the Deutsche Bank, and American and French banks to set out their individual proposals on the creation of an international market in Tokyo.[1]

The British contribution to the process of change was mostly made indirectly through the first and second of the above means, though British governments intervened to bring pressure at times. Although the process of internationalization was an internal one of amending Japanese law and regulations, a short account is necessary in order to understand how the relationship between London and Tokyo has developed. The first stage, up to 1972, which has been described in chapter 10, was marked by such advances as foreign access to the call market, the bill discount market, foreign exchange operations, portfolio investment, and so on. The growing strength of the economy permitted the first outflow of capital, in fact a freer movement of capital in both directions. These developments were held up and, at times, even temporarily reversed by such outside events as the 'Nixon Shock' and the first oil crisis. For several years there remained a vast array of restrictions and prohibitions; for example, in the 1970s foreign banks still had to sign undertakings not to solicit any deposits. What follows concerns the period from 1979 onwards.

The Establishment of a CD Market 1979

In 1970 a group called the Committee on Financial Systems Research were asked to report to the government on structural reforms. One of their recommendations was against the creation of a market for Certificates of Deposit. Japanese banks, on the other hand, were pressing very hard to be able to issue CDs. They were raising funds for their clients on the Eurodollar market where maturities were short. The clients were pressing for longer maturities. Their wants were increasingly supplied by foreign banks with access to the dollar-based CD market in London, which had been open since May 1966 and offered longer maturities. The Japanese banks therefore found themselves at a disadvantage to their foreign competitors. In 1972 the Ministry of Finance adopted a compromise, allowing the banks to issue CDs abroad but not at home. Their fears that this might cause a

massive inflow of funds from London and put pressure on the
yen were not realized and all controls on this activity were lifted
by the end of the year. But it was still forbidden to foreign and
domestic banks alike to issue CDs in Japan.

By the late seventies there was an imbalance in the holding of
liquidity. Corporations were increasingly turning to the issue of
equity instead of bank borrowings. The high valuations now
being put on Japanese companies made these flotations very
successful and the companies were flush with funds. The banks,
by contrast, were short of liquidity, having been obliged to spend
their reserves on the trillions of revenue bonds flowing from the
government's deficit budget financing. To remedy this the government at last decided to permit the issue of CDs. In spite of strong
opposition from the securities houses, the Tokyo CD market was
opened in May 1979. Secondary trading in these instruments was
permitted from April 1982.

Foreign participation rose rapidly after the first year. In 1981 it
was at 18.5 per cent of the market. It has fallen off since then,
with foreigners raising money or lending it between the CD,
discount, call, and *gensaki* markets. As R. A. Feldman puts it:
'One may conclude that foreigners played a growing role in
Japanese money markets in the 1970s, becoming aggressive arbit-
rageurs in the 1980s.'[2]

REVISION OF THE FOREIGN EXCHANGE LAW 1980

The flooding of Japan with government bonds was not the only
reason for having to make changes. Capital movements in both
directions had begun to increase at an enormous rate. The existing mass of restrictions and regulations was a jungle for
Japanese and foreign operators alike. Perceiving that Japan was
on the verge of becoming a major exporter of capital, the Americans wanted to know how she proposed to accommodate herself
to the world scene. The fact that Japan, after surmounting two
oil crises, still had adequate reserves of foreign exchange, deprived the no-change party of their ability to frighten their

colleagues with fears of a shortage of capital at home. In any case, ample funds for corporate development were coming from the Euromarkets.

The New Foreign Exchange Law swept away some of the foreign exchange provisions of the 1948 Law and a host of minor regulations that had grown up since. Chapter 4 dealt with capital transfers and chapter 5 with direct investment. The approach at least was certainly novel, in that it was based on the principle of freedom with some regulation rather than, as heretofore, on regulation with some freedom. Restrictions were removed on impact loans but this, as we have already seen, enabled Japanese banks to enter the market and displace the foreign banks. Foreign exchange could be freely converted into yen and foreign investment in the stock market increased sharply, perhaps as much in anticipation of a stronger yen as because of the merits of the stocks.

Nevertheless, there were still numerous limitations affecting capital movements. These took the form of requirements for approval or for registration of all sorts of capital transactions. For example, transactions in Euroyen bonds and all foreign exchange business had to be registered. Some other kinds of business were subject to 'qualified registration requirements'; in other words, the authorities should have time to make enquiries and demand changes. Notwithstanding, the operations of the markets had been effectively simplified in many respects.[3]

AMERICAN PRESSURE: THE YEN–DOLLAR COMMITTEE 1984

Improving the regulations in 1980 certainly had no effect on the principal problem with which the Americans and Europeans were concerned – the enormous size of Japan's trade surplus. The general view was that the exchange rate for the yen, which had scarcely shifted since the currency was floated in the wake of the 'Nixon Shock', was artificially low. Certainly the yen was not behaving like other international currencies, since it failed to respond in any way to favourable trade balances. But then, nor had the dollar responded to unfavourable trade balances – it just got stronger every year. Those who felt that the problem was entirely due to the hidden intervention of the Japanese monetary authorities, received a shock when Mr Beryl Sprinkel, Assistant Secretary of State for Monetary Affairs, announced that a US Treasury study had

> found no evidence to suggest that the Japanese authorities were manipulating markets to weaken the yen. On the contrary, Japanese macro-economic policy objectives, foreign exchange market intervention and reluctance to lower the official discount rate, all suggested that the Japanese authorities sought a stronger yen.[4]

In fact, the Japanese authorities had little cause to intervene one way or the other. The outflow of capital from Tokyo was in full tide and Japan was about to begin its regular financing of the American budget deficit. The Japanese life insurance companies were shipping their reserves to New York to buy US Treasury bills. Japanese corporations were beginning to buy industries and real estate on the West Coast of the USA. Even Japanese individuals were eager to get their funds to America. (A curious impulsion was given to this when the revenue authorities announced that they were about to launch a campaign against tax evasion through the holding of multiple savings accounts by the introduction of 'green cards'.)

The argument became somewhat academic as the trade figures rolled in. The US deficit with Japan was running at nearly $20 billion a year by the second half of 1983 and projections showed a likely doubling by the end of the year to come. President Reagan took a personal interest; he was due to meet Mr Nakasone in November and he put this problem at the top of his agenda. At the same time, American banking interests persuaded the President that an opening of Japan's capital markets would not only help to internationalize the yen, but would also enable the United States to make important invisible earnings in Japan. As a result of this meeting, the two leaders announced on 10 November 1983 that they had agreed to set up 'The Yen–Dollar

Working Committee' to recommend how best Japan's capital markets might be opened up and how international use of the yen might be increased. The Committee reported on 29 March 1984. They made far-reaching recommendations on every matter of dispute. The internationalizing of Japan's financial markets had begun in earnest.[5]

In so far as the Tokyo financial market was concerned, one of the most fundamental matters discussed was the deregulation, or freeing to competition, of interest rates. The existing refusal to allow competitive quoting and the imposition of minimum offering levels had been a means of restraining the foreign banks in a market where, as strangers, they were already at a disadvantage in most other respects. An agreement was reached in May 1984 which represented a major concession by the Japanese, considering that for forty years they had been operating a system in which, as Aron Viner so picturesquely expressed it, the authorities were: 'accustomed to a political economy in which market forces have been in a perpetual state of house arrest.'[6]

Under the terms of the new agreement the Ministry of Finance allowed banks to quote free and competitive interest rates on deposits of 1 billion yen and upwards. This, of course, excluded any foreign banks since they were unlikely to have any deposits of this size. The same deregulation was applied to CDs and also to Monetary Market Certificates, for which a market was opened in March 1985. In April 1986 the level for free interest on all these forms of deposit was lowered to 500 million yen, in October 1986 it was reduced to 300 million yen, and in April 1987 it fell to 50 million yen, a level at which foreign banks might hope to profit. At the end of 1988 it was expected to fall even further. At that point, free interest yen probably represented about 40 per cent of total yen funds in the City Banks. This clearly must have produced serious problems for the many smaller co-operative banks and credit institutions. An official of the Sumitomo Bank was quoted as early as April 1987 as predicting that many of them would be forced into mergers with the City Banks as they would be quite unable to sustain such competition.[7]

As regards capital inflows, many of the obstacles had already been cleared away after 1980. Quantitive restrictions, however, had survived on the proportion of foreign ownership in certain industries like silk or petroleum products and these were now removed. It was also made easier for foreigners to purchase real-estate, if they could afford it. But what the Americans had principally been after had been the freeing of capital outflows. Commenting on the meeting of the President and Prime Minister Nakasone, Secretary of the Treasury, Regan had said: 'So what we are saying is, open up your capital markets and learn to share. And that way you will help to strengthen your yen and our dollar won't be nearly so strong.'[8] This statement is too imprecise for the logic to be obvious, but important results were achieved. First, the Ministry of Finance and the securities houses reached early agreement on the freeing of the market in Samurai bonds. Restrictions on eligibility, credit ratings, size of flotations, and intervals between applications were all relaxed. Second, administrative guidance governing overseas lending by Japanese banks was reviewed. Not surprisingly, in the wake of the 1982 Third World debt crisis, the Japanese authorities had exercised strict control on lending abroad. It was now recognized that any such controls were to be purely 'prudential' and not in any way used to control the yen rate. Third, there were relaxations in the domestic CD market; the minimum size of units was reduced and the amount which any one corporation might issue was increased. At the same time, permission was given for Japanese banks to deal domestically in foreign commercial paper issued abroad. Finally, restrictions were relaxed governing the deposits of Japanese citizens in foreign financial institutions, making it easier for them to invest abroad. It can be noted also that it was only after this stage that foreigners obtained their first seats on the Tokyo Stock Exchange and that the issue of banking licences became easier.

This was a period of more rapid movement than had been seen since the end of the war and the Americans continued to press their advantage. On 30 July 1985 the Japanese government announced a three-year 'Action Programme for Improved Market Access' and the appointment of an Action Programme Promotion Committee which would actually be responsible for supervising the new regulations and practices under the programme. Financial and capital markets and services were included in the remit.[9]

Revaluation of the Yen: the Maekawa Report 1985/6

Although the Yen–Dollar Committee had helped to set going many of the above developments, its main task (as its name implied) was to tackle the yen–dollar exchange rate. The Americans were now convinced that the 'low value' of the yen, rather than lack of competitiveness in their own industry, was the main reason for the US chronic trade deficit with Japan. Second, despite anything that Under-Secretary Sprinkel might have said, they considered that the Japanese authorities were in a position to bring about a very substantial revaluation of their currency. The views of the Europeans were the same, though the British laid more emphasis on the 'impenetrability' of Japanese markets and lack of reciprocity. What appears strange is that neither the European Community nor its individual members pressed for a parallel body to the Yen–Dollar Committee and that they were ready to leave everything to the Americans. They might have foreseen that the latter would pre-empt for themselves most of the advantages to be gained from Japanese concessions.

One of the main points made by Japan's trading partners was that Japan invoiced an insignificant proportion of her foreign trade in her own currency, thus artificially restricting demand for the yen. Equally importantly, the yen was not used at all in third-party trade. Much thought was given to how greater use of the yen could be made for trade finance — the 'yen shift' as it was called. Some of the conditions for it existed already. For instance, yen interest rates were below dollar rates and the import finance facilities offered by the Bank of Japan were cheaper than dollar financing. Yen credit was fully available. What was preventing the shift was the perceived likelihood that the yen would appreciate and increase the costs of repayment or hedging. Until that revaluation took place, use of the yen would not increase. It was a chicken and egg situation.

Nevertheless, a few improvements were made at this stage. In April 1984 the Ministry of Finance withdrew its 'real demand' rule, whereby foreign exchange facilities were only permitted for bona fide transactions and not for 'speculation' or arbitrage. In

April 1985 a market was set up in yen-denominated Bankers
Acceptances. The growth was disappointing, only reaching about
30 billion yen a month.

The reforms of 1984/5 and the discussions of the Yen–Dollar
group had clearly failed to solve the basic problem. The showdown came at the Plaza Meeting of the Big Five in New York in
September 1985. The Japanese were told that if they did not take
their own steps to revalue the yen the other governments would
start buying that currency on a huge scale to force up the price.
The Japanese government were by now also fully aware of the
political implications of their trade surplus, which was accompanied by the closing down of whole industries in the United
States and Europe and the loss of employment by thousands of
people there. They were becoming acutely aware of their vulnerability to protectionist reprisals. Although the Japanese claimed
that they had done everything possible and that they were the
victims of unjustified Japan-bashing, which might well prove
counter-productive, they nevertheless agreed to a formal com-
muniqué which said that the yen would be allowed to strengthen.
The truth was that Prime Minister Nakasone was now fully
convinced that action was essential and, on his return home, he
was able to achieve enough support among his ministerial colleagues and in the hierarchy of the Liberal Democratic Party to
lay the basis for a consensus. The former Governor of the Bank
of Japan, Mr Haruo Maekawa, was asked to head a Commission
to prepare a report on Japan's trade and financial dealings, with
a view to 'harmonizing Japan's economic relations with other
countries'. Mr Maekawa's remarkable report was released in
April 1986. It suggested that the Japanese nation must change its
whole way of thinking and recognize that it had become a major
member of the world community. The old inward-looking, self-
protective attitudes must go. Japan would have to live with a
currency which reflected the strength of its economy.[10] This was
not a popular point of view. Many in Japan argued that Maekawa had caved in to American pressure, that his views did not
represent any sort of consensus, and that *nemawashi* had been
ignored. It was asserted by some that the report was an internal
memo for the Prime Minister and was in no way binding on the
Japanese nation. Mr Nakasone, however, stated publicly that he

welcomed its findings and would follow its recommendations. He then proceeded to win a resounding election victory in July 1986, which made it possible for his pledge to be carried out. The Action Programme Promotion Committee was expected to include appropriate recommendations of the Maekawa Report among the measures which it was implementing.

Since 1986 the yen has found a truer value, not by any official revaluation but by being allowed to float gradually towards its present level. The initial result was more formidable than any Japanese opponent of liberalization could have foreseen. From a rate of 217 yen to the dollar at the time of the Plaza meeting it moved in three years to 125 to the dollar. This state of affairs is known in Japan as *endaka* (from '*en*', a variant of 'yen' and '*taka*', meaning 'high'). Its effect on Japanese industry must have been frightening and extremely taxing for managements. Nevertheless, just as it surmounted the 'Nixon Shock' and the two 'oil shocks', Japanese industry has ridden over the problems of *endaka* with less than substantial damage to its economy. Exports, although they continued at first to rise in dollar terms, have fallen in yen terms. Between 1985 and 1987 imports of manufactured goods rose by 64.3 per cent in dollar terms, but from a very low base. The trend continues at a slower rate. There is still a massive surplus of physical trade, but it is more than wiped out by capital exports. By 1989 both the surplus and the yen–dollar exchange rate had started to come back.

THE TOKYO OFFSHORE MARKET 1986

The possibility of instituting offshore banking activities in Tokyo had traditionally been opposed by the Ministry of Finance on the grounds that it would cause them to lose control of domestic interest rates. But the same arguments had been used against permitting the secondary bond market in 1977 and the CD market in 1979, without proving justified. During the discussions of the Yen–Dollar Committee the Americans had pressed hard for the establishment of an offshore market on the grounds that it should increase international demand for the yen. In April

1982 the Ministry of Finance sent a team of thirty-three members, drawn from the Ministry of Finance, the Bank of Japan, the securities houses, and Japanese and foreign banks, on a tour of the world's offshore banking centres. Although the party were unable to reach a consensus, the evidence which they brought back enabled the Ministry to overcome some of its fears. The market was eventually opened in late 1986.[11]

One hundred and twelve Japanese and sixty-nine foreign firms immediately acquired licences. All the same, ten foreign banks, including the Hong Kong and Shanghai Banking Corporation, declined the invitation. They may have felt that it was too hedged around with restrictions. It certainly got off to a slow start. Aron Viner, writing about the Tokyo Offshore Market only a few months after its inception, commented that it had become: 'a facility for accepting deposits rather than a market place for raising funds and trading instruments',[12] which was, of course, the opposite of what the Americans had required of it. The manager of the Tokyo Branch of Credit Suisse complained that it offered nothing that was not available at lower cost elsewhere. Others claimed that the market was being stifled by the amount of paper-work required by the authorities to satisfy them that there was no leakage from offshore into the domestic market. But what those who complained were watching was a classic case of the Japanese method of proceeding by easy stages. As the *Far Eastern Economic Review* noted: 'The position taken by Ministry of Finance officials is that the Government is ready to do what is necessary to make the offshore market grow after watching its progress during the next few months.'[13] The authorities had nudged some of the leading Japanese banks into the market. For example, the Sumitomo Bank and the Long-Term Credit Bank of Japan transferred all their relevant business into it. Within a year the new market had grown out of all recognition.

By 2 June 1988 the *Far Eastern Economic Review* could report that the Tokyo offshore market, although still behind Hong Kong and Singapore, had reached the same size as the New York market established more than six years earlier. Moreover, it appeared that it was beginning to exercise an attractive force over the Hong Kong market. By the end of 1987 outstanding lending from Hong Kong to Japan had grown to $266 billion, of which interbank lending accounted for $125 billion. It has been suggested that the cause for this was not so much a response to a genuine call for funds as the attraction of arbitrage between the controlled (domestic) yen and the free (offshore) yen. In 1987 yen lending accounted for nearly 30 per cent of all new lending by industrial countries. The two largest sources were now the Euroyen market and the Tokyo offshore market. Here again there appears to have been arbitrage between the two.

By 1989 the Tokyo offshore market had been in existence for less than three years and it was too early to say what its long-term character would be. *The Economist* on 2 December 1988 suggested that its spectacular rise has been partly due to the immaturity of short-term money markets in Japan. It alleged that the offshore market was being used simply for interbank facilities and that ten trillions of yen had been transferred into the domestic market in this way. This may be, but, if so, the authorities will have been watching, as always, and will decide how much they mind.

AN UNFINISHED PROCESS 1988

The opening of Tokyo's financial markets is certainly not complete. 1988 saw a considerable number of important steps taken by the authorities. The Action Programme Promotion Committee noted in its final report of August 1988 that the ceiling for free interest rates would shortly be lowered again for time-deposits, CDs, and MMCs. A Financial Futures Trading Law was approved in May 1988 to allow this branch of financial activity. Other measures were announced in 1989. The process will never be complete. But in less than twenty years, in spite of all the fears and habits of mind of Japanese officials, the country has come a very long way towards creating an international financial centre in Tokyo. Much more is needed; only now there is a difference. Whereas in the seventies and eighties the foreigners pressed specific demands for liberalization, it has since become more difficult for them to think what they want to ask for next. Indeed, they must expect that change in the future is as likely to come from the initiative of the Japanese themselves as from response to the complaints of outsiders. Japanese financial institutions may now have as much of an interest in liberalization as foreign ones. If in the past they looked to their government to maintain restrictions to protect them from foreign competition, they may now require that government to remove any impediments to their power to compete world-wide.

The whole course of liberalization has been perceptibly accompanied by a course of deregulation of the banking system, breaking down the detailed distinctions between all the archaic structures of the different institutions, freeing them and allowing them to grow into new creatures, able to go out and take on the Americans, the British, the Germans, the Swiss, and the French all over the world. We have seen too, how the banks were able to begin to break into the field of underwriting and securities business, thereby frustrating the intentions of Article 65 of the Exchange and Securities Law which had been the bedrock of financial regulation since 1948. How much of Article 65 remains today? It might certainly vanish overnight if the Glass Steagall Act were ever invalidated or repealed in the United States. Finally, when one looks at the complexity and multiplicity of free and controlled interest rates in Japan, might not the Bank of Japan itself have an interest in liberalization of the field?

One last point may be worth discussing. Both Japanese and foreigners have accepted that the latter have, up to now, happened to have by far the greater experience of international finance and that they have been the inventors or originators of all the new ideas and practices by which international finance has advanced since the Second World War. There has therefore always been a tendency for foreigners to think that by opening up financial markets in Japan they would be unsealing a cornucopia of riches. Certainly the bankers who pressed President Reagan to take up their cause foresaw an absolute bonanza. But things have not worked out in that way. Foreign banks and securities houses now have some profitable business in Japan, but, in spite of their technological lead, they have not been able to corner any field for themselves. The one exception, the enjoyable spree with impact loans, is unlikely to be repeated.

No one who has read Part I of this book will be surprised by this conclusion. The rate at which each new form of financial activity has been permitted in the Tokyo market and the manner of its introduction have always been such as to allow Japanese financial institutions to master its use before being exposed to foreign competition. It has never been the Japanese practice, and never will be, to have other people doing things for them in their own markets which they can learn to do for themselves.

NOTES

1 Information kindly provided by Mr Collin Stevens.
2 Robert Alan Feldman, *Japanese Financial Markets: Deficits, Dilemmas and Deregulation* (Cambridge, 1986), pp. 163–6.
3 James Horne, *Japan's Financial Markets: Conflict and Consensus in Policy-making* (George Allen & Unwin in association with the Australia–Japan Research Institute, Australian National University, Sydney, 1985). pp. 142–7.
4 Jeffrey A. Frankel, 'The Institute for International Economic Policy', in Policy Analyses in International Economics, 9: *The Yen–Dollar Agreement Liberalising Japanese Capital Markets* (MIT Press, Washington, Dec. 1984), Appendix A.
5 Ibid., pp. 1–10.
6 Aron Viner, 'Inside Japan's Financial Markets', *The Economist* (1988).
7 *Far Eastern Economic Review* (9 Apr. 1987).
8 Frankel, *The Yen-Dollar Agreement Liberalising Japanese Capital Markets*, p. 27.
9 Ibid., pp. 27–32.
10 The Maekawa Report available from the Japanese embassy in London.
11 Takeshi Hosomi, *Tokyo Ofushoa Shijo: Sekai Sandaikoku Kinyu Senta no Tembo* (Toyo Keizai, Tokyo, 1985).
12 Viner, 'Inside Japan's Financial Markets', p. 184.
13 *Far Eastern Economic Review* (9 Apr. 1987).

14

JAPAN IN THE CITY OF LONDON
1972–1988

THE BIG MIGRATION

In chapter 10 (p. 139) it was noted that, by 1972, the Japanese financial community in London had grown to comprise fourteen banks, five securities houses, and nine insurance companies and that it was the next largest foreign group in the City after the Americans. The following year was to see the beginning of an explosive growth, for it was in 1972 that the Ministry of Finance gave permission for Japanese banks to lend to foreign entities and to take part in the international syndicated credit market. At the time of writing there are 52 Japanese banks with branches or representative offices in the City of London. These include all thirteen City Banks, the seven Trust Banks, the three Long-Term Credit Banks, and many others. There are also merchant banking subsidiaries (see chapter 11, p. 149). In 1987, the assets of all these banks represented a quarter of the total sterling and foreign currency assets combined of all the banks in the United Kingdom, while their international assets in London represented 36 per cent of those of all UK banks combined. The Japanese had overtaken the Americans as the largest foreign element in London and London had become the largest area of overseas activity for Japanese banking. They employed over 2,000 people, of whom only about one-quarter were Japanese.[1]

The nature of the Japanese banking presence has also changed as significantly as its size. Before the 1970s the principal activity was trade finance; now they are fully engaged in a huge range of activities of which the more important will be discussed below. Furthermore, the London office of a bank has often become the centre of activities relating to other countries. Instead of just being Japanese banks operating in London, some have become international banks operating overseas. These developments have been pursued with careful forethought. As the General Manager of the Sumitomo Bank in London said in 1985: 'It is our intention to become a fully diversified universal banking organisation.'[2]

A similar immigration of securities companies has occurred. In 1988 there were at least fifty-eight Japanese securities houses in London, representing 30 per cent of all such foreign institutions. Of these, fourteen firms had seats on the London Stock Exchange, as compared with forty-eight American houses.[3] They are even bigger employers of labour than the banks. Nomura alone in 1988 employed 750 people in their various offices and of these 85 per cent were non-Japanese, with this percentage rising.[4] The larger securities houses have set up banking subsidiaries in London. Having long ago lost the battle to maintain Article 65 fully in force overseas and having lost so much of the underwriting and lead-management business to the banks, they are now carrying the war into their rivals' camp.

While the Big Four: Nomura, Daiwa, Nikko, and Yamaichi are well known in Britain and the size of their operations has become famous, people who are not closely concerned have little knowledge of the intense activity of houses in the second rank. These are sometimes offshoots of the financial managements of large corporations. Typical examples are NKK, Okasan, New Japan, Wako, and Sanyo. Most of their foreign business is carried on in London and in South East Asia. In July 1986 it was estimated that 15 per cent of their total net profits were made from these overseas operations. They expected this to rise to perhaps 25 per cent within five years, but it is interesting that Nomura claimed to be earning 20 per cent of its total annual profits overseas in 1988.[5]

There are also in London numerous financial affiliates of the Japanese trading companies and insurance companies. And finally there are the many trusts set up to manage *zaiteku* money, a subject which will be discussed below.

The Choice of London

The reason why London was to become the second financial capital of Japan needs some explanation. The first and most obvious reason is that when the Japanese banks were permitted to operate in the international bond business in 1972, they had no international market of their own. Since London was already much the largest centre of Eurocurrency, and particularly Euro-dollar business, that is where they went. They arrived in time to join in the major activity of recycling the OPEC petro-dollars. Once they had settled in London, they soon discovered many other kinds of profitable business in which they could engage. Mr Hirokazu Ishikawa, deputy general manager of the Mitsui Bank in London, was later to describe the process very well as: 'The non-Japanisation of the broad areas of our business, especially here where we can efficiently utilise our wide European contacts and benefit from the innovatory nature of this banking centre . . . '.[6] The last seven words of this quotation point to a second factor. As Japan's financial activities became more complex and less self-contained and Japanese corporations of all kinds became increasingly involved overseas, the banks needed to learn many new skills. The securities houses also needed to learn how to cope with the increasing securitization of Japanese companies, the investment of their liquid funds, and portfolio management over-seas. London provided the perfect training-ground. In a recent statement, Mr Raymond Wareham, an executive director of Morgan Guaranty in London, said: 'Like the US banks, the Japanese banks are using London as a laboratory to develop their securities business, because they cannot yet do securities busi-ness at home.'[7] In other words, both banks and securities houses in London have been learning what lies on the other side of the Article 65 divide and what are the latest practices overseas.

A third factor has been the vast and rapidly growing export of capital from Japan. As this has regularly exceeded the trade surplus, Japan has been in the odd position of having to re-import capital. The Japanese banks have ridden out on the wave of capital exports and then clawed back the capital imports. For instance, in 1986/7, Japan's net borrowing was $48 billion, of which half was raised by banks in London.[8]

Fourth, Japanese banks and securities houses were eager to escape from the over-regulation and structural disabilities from which we have seen them suffering at home. Moreover, they were engaged in frantic competition to see which could grow the largest balance sheets. The attitude of the British authorities towards offshore banking, the relaxed climate of the City of London, and the strict but non-interventionist control of the Bank of England to maintain standards offered them business opportunities which they could not hope to find elsewhere. As Mr Koichi Kimura, Managing Director of Daiwa Securities in Tokyo has said: 'Tokyo is supplying the funds, New York is supplying the product. London is where a lot of the deals get done.'[9] In fact, in this trilateral relationship, quite a lot of the products originate in London as well.

Finally, the rapidly growing investment by Japanese corporations overseas, their purchase of foreign companies and building on green-field sites, their acquisition of office blocks and hotels, have encouraged their Japanese bankers to be present in London to prevent all this business from falling into the hands of others.

The overall situation may be summed up in the words of Mr Eiji Seiki, Managing Director of the Bank of Tokyo's London office:

> London will remain one of the biggest financial centres, where we can expand our Euroyen business and reduce the cost of our banking funds. It is also necessary for us to develop the new techniques which will enable us to compete in a more complex trading environment.[10]

In short, to quote the *Bank of England Quaterly Bulletin*: 'The primary role of the Japanese banks in London is to carry out international business.'[11]

This will be clearly illustrated by the following account of some of their principal activities and those of the securities houses.

Treasury Activities

Japanese banks in London have been net borrowers of funds. Their outstanding liabilities at the end of 1987 were $81.5 billion. They have borrowed, of course, to meet their own requirements, but their principal call has been for their main offices in Japan. At the end of 1987 the outstanding claims of the London branches on their own head offices had risen to $144 billion. It might be thought that most of this was being raised in the London market, but that is not the case. In 1987 about one-half of the total amount borrowed came from banks outside the UK. Roughly one-quarter came from the interbank market. This demonstrates the interesting situation in which, in spite of the immense resources behind them, the Japanese banks in London are borrowers on the interbank market and are a means of syphoning back to Japan part of its immense capital outflow.[12]

Naturally, Japanese banks also undertake Treasury business for their corporate clients. This, not surprisingly, has shown a better return than the inter-office business described above. They have also been active in the foreign exchange market, mostly in yen–dollar business, but their daily turnover in 1986 only represented 7 per cent of the market and has remained fairly constant.

The UK Interbank Market

As noted in the section above, Japanese banks are net borrowers from the interbank market. In the year to September 1987 they accounted for 39 per cent of all borrowing from this market and for 24 per cent of all lending to it. The trend has been for them to depend progressively less on this source and to borrow increasingly from outside the UK.

An interesting aspect is the extent to which the Japanese banks depend on one another within the interbank market. This varies, apparently, according to how the consideration of safety with one's associates (whose margins are very fine) is weighed against better returns from correspondents with more generous margins.

Some Japanese banks do as much as 70 per cent of their inter-bank business with their compatriots. They also tend to favour very short maturities; at the end of July 1987 about half of all the sterling and foreign currency deposits of Japanese banks in the London interbank market were at maturities of less than one month.[13]

LENDING TO NON-UK RESIDENTS

In September 1986 the Bank for International Settlements reported that Japanese banks accounted for around one-third of all international banking business in the area under its surveillance. Of this, about one-third again was booked with Japanese banks in London. There are a number of distinctive features which characterize this massive programme of lending.

First, there is little sovereign lending to Governments, the amount having declined sharply since the international debt crisis of 1982. Eastern Europe is the only area where the Japanese commitment has been increased in recent years. Second, only a very small proportion of this business is done in sterling; indeed 98 per cent has been in foreign currency. While the majority of loans outstanding, which stood at $293.8 billion in mid-1987, were in dollars, the proportion of yen lending has been rising, chiefly through smart activity on the Euroyen market. Eighty per cent of all these transactions are through direct lending overseas and 15 per cent through the interbank market. Third, about 10 per cent of this large volume of money is going to non-banking organizations. These are mostly client corporations at home in Japan but include companies in Europe and the United States. Japanese bankers seem to have been impressed by the advanced state of aircraft leasing abroad and an interesting loan is that to GPA of Shannon, perhaps the leading world practitioner in this field, in which both Mitsui and Mitsubishi companies hold substantial stakes. Finally, Japanese banks have been busy in the London acceptance market where they accounted for some 9 per cent of all acceptances outstanding in 1987.[14]

As might be expected from such a pattern of activity, nearly all of the assets of Japanese banks held in London are international assets. At mid-1987 these stood at $363 billion, representing 36 per cent of all the international assets in the UK.

FLOATING RATE NOTES

Floating Rate Notes were to become rather a speciality of Japanese banks. In July 1987 they held $20.6 billion (or 60 per cent) out of a total of $34 billion held by all the banks in the UK. These seem to have been acquired as a way of sustaining growth when sovereign lending had fallen off in the mid-1980s. One might have the impression that the vendors were happy to find such ready takers. They have proved to be a very slow trade and the Japanese holders often had to hold on to them.[15]

THE SWAP MARKET

There has been keen competition among Japanese banks for both interest rate and currency swaps. At the end of 1986 they accounted for 15 per cent of the outstanding value of interest rate swaps on the market, while currency swaps amounted to about two-thirds in value of the interest rate swaps.[16] The volume of this business has been buoyed by increasing interest between institutions in London and Tokyo in taking advantage of arbitrage opportunities, but much of it has arisen from the activities of the Japanese merchant banks in underwriting issues in the Euroyen market. Where non-Japanese clients are concerned the issues are normally linked to a currency swap arrangement which is passed by the merchant bank to its associated bank branch in London. Japanese business in the swap markets continued to increase steadily as awareness grew of the many opportunities which it offers for profitable exchanges or for access to some types of loans from which banks in Tokyo are still debarred.

INVESTMENT BANKING

It is in the field of investment banking that Japanese banks and securities houses have attempted to escape most completely from the restraints of Article 65 and compete openly with each other for business. It was noted in chapter 11 (p. 149) that the first Japanese merchant banking subsidiaries were set up in the early 1970s to enable the parent banks to engage in securities business in the Eurocurrency markets. This inevitably led to disputes and complaints. The situation was stabilized by administrative guidance in August 1975, reached through discussion between the Banking Bureau, the International Finance Bureau, and the Securities Bureau of the Ministry of Finance and known as the Three Bureaux Agreement. This ensured that securities houses would be the book runners in the case of any Japanese corporation making a bond issue abroad and that banks could not have precedence in such cases. Margins in these markets and particularly the Euroyen market, largely due to the competition between the Japanese houses themselves, have become very fine. Even when the margin on the swap transaction is added, the possibility of financial loss may sometimes have to be weighed against loss of the client. Although they have been successful with issues for non-Japanese residents, the merchant banks have therefore been anxious to find other business. For example, they have been developing comprehensive services which the London branches of the parent banks cannot give, such as new funding techniques, investment management, new financial services, leasing, and so on. They are keen to attract clients directly and some have applied to the Ministry of Finance to open offices at home in Tokyo.[17]

As for the securities houses themselves, their leading performance in Eurobonds has been discussed in chapter 11. It must be said that the intense competition which has brought them to the top of the league table has caused some domestic and other foreign operators to pull out of the market. While this could have given rise to great resentment, it is wise to keep a sense of proportion. Considering their enormous resources, there was no great disparity in 1987 between the fact that the Japanese were responsible for 22.1 per cent of the borrowing in Eurobonds and for 26.6 per cent of the book-running.[18] While there is no compelling reason in either logic or equity why these two figures should be close to one another, it is not particularly surprising or disturbing if they are so. This is especially the case when one takes into account the fact that the Euroyen market is so largely a Japanese preserve.

CORPORATE LENDING TO UK RESIDENTS

With all of this international business in hand, Japanese banks have not overlooked the domestic market in the UK. In the long run this is an exceedingly important area for relations between the two countries. If more Japanese capital is diverted from the United States to Europe, the amount which reaches the UK and the manner in which it is absorbed will have a profound effect.

The Japanese have not found it easy to get going, and lending to UK residents has advanced very slowly. At August 1987 it represented only 3 per cent of all sterling loans made in the UK over a period of four years; presumably British finance directors could see no reason to go to a Japanese bank to borrow pounds. But foreign currency is a different matter and when all loans are taken together, both sterling and foreign, the Japanese share is 8 per cent, certainly a significant amount.[19]

The recipients of these loans make interesting reading. In a few sectors the Japanese have carved out an impressive percentage of the whole. Leading examples by 1988 were wholesale distribution (37 per cent), water companies (34 per cent), building societies (34 per cent), central and local government services (30 per cent), and securities dealers (27 per cent). Clearly, in both the wholesale and securities dealing sectors, the local subsidiaries of Japanese firms are important borrowers. Nor can it be said that this was all equally attractive business, much of the local government lending being to 'Red Boroughs' in inner London against the security of municipal offices and so on.[20] Moreover, the legality of some municipal dealings has since been called into question. Generally speaking, Japanese banks tend to discount the big multinationals, who can insist on very competitive rates, and look to medium-sized companies to provide future business. Four banks have already set up branches in industrial areas outside the south-east of England to contact such enterprises. They are also actively looking at construction and property development, usually in partnership with British companies.

SECURITIES TRADING

In October 1987 there were seventy-four Japanese houses authorized under the Prevention of Fraud (Investment) Act 1958 to deal in securities in London. This figure included those with the exempted status granted to organizations which already have a banking licence and those which had received authorization automatically because they belong to the UK Association of Tokyo Stock Exchange members. These were by no means all 'securities houses' in the Japanese sense; a number of them being special overseas subsidiaries of Japanese banks or trading companies. As we saw at the beginning of the chapter, fourteen of them have seats on the London Stock Exchange. This compares with six British firms on the Tokyo exchange, probably soon to rise to 8 (see pp. 174–6).

It is difficult to know how much business is accounted for by these companies. The Bank of England estimate for 1986 was that Japanese securities houses were responsible for $13 billion in bonds and $1 billion in equities, but these figures do not distinguish between domestic and international securities. The figures for the year to the end of the bull market in October 1987 were said to be very much higher.

The great size of the Japanese firms causes anxiety. It is well known that Nomura is by far the largest securities company in the world. Although it is usual to talk about the Big Four, Nomura and Daiwa have drawn well ahead of the other two. Indeed, the former claims that one of its subsidiaries, Kokusai, is itself now bigger than Yamaichi. It has become part of the lore of the London Stock Exchange that, within half an hour of joining, Nomura had driven up British Telecom from 205p to 214p. One broker commented: 'Nomura obviously wanted to build up its inventory, but it could have done that slowly. The fact that it chose the biggest stock on the market is no coincidence; they did it to show that they could move the market.'[21] That is a matter of opinion, but clearly a buy-recommendation from such an enormous punter is likely to move prices up, while a New York style computer-triggered sell-programme could one day provoke a disaster. In fact, the Japanese share of the market is still small;

Japanese houses have trodden carefully and they have acclimatized well to the London scene. One British merchant bank gave as its opinion that Nomura is always reluctant to do unprofitable business and that its strength lies in its unrivalled ability to distribute securities quickly to a huge network of Japanese and foreign investors.

Fund management on behalf of Japanese investment trusts, funds, and corporations in search of overseas bonds, equities, and financial instruments of all kinds is a major activity. Lack of experience and skilled personnel has been evident in some firms. The *Bank of England Quarterly Bulletin* for November 1987 contained the firm expression of view that:

> Apart from the international money management subsidiaries and departments of the Big Four securities firms, the experience and performance of fund managers in Japanese trust banks lagged far behind that of the UK and USA money managers.

Nevertheless, the immense capital resources available to Japanese houses of all kinds, their great capacity for selling a product, and their invariable commitment to growth and success are sure to carry them forward. They will be looking for foreign clients as much as for Japanese. Some are extending their capability by joint participations. While there has been no equivalent in London for the purchase in New York of 12.5 per cent of Goldman Sachs by Sumitomo Bank, there are modest co-operative ventures by Japanese insurance companies and securities houses. For example, Sumitomo Life has invested in Ivory and Sime, Daido Life and Mitsui Life have invested in MIM Britannia, and Yamaichi has established a Channel Islands trust with Murray Johnstone to tap the UK retail savings market.

ZAITEKU

Zaiteku[22] is the term used to describe the financial dealings by the treasurers of Japanese corporations, outside the scope of their normal corporate business. There had been a tendency for some years for those companies which had any liquid funds to play around with them to best advantage, when an impulse was given to the practice by the revaluation of the yen in 1986. The onset of *endaka* presented the threat of serious loss of profits to manufacturing companies. This was something which no Japanese board of management would wish to contemplate. At the same time, the process of strengthening the Asset–Debt Ratios of Japanese companies through securitization had revealed the enormous values locked up in the potential assets of the companies, due to the high level of the stock market. This permitted 'them to unload a plethora of low-cost, equity laced financial packages on the world's investment community.'[23] The proceeds of these issues could be used in a series of arbitrage games to yield extremely satisfactory returns to the annual profit and loss account. Indeed, *zaiteku* may be seen as a high-tech version of the more staid *tokkin* discussed in chapter 12 (p. 174). Since 1984 Japanese companies have been permitted by the Ministry of Finance to engage in swaps. Furthermore, the warrants which were now such a popular feature of bond issues (see chapter 11 pp. 155–6) also offered opportunities. Some British merchant banks in Tokyo were able to lead the way into the maze of dealings and arbitrage available for these funds and Kleinworts and Schroders in particular are said to have been very successful at arranging deals.

There are clearly dangers involved in these practices. Money diverted in this way contributes to the 'hollowing-out of the Japanese economy' – the Japanese counterpart (though not equivalent) of 'de-industrialization' in the West. There was a perception that the practice should not be carried too far. Mr Yuichiro Tani of the Kirin Brewery Company put it: 'We are a manufacturing company, not a finance company. We started investing overseas recently because yen interest rates have come down. But we have been careful to increase the amount of yen investment slowly.'[24] In fact, certain distortions began to appear in the bond market also as companies prepared their ground for *zaiteku*.

Most of the operations involved have to take place overseas and this has brought *zaiteku* to London where, not surprisingly, it becomes *eurozaiteku*. The returns are made principally by swaps and speculation on interest rate and currency movements, and are therefore very dependent on operations in the London eurocurrency markets. London has been the essential focus for the trade. 1985 saw a boom in Sushi bonds. These are Japanese bonds which can be issued by institutions or corporations and which were for a while selling at interest rates below those for eurobonds. Subsequently, a favoured instrument has been euro-commercial paper. Since this is rather strictly controlled in London, dealing has been shifted to other European centres, particularly the Netherlands.

Amongst Japanese corporations, those which have naturally had the most experience of overseas financing have been the trading companies. A very clear account of what is involved has been given by Mr Simon Narroway of Kleinwort Benson in Tokyo, describing the activities of a company called Notis. This is a joint venture, incorporated in Rotterdam with an initial capital of $200 million to carry the *eurozaiteku* of the Nichimen Corporation. Kleinwort Benson have a 10 per cent stake in Notis and it is managed from their London head office.

> Its aim is arbitrage between a wide variety of banking sources, including bankers-acceptances and multi-currency lines, often combined with interest and/or currency swaps. Public bond issues, private placements, loan sub-participations and other investments are also used. The idea is to make a spread on a matching basis, taking a risk on the underlying asset.[25]

That was in September 1985 at a pioneering stage. Since then, many other companies have moved into the field, some at the high-risk end and some in a more conservative way. As one Japanese executive put it: 'Some financial companies set up by trading firms are almost undertaking banking business here in London. Trading profit is declining so they are using their credit standing to boost profit.'[26]

One can say that these activities were seen by some companies as exciting, by some as a desirable supplement to normal trading, and by others as a disagreeable expedient in hard times. But a very large number of corporations have been involved. With its traditional suspicion of any activity which smells of speculation, the Ministry of Finance, while understanding the financial imperatives of *zaiteku*, cannot be very enthusiastic.

NOTES

1 R. J. Walton and Dermot Trimble, 'Japanese Banks in London', *Bank of England Quarterly Bulletin*, 27/4 (Nov. 1987).
2 *Euromoney* (Apr. 1985).
3 Information provided by the London Stock Exchange.
4 Information kindly supplied by Mr Howland-Jackson of Nomura.
5 Ibid.
6 *Euromoney* (Apr. 1985).
7 Ibid. (Apr. 1987).
8 Walton and Trimble, 'Japanese Banks in London'.
9 *Euromoney* (Apr. 1987).
10 Ibid. (Apr. 1985).
11 Walton and Trimble, 'Japanese Banks in London'.
12 Ibid.
13 Ibid.
14 Ibid.
15 Ibid.
16 Ibid.
17 Ibid.
18 IFR Global Financing Review.
19 Walton and Trimble, 'Japanese Banks in London'.
20 Information supplied courtesy of Guinness Mahon.
21 *Euromoney* (Apr. 1987).
22 This hybrid is formed from *zai*, the first syllable of zaimu, 'finance', and 'tek', a transliteration of the first syllable of English 'technology'.
23 *Euromoney* (Nov. 1986).
24 Ibid.
25 *Euromoney* (Sept. 1985).
26 Ibid.

15

TOKYO AND LONDON COMPARED
1988

Tokyo

In little more than 100 years since the Act of 1882 laid the foundations for Japan's present financial system, Tokyo has changed from an almost medieval, wooden city into a metropolis of concrete and glass. But we have seen in chapter 13 that it was only after 1970, and as a result of nearly twenty years of struggle between foreigners and different factions of Japanese thought, that it also began to evolve as an international financial market. Has it really done so and can Tokyo, at the end of 1988, be called a truly international centre?

A contemporary Western view of what constitutes such a centre might be a market, or rather *congeries* of markets, providing all those facilities for every kind of financial dealing which are to be found in London or New York and differing from those centres only in its time zone. In other words, the Tokyo markets would become integrated into newly globalized markets in which multinational houses would conduct twenty-four-hour, round-the-clock trading in bonds, stocks, shares, warrants, options, futures, swaps, foreign exchange, commodities, and everything else. The old independent centres would be no more than time windows on a world market.

This uniform state of affairs certainly does not yet exist, if it ever will. Nor is Tokyo yet the same sort of place as London or New York. The Japanese authorities have a good right to claim that they have moved a very long way to deregulate and liberalize

Tokyo financial markets and to free the yen, particularly since 1985, yet important limitations remain. The Japanese are aware of these and like to describe them as 'cultural differences'.

Perhaps one of the more important differences between the three major world financial centres is not really a 'cultural' difference but reflects their different historical development. London was already an international financial centre by the beginning of the nineteenth century and New York has been one ever since 1911. Both have developed as sponsors of third-party trade and providers of services to third parties; Tokyo has not. From 1945 the function of the Japanese financial system was uniquely to promote the growth of Japanese industry and trade and to defend them from injury or crippling competition. In the seventies a secondary requirement arose – the orderly export of capital – but this too was tied to the problem of maintaining a favourable value for the yen in support of the Japanese export trade. It is only from 1980 onwards that wider considerations began to play a part. That is not very long ago and we have seen how the Japanese banks and securities houses still have to go abroad to take even a small step across the Article 65 divide, still prefer to raise yen in London through the Euromarkets rather than in Tokyo through domestic bonds, still have to take such novel requirements as *tokkin* and *zaiteku* abroad rather than conduct them from home. *A fortiori*, if they are not meeting their own full range of financial requirements they are certainly not yet providing them for third parties. The beginnings of real change in this respect have appeared in the Tokyo offshore market and Tokyo may be developing an edge as an East Asian regional market, but it is certainly not yet as truly international as London or New York.

The second traditional difference of importance concerns the exercise of authority by government in the private sector, the degree of regulation, and the implacable nature of administrative guidance. This reflection of respect for authority, requirement of group solidarity, and need for consensus agreement and action is certainly cultural. We have seen the difficulties and frictions which it has caused for foreign financial institutions trying to enter its domain from abroad and for Japanese institutions trying to escape from its domain to overseas. Now that so many of the formal controls and regulations have been lifted and that more are certain to go, what will happen to administrative guidance? It will surely not vanish and, with the abandonment of structural safeguards for Japan's interests, it may well become more important. But, for the present, it is less obtrusive than before and, as one British banker with much experience of working in Tokyo said, in his opinion the nature of guidance had changed since 1986; it had become less a system of prohibitions and more a matter of nudging in the required direction. Nevertheless, in times of future depression, crisis, or mere change, the voice of administrative guidance will be strong.

A third factor is the familiar preference of Japanese people for dealing with each other rather than with foreigners. The internal loyalties imposed by membership of *Keiretsu* or by past business association make it difficult for the foreigner to break in. It can be said, however, that this factor can also act eventually to a foreigner's advantage. Every British businessman in Tokyo who has been consulted has stressed the importance of long-standing connections with Japanese companies and has acknowledged that business has often come his way as a reward for past favours.

Against this rather unpromising background one might wonder whether, from the Japanese point of view, there was ever any need for the presence of foreign banks in their primary function, that is, of acting as bankers. The answer may be: only sporadically. It has been at times when there has been a shortage of liquidity or of foreign exchange in the Japanese economy that foreign banks have been fully utilized within the restrictions imposed upon them. At other times it has been the secondary functions which have kept them going – the provision of contacts and services abroad, the introduction of foreign borrowers to the Tokyo market, advice and assistance to corporations about raising money overseas. Not least, foreign banks and securities houses have had a vital role in introducing and demonstrating new skills and methods – but the effect of that is more conveniently discussed at the London end in the next section.

One may take the view that the foreign houses have had a very hard time of it or one may take the view that it is remarkable that they have done as well as they have. Leaving aside the fortunate episode of the impact loans, we have seen foreign participation in various markets and activities usually fluctuating between zero and 10 per cent. An overall figure for foreign activity in the financial sector is probably meaningless, but if it existed it would be unlikely, according to Mr Satoshi Sumita (Governor of the Bank of Japan) to be as much as 2 per cent of the whole for all the foreign banks put together.[1] The British share of the overall market is therefore small indeed.

Against this, we have found only two cases of British banks withdrawing from Tokyo, and one of those has gone back again. The others profess themselves reluctantly resigned to those activities which they have selected as worthwhile. Very few British banks cover a full range of services in any depth. The commercial banks come nearest to it. While Kleinworts perhaps operates the most fully as a merchant bank, the tendency was noted in chapter 12 to withdraw into 'niche banking' or 'boutique banking'. The trouble about boutiques is that they deal in fashions, and fashions constantly change. Once a new idea has caught on there is always the certainty that others with greater resources will move in and drive out the profit. So constant renewal is called for. One very experienced British banker complained that he could no longer understand the new financial products which his colleagues were devising for Japanese clients, so far-fetched had they become.

An important measure of the level of international business must be the number of foreign banks present in Japan. In mid-1988 there were eighty-one such banks operating through 119 branches.[2] This figure is far below the total of foreign banks to be found in the United Kingdom and United States and the majority of them will only be able to operate at a much lower level of business than Japanese banks abroad. Nevertheless, the figure reflects an increasing use of Tokyo as a base for international business. Nor, in spite of all the delays, discouragements, and difficulties of setting up in Tokyo, is the number now artificially determined. In giving evidence to the House of Lords Mr Alan Loehnis of the Bank of England said that he had no knowledge of any case in which permission to operate had been refused.[3]

Securities dealers in Tokyo speak in much more sanguine terms. Not only have they had an unbroken record of success with their Japan or Pacific investment trusts, but recently they have at least seen new opportunities of acting for Japanese clients and funds. However, while some British companies are enthusiastic, another, as we have already heard, has described the business as 'the crumbs which fall from Nomura's table' and when asked what the influence of British companies has been, one American broker is said to have replied: 'They have very much improved the sandwiches eaten around the Tokyo Stock Exchange.'

One way of judging how well an efficient company is doing is to discover the size of its staff. The merchant banking and investment arms of each house are in separate companies because of Article 65 requirements, but the following approximate figures (taken as random examples in 1988) cover both, as well as any staff engaged in offices outside Tokyo: National Westminster/County NatWest, 280; Barclays/BZW, 500; Barings, 285; Jardine Fleming, 210.[4] In every case the securities business employs far more than the banking side and the proportion of locally engaged employees is very high; there are usually only one or two British in each division. These figures are modest compared with the numbers employed by Japanese companies in London, but they do indicate a much higher level of activity than would have been thought possible a few years back. This is also reflected in the growing number of foreign securities companies which have thought it worth their while to open offices in Tokyo. The figure increased from ten firms in December 1984 to forty-five firms in July 1988. Four of these also have branches in Osaka.[5]

The position of British financial houses in Tokyo today may be described as adequately satisfactory to justify their continued presence but very disappointing when measured against the size of the markets. In the year ending March 1988 the five branches of British commercial banks in Tokyo had made a combined profit before tax of only about £4 million, a distinct improvement on the preceding year but still a very poor return. Nevertheless, lending opportunities for British banks look as if they are improving and further steps are expected in extending interest deregulation on time-deposits and MMCs. The foreign securities houses have never really recovered from Black Monday, which hit the Tokyo Stock Market before they could gain the confidence of Japanese investors. Current financial results are not encouraging and the foreign members of the exchange may all be suffering losses. The situation is made worse by the presence in Tokyo of the forty-five foreign houses with securities licences so that now overcapacity has replaced under-representation.[6] One encouraging factor is that the *Kisaikai* have conceded a substantial increase to the allocation of securities to foreign houses in the domestic bond market (see pp. 168). Negotiations are also slowly proceeding for foreign companies to engage in pension and investment fund management in a meaningful way.

LONDON

In chapter 14 the enormous weight of the Japanese presence in London was described. But it is not just the total number, it is also the size of the individual units that impresses. Among the Japanese banks in the City of London are the five largest banks in the world (in terms of net assets) and nine of the largest ten. Nomura is said to have assets ten times bigger than Merrill Lynch, the next to rank in the world order of securities houses. The Japanese in London dispose of far greater ultimate resources than their British hosts, the opposite of the situation of British companies in Tokyo. This causes many people in the City to have genuine fears about how this financial power will be used and some in politics or the press to echo them. For example, Japanese houses have swallowed nearly two-thirds of the market in Floating Rate Notes and completely dominate all transactions in Euroyen. So what next?

One might point out that the Japanese experience with FRNs has been a disappointing one and that they have almost squeezed the Euroyen market dry of profit. That has no doubt left its mark on those responsible. But fears continue that the muscle of the Japanese houses will be used to force down margins to the point where competition is eliminated or loss-leading offers are used to buy up the whole of the market. Japanese management has now for some time been aware of these fears. Three years ago, when asked about this matter, Professor Saburo Okita, Chairman of the Tokyo Institute for Domestic and International Political

Studies, said: 'We all remember what the Japanese motorcycle industry did to the British motorcycle industry. We do not want that to happen again.'[7] This was natural, coming from a public figure, one of whose main tasks for many years has been to reassure the Americans. But there are also practical influences at work. Much attention has been paid to the deliberations of the Cooke Committee. When its recommendations, as seems likely, become European Community Law, all banks will be required to have a Capital to Risk-weighted Assets Ratio of 8 per cent and the BIS already has similar requirements. The average for a Japanese bank in 1988 was 7.2 per cent. Even though the Sumitomo Bank can show a ratio of 8.2 per cent, these high levels have only been achieved by raising additional equity and constantly realizing profits on securities, a measure only consistently possible in a bull market. If such a ratio has to be maintained, present profitability may not be enough to finance anything more than a slow growth of business. So how can profitability be improved? Deregulation of interest rates at home is eating into domestic profits, while we have seen that some formerly profitable sectors in London have collapsed under intense Japanese competition. In these circumstances high quality investment becomes more attractive and mass under-pricing cannot sensibly continue. Whether this apparent logic of the market-place will assert itself remains to be seen, but it is certainly being discussed. There is little evidence that Japanese companies seek to do unprofitable business, only that they are accustomed to working on lower margins than the Americans and British.

The size and splendour of their offices announce that the Japanese banks, securities companies, and finance-houses have come to stay. Indeed, their search for accommodation has been a major factor in driving up the cost per square foot in London to be the second highest in the world – after Tokyo. Inside these palaces the occupants are trying to assimilate their organizations to the character of the London market. Some of them have realized that the 'cultural differences', about which their own Ministry of Finance likes to speak, imply a need to adjust to the culture of the City of London. Mr Tabuchi, the President of Nomura, used to refer to this process from time to time when giving interviews to the press, as *dochakuka* or 'localization' (from '*do*', meaning 'earth, soil' and '*chaku*', meaning 'attach to or fix to'). It means not only increasing the numbers of local staff, but integrating them closely into the management and decision-making life of the company at all levels. The end-product should not just be a Japanese company operating in London but a London company with Japanese ownership. Such companies may have an increasing proportion of their assets generated locally, but it seems unlikely that any of them would slip out of Japanese control. In any case, there will be many companies that prefer to keep an uncompromisingly Japanese character to their operations.

In chapter 14 foreign sources were quoted which stressed the importance of London as a centre in which to learn the most up-to-date methods of banking and asset management. Certainly, London has played a key part in the explosion of learning that has taken place in Japan in this field since the war. For instance, in 1988 BZW brought no fewer than twenty-five Japanese trainees to work in their London offices, despite initial reluctance on the part of the Home Office to grant permits.[8] Such *White Adder Tours*, as they might be called on the analogy of 1859 (see p. 14), are programmed by a number of British companies.

If there is still a very long way to go before Tokyo has been internationalized as a financial centre, there can be no doubt that the operations of the Japanese financial houses abroad have become mostly internationalized. This will certainly make them better performers and more competitive, but the extent to which it will affect the composition and attitudes of senior management is not yet clear. Is it only a matter of personnel learning new skills and techniques or is there a process whereby '*localization*' flows back to head office? Will the new roots send sap to the tree? It is known that there has been an attitude of mistrust in Japanese society towards those of its members who have been 'tainted' by life abroad. It is said that employees returning to Japan after a period of service in Europe or America are often considered as no longer 'one of us' and that they, their wives, and children are in for a hard period of re-education. But while this attitude may persist in manufacturing industry, it will have become harder to sustain in financial services and trading. There must be fewer and fewer men in the ranks of middle management in the head offices

of Tokyo banks, securities houses, and trading companies who
have not had experience overseas and been affected by it, so that
the time is near when a high proportion of those at the top will
have spent a formative part of their careers in London and New
York.

The open nature of the London market has enabled the
Japanese financial institutions to move into every field as fast as
they could acquire adequate understanding of it (sometimes, alas,
before doing so) or recruit adequate experienced staff. The latter
has not always been easy, particularly during the period after Big
Bang and when the bull market was still running, though there
will be more qualified people looking for jobs today. Nor have
relations between Japanese management and local staff always
been very easy in those firms where 'localization', or some
variant of it, are unknown. But the range of Japanese activities
has extended with only occasional friction or restraint. In 1985
the Japanese banks complained that the Bank of England was
refusing to allow them to lead-manage Eurosterling issues. In
1987 there were the much more serious problems (referred to in
chapter 12 pp. 175–6) caused by the reluctance of the Japanese
authorities to grant licences or remove restrictions on British
banks in Tokyo, the non-admission of British companies to the
Tokyo Stock Exchange, and the dispute over the rights of Cable
and Wireless. At that time the Prime Minister referred in parliament to the power to revoke the licences of foreign banks in the
UK under the Financial Services Act of 1986 and the Bank of
England held up the applications of a couple of Japanese securities houses. In spite of such occasional hitches the Japanese
presence in London has been established without difficulty.
Moreover, as the threat referred to at the beginning of this
section that its presence would be dangerously overwhelming
has failed to materialize, the British financial community has
accepted that the enormous increase of money and activity
brought to London by the Japanese has been to everyone's benefit. A British banker summed up the situation by reflecting that
it didn't matter how many Japanese firms there were in the City
or how big they were – they were very very important customers.
None the less, the presence of too many banks in London can cut
down everyone's share of the cake.

To watch over this whole situation the British Invisible Exports Council established in 1988 a permanent Japan Committee. The membership is drawn from the Bank of England, Treasury, Department of Trade and Industry, and Foreign and Commonwealth Office, on the one side, and banking, securities, insurance, and related financial services and professions, on the other. Their tasks might be described as acquiring full information on the Japanese presence in London and elsewhere overseas and ensuring that the situation runs as smoothly and amicably as possible and to make Japanese companies feel welcome. However, a situation could arise in which the Bank of England or the BIEC would come to the conclusion that there were enough banks of all kinds in London and that the presence of yet further numbers, such as Japanese regional banks, would have little justification in itself and could spoil the market. It is unlikely that the Bank of England would alter its traditional habit of issuing a licence to any bank meeting its requirements but the Japanese, in such a situation, might find themselves faced with the British equivalent of their own administrative guidance.

To conclude, the most significant comparison between the states of play in Tokyo and London today is contained in two figures which have appeared in this book – the estimate of the Governor of the Bank of Japan that all foreign institutions together are responsible for less than 2 per cent of the financial activity in Tokyo and the estimate of the Bank of England that in 1987 the Japanese banks in London accounted for 36 per cent of all international assets of UK banks.

NOTES

1 Aron Viner, 'Inside Japan's Financial Markets', *The Economist* (1988), p. 229.
2 'On the move', Final Report of the Action Programme Promotion Committee, Aug. 1988, p. 14. Issued by the Japanese Embassy, London.
3 House of Lords, Select Committee on the European Communities, 13th Report (London, HMSO, 27 June 1989), Appendix 2, p. 60.
4 Information supplied courtesy of the banks mentioned.

5 'On the move', p. 14.
6 Information kindly supplied by the Ministry of Trade and Industry.
7 *Euromoney*, April 1987.
8 Information kindly supplied by Mr John Cousins of BZW.

PART III

PAST, PRESENT AND FUTURE

16

PAST

A cursory survey of 130 years in the financial relations between Britain and Japan has now been completed. There are no historical lessons' to be learnt from this but there are certain patterns of behaviour or persistent trends which are interesting to contemplate.

JAPANESE PATTERNS

It is impossible not to be impressed by the Japanese capacity for study, selection, adaptation, and improvement of new ideas. Most of the ideas considered in this book were foreign ones. The readiness to treat these with seriousness and respect and to make them the subject of exhaustive study is peculiarly Japanese. English people seem to be surprised, and even amused, by the Japanese practice of taking detailed notes on even the most commonplace things and of arriving in a group of five or six persons when one or two are expected. It is all part of the process of making sure that information is complete, that nothing has been overlooked or misunderstood, and that enough minds have been engaged to ensure a really searching consideration of the whole matter. Who would dare to say that it does not produce remarkable results? For the outcome of all this information-gathering, study, and discussion is the advancement of the company at the immediate level and of the country itself at the ultimate level – in other words, adaptation to Japanese purposes.

These habits of mind must already have been formed by the educational methods of Tokugawa times for the Japanese sprang ready into action almost at the instant of the Meiji Restoration. At that stage, they already had a remarkably high rate of literacy. We have seen how very quickly they realized a modern industrial state with all its necessary institutions. Those first forty years provide one of the most remarkable chapters in history and the last forty years are equally astonishing. What happened in between those two periods? Nothing fundamental can have changed very much, but it gives a feeling of an age in which dreams of military and political grandeur led the nation away from its real genius. At any rate, the explosion of energy and achievement after the Second World War takes up the same drive as that in the early chapters. This time the aim was to create a more advanced industrial society, based on applied science, extensive research, high-technology, and excellence of products, but the method of intellectual approach had not changed. Furthermore, this habit of mind is not confined to a small managerial and administrative elite. A very striking feature is the high degree of what might be termed 'industrial literacy' on the shop-floor or in the office, which enables a large proportion of employees to contribute to the life and advancement of their company with full understanding of its aims and nature.

The Japanese approach has not been quite as rapid in the field of finance as it has in manufacturing or buying and selling. Finance is a matter of ideas and concepts and it may be that the mode of thought we have been discussing works best on practical problems.

The second pattern to emerge is one that is so well known that one hesitates to mention it. This is the extent of Japanese self-discipline, both personal and social, reflected in the work-ethic on the one hand and group-attachment on the other. The only reason for referring to it here is that it does tend to be misunderstood. Many Westerners express their view of Japanese solidarity by the journalistic phrase 'Japan Inc.'. While this cliché can be convenient, it hides half the reality. Opposition and friction are as much part of life in Japan as they are anywhere else. Government complains about business and business complains about government. Politicians complain bitterly about newspapers and newspapers complain bitterly about politicians. In these pages we have traced a dispute over a period of forty years within the administration about whether or not the financial system should be liberalized. This will have generated a good deal of internal heat. The Japanese have developed systems of controlling and resolving conflict so as to ensure that the energies of person, family, group, or nation are wasted as little as possible. The ultimate expression of these systems is *nemawashi*, the process of reaching consensus. But foreigners do not realize how incredibly difficult it often is to achieve such consensus and how much effort and time goes into it. Consensus is perhaps the highest of all expressions of self-discipline.

A special case of this acceptance is the much greater role of the administration in the day-to-day affairs of business than any-where in the West. British and Americans who are exercising responsibility almost invariably resent state intervention or direc-tion. The Japanese accept it as an inevitable part of the national consensus and they know how to get the best from it. Foreigners working in the financial sector have often chafed under the com-plex regulations and the irksomeness of administrative guidance. At the same time, they have played a part in clearing some of them away.

These two aspects of intensely applied thought and disciplined consensus help to explain a third pattern that may have emerged from the book. This is the astonishing ability of the Japanese to overcome disaster or set-back. It is one thing to deal with a great earthquake or defeat in war; people have little alternative but to get on with it. Lesser crises can be more difficult precisely because not everyone is so intensely aware of being directly affected. The first 'oil shock' of 1973, for instance, presented the country, which imported 95 per cent of its energy requirements, with a multiple increase in its cost of energy imports overnight. Again, the revaluation of the yen from 1986 and the problems of *endaka* almost doubled the dollar costs of some products. Yet in both cases, as in so many other times of difficulty, after a while everything seemed to be under control again and the economy had suffered only one year's serious check. It can be seen from such performances that the country has developed strongly reac-tive mechanisms to deal with crises. Where others might be inclined to plug a hole, the Japanese will look further ahead and recognize the need for a new dyke. Straightforward projections may be shown to be inadequate because the Japanese will attack and alter the circumstances which gave rise to that projection or engage in new forms of activity which make the circumstances less relevant. We read increasingly now about how the Japanese are not going to be able to deal with the problem of affluence, or how they will be brought down by the demographic problem of an ageing population. One does at least know that they will react strongly to these challenges and that there is no obvious reason why they should not deal with them as effectively as with past difficulties. Foreigners, faced with Japan's extraordinary success, find it hard to remember that behind all this activity lurks a sense of danger. The spectres of lack of natural resources, past poverty, and disaster have never been banished. This is one of the reasons why the Japanese have been so slow to relax in their new, affluent circumstances. Few Japanese, until the last year or two, have felt rich.

There are some patterns of Japanese behaviour which foreigners have found it difficult or unpleasant to deal with. It is the very deliberateness and thoroughness of the Japanese method that creates problems for others. There is a steady sectoral progression. Steel is selected first, then shipbuilding, motor-cars, communications, computers. Mergers are suggested, but the right competitive level maintained. Scarce resources are allocated: capital, raw materials, and preferential finance. Protection through tariffs, quotas, and standards is maintained until manufacturing capability has been established on the basis of an assured and impenetrable domestic market. The second stage is careful study of the export market. An assessment is made of the modified requirements for the product in each geographical or social area. The share of the market required to justify costs of penetration is calculated and the price fixed at which such a share will inevitably be acquired. The initial price will usually be just about economic because anti-dumping proceedings are to be avoided whenever possible. Then it all happens. Japanese exports in the sector climb at an astonishing rate. Factories and whole industries are closed down in the receiving countries. Unemployment ensues. A model exercise has been carried out but the social and political consequences have far exceeded anything within the brief of the planners.

This pattern typified the seventies and early eighties. The Keidanren had for some years understood the ultimate implications of such policies, but the individual member companies did not easily respond to calls for moderation. Foreign competitors could see few signs that Japan was really addressing itself to the matter with more than fair words. The problem was how to rein in well-conceived and successful Japanese enterprise to the advantage of uncompetitive industry overseas. One device adopted in the late seventies and early eighties was the 'voluntary restraint agreement' by which certain Japanese industries such as television tubes, automobiles, ball-bearings, or VTRs would agree to a limited quota of exports while native industries in Europe or America would have time to reorganize. This device has not always been successful; the breathing space has not led to noticeably deeper breathing. The British government has been attracted by the alternative solution of allowing the Japanese manufacturer to produce within Britain, using British labour and British or EEC components. Meanwhile the pressures on Japan described in Chapter 13 have effectively reduced most of the tariff and many of the non-tariff barriers in Japan, as well as the more obvious financial aids.

This rough analysis of industrial experience is offered because it has been feared that it gives a pattern for financial activities also. In Chapter 14 we noted that such fears had been widespread as the size and financial weight of the Japanese presence in London became apparent. There is not the slightest doubt that, with the funds at their disposal, the Japanese banks or securities houses could buy up certain sections of the market. They have certainly taken over the Euroyen market and dominated the market for floating rate notes, as we have seen. But the profitability of both these sectors diminished or disappeared with Japanese domination. There is little attraction in a scorched-earth policy for sophisticated managers in a sensitive environment who need to build profits. One must hope that the logic of this is holding against the temptation to dump financial products.

Perhaps the real problem lies not in aggressive conduct but in comparative staying power. With 'Big Bang' and the arrival of the Japanese as leading players, there has been a fundamental restructuring of the gilt-edged market in London and the treasury market in New York, with a limited number of primary dealers participating in each. Similarly, the equity markets have been recast with a number of big market-makers in the different sectors. The Japanese houses were encouraged to take up these roles in order to attract Japanese funds. After little more than a year, some British and American banks were already finding the system too competitive and therefore too costly. There have been quite a surprising number of withdrawals; for instance on the London gilts market the number of primary dealers has fallen from twenty-seven to nineteen and more withdrawals are expected. In 1989 there have already been withdrawals from other markets, the National Westminster, for instance, pulling out of the New York Treasury market in January. Not one Japanese firm has withdrawn from any of these positions. With such huge resources they may be prepared to wait until much reduced numbers leave a profitable market share to the survivors. Sitting it out is a marked pattern of Japanese behaviour. Such a 'no surrender' policy may be expected to leave the Japanese with a very large share of world securities markets.

BRITISH PATTERNS

Any patterns of British behaviour to emerge from this text are less clearly defined than Japanese ones. This is partly because British behaviour is more aberrant than Japanese and far more likely to be an expression of the cult of the individual than in Japan. The supposedly deadening effects on British people of public school education or middle-class conformity are not very visible in the City of London. A second factor is the way in which the British have reacted to change. Faced with a fundamental challenge, the Japanese have tended to intensify and apply their patterns of behaviour; the British have tended to rethink theirs. After the Second World War, loss of Empire, loss of Great Power status, loss of a leading share in world trade, and loss of industrial power have eventually left the British living by their wits and ingenuity, while trying to work out a new and secure role for British industry. This has required both old qualities and new ones.

In Part I of this book, we saw Britain at the turn of the century functioning as the principal centre of international money and as the natural place to which Japan went to finance its industrial expansion and its imperialist wars. The old City showed itself extremely competent in organizing sovereign lending for Japan. But corporate lending was a different matter. The City of London had built as much of its success on caution as on enterprise, but here one begins to get a feeling of super-caution, of attachment to the 'fat option'. Perhaps one can see over this period a very gradual fading of entrepreneurship in British financial circles, and a growth of the old British tendency to relax when opportunity offers. At the same time, one must not overlook the fact that all over the Far East, in China, South East Asia, Borneo, or even Manchuria, branch managers, with sometimes little encouragement from Head Offices, were scraping away to make the small profits which, added together, would supply the very satisfactory earnings of the British overseas banks and trading companies.

During the first twenty years after the war, the City of London played a marginal role as a world financial centre outside the sterling area. It was only in the mid-sixties that a combination of luck, opportunity, and enterprise enabled London to re-acquire rapidly its significance as a major international centre. At this point a quite different pattern emerges of originality, imagination, and inventiveness. Moving away from the strict fields of commercial banking and stock-broking, financial houses developed an endless fund of novel techniques, instruments, and dealings in allied fields of bonds, interest rates, foreign exchange, and asset management. It is this quality that has made it the major financial centre for Japanese companies overseas.

It is also this pattern which has shown itself in the readiness with which British merchant bankers and others have taken up niche or boutique roles. While this is sometimes a necessary consequence of lack of financial power, in Tokyo it has usually been the result of restrictions and prohibitions by the authorities. Now that these are being removed, it will be seen whether the field is really free enough for the British to come out of their niches. For several decades we have been contemplating the exceptional inventiveness of British scientists, the high proportion of Nobel prize-winners, the numbers of advanced materials, processes, drugs, engines which are invented in the UK, and we have lamented the failure to turn them into production and mass-marketing. One would hope to avoid any parallel in financial products.

A final pattern of the greatest importance is the relationship between the Bank of England and the institutions and companies working in the City. By contrast with the authorities in Tokyo, the Bank of England has pursued a policy of *laissez-faire* in the positive sense of the term; that is to say, the Bank only interferes when there is real and justified cause to do so. While the authority of the Bank has been exercised within the policies of British governments of the day, which have sometimes been highly interventionist, the institutions in the City have had great freedom to operate within those limits. This has encouraged the remarkable regrowth of London as the European financial centre in recent years, as opposed to Frankfurt, which might otherwise have seemed a more natural choice in view of the economic strength of the Federal Republic and the important international role of the Deutschemark. The relationship is a delicate one which could be disturbed if government interposes itself between the Bank and the institutions by over-active legislative intervention in the powers and functions of the self-regulatory bodies.

In spite of the occasional friction described in the last chapter, the Japanese have benefited enormously from this freedom enjoyed in the City of London. Nor has the Bank of England had any cause to worry about the presence of Japanese banks from the prudential point of view. Japan has only had one bank failure since the War, a record which contrasts well with what happened during the secondary banking crisis in the UK or the recent wave of insolvencies in the United States. The problem will be to watch for any abuse of size or strength which would distort the free functioning of the London markets.

17

PRESENT

There are a number of special features and problems today in the economic field which, although outside the immediate area of Anglo-Japanese affairs, deeply affect the financial relationships of all the major industrial powers and provide the background to much activity, decision, and planning.

SURPLUS AND DEFICIT

The most worrisome macro-economic feature of the last fifteen years has been the persistent trade surplus earned by Japan. The post-war system of world trade has been based on the GATT Agreements. These enshrine the principal of free trade and, in round after round of negotiations, efforts have been made to reduce tariffs, to abolish non-tariff barriers, and to extend free trade to agricultural products and services. In any system in which free trade is genuinely practised there will always be surpluses and deficits. To attempt to abolish such irregularities would be the very denial of free trade. A conflict between interest and ideology therefore arises when a chronic surplus/deficit reveals a structural imbalance in trade. Moreover, such a structural imbalance becomes dangerous to international society when the benefits to be derived from the world's system of trade flow overwhelmingly in the direction of one country or area for a long period of time. This is precisely what has been happening with Japan.

Many of the developments described in Part II of this book have been the results of direct attempts to deal with this problem. The most important were the freeing of exports of Japanese capital, the measures flowing from the Maekawa Report, and the revaluation of the yen. The last two of these, as explained in chapter 13, followed the Plaza Meeting in September 1985. In the minds of the Japanese they were intended to reduce the US deficit, but they have done so only to a very limited extent. In dollar terms the deficit fell from 59 billion in 1986 to 55 billion in 1987 and 43 billion in 1988 but shows little sign of a further downward trend.[1] As for Japanese trade with the outside world as a whole, the surplus continued to rise, reaching a peak of nearly $80 million in 1987 and falling only to $77.6 in 1988.[2] Thus, while Japan's exports to other industrialized countries, including Britain, have been contained and even slightly reduced, the country is still proving to be a very difficult market for the import of manufactured goods. The disturbing fact is that none of the measures taken to date has given adequate results and this is putting a tremendous strain on the relations of the United States, not only with Japan, but also with all the other trading partners with which she is in deficit.

There is also a second unsatisfactory feature. Hitherto, Japan has always run a large deficit in invisible trade, particularly with the United Kingdom. This has helped to offset, but not to wipe out, the large Japanese surplus in physical trade. This situation is now changing. The enormous exports of capital from Japan in recent years are beginning to earn increasing annual sums in interest payments. Furthermore, the earnings of Japan's financial services abroad are becoming important. We have noted that securities companies are talking of making 20 per cent of their profits overseas. So, although Japanese people are spending more every year on foreign travel, it is to be expected that invisible trade in future, instead of diminishing the Japanese surplus, will have little effect on it or, in some sectors, could even substantially add to it. This trend is clearly shown by the fact that Japan's share of the world's invisible receipts has been rising steadily and by 1988 had reached 10.8 per cent compared with the UK share of 14.5 per cent and the US share of 19.2 per cent.[3] There is no early prospect of abolishing a double surplus by any method which would not be very disruptive to world trade.

THE CONCEPT OF RECIPROCITY

In such a situation it is natural that the deficit countries should start talking of the need for reciprocity. There are two kinds of reciprocity. One is a balance of the goods and services exchanged, resulting in a nil transfer of payments between two trading partners. The second is an equality of access to and opportunity in the respective markets of two trading partners (this is what the Americans call 'the level playing field'). The first of these concepts is not a necessary or proper feature of free trade. As suggested in the previous section, pursuit of such an aim can only lead to the restriction of free trade and to stagnation; it is contrary to the obligations of GATT. The second kind of reciprocity is, however, an absolutely reasonable one and any British government would certainly fight to achieve it. It is unfortunate that the Americans quite often confuse these two issues. For instance, during the lengthy debates in the US Congress on the Foreign Trade Bill of 1987, many Senators and Congressmen called for retaliatory measures against imports from any country which consistently ran a surplus in its balance of trade with the United States. At the same time they understandably called for 'the level playing field'. In this way, by confusing the two issues, the Americans give the impression that all trade imbalances are the result of discrimination. This is not the case, but it is presumably what President Bush meant when he said, during the run-up to his election campaign on 14 March 1988: 'Today we are in a global economic battle with Japan, Europe and the emerging nations.'

Successive British governments have always demanded reciprocity of opportunity in the United Kingdom's financial relations with Japan. This is why they have supported American demands for the internationalization of the Tokyo market. It is also why, in the last three years, they have put so much direct pressure on

the Japanese government to expedite the grant of banking licences to British banks or to ensure that seats on the Tokyo
Stock Exchange are made available to securities companies. But
this has nothing to do with mathematical equality. All those
British firms who are ever likely to wish for seats on the Tokyo
Stock Exchange have already applied. There will probably not be
any more. They are outnumbered by the Japanese with seats on
the London Stock Exchange. The only way to get numerical
equality is to remove Japanese memberships. That would not be
a sensible sort of reciprocity.

Absorbing Chronic Imbalances

The Japanese are not the only people to have ever earned a
persistent trade surplus. Britain had such a surplus for part of the
nineteenth century and the United States for a good part of the
twentieth century. West Germany is running one now and may
even overtake the Japanese. Attempts in the past to deal with
such situations by imposing tariffs and other protective measures
have always been liable to produce unforeseen and undesirable
consequences. Since the rise of capitalism the classic manner of
dealing with a chronic surplus has been to re-export it in the
form of capital investment. A secondary channel is also available
today in the form of Overseas Aid. This is precisely what the
Japanese have been doing since 1984; after taking their capital
exports into consideration, they have shown a considerable
annual deficit on current account.

When the British were exporting capital in the nineteenth century, they met with little difficulty. They disposed of sufficient
navies and troops all over the world to kick open any door that
did not open of its own accord. They were also in a position to
protect British lives and property anywhere abroad, though
Japan proved to be the interesting exception. The United States,
exporting capital in the twentieth century, has been faced with a
more difficult situation. Whereas American investment has been
generally invited and welcomed by governments in Western
Europe, in other parts of the world it has been greeted with cries

of 'Coca-Colonialism' or 'Dollar Imperialism'. Indeed, these slogans have provided rallying cries for anti-Americanism in Europe and the Third World alike. It is not to be supposed that the absorption of immense amounts of Japanese capital will not also provoke hostile reactions of some kind. Animosity is already visible in such totally different situations as South East Asia and the West Coast of the United States. The one country which has so far shown almost unlimited enthusiasm for Japanese inward investment has been the United Kingdom, and this fact is very well known in Japan.

JAPAN'S CAPITAL EXPORTS

In 1986 Japan's net capital outflow (excluding banking funds) was $131 billion. In 1987 it was $137 billion.[4] These huge transfers can be looked at under the following different heads.

Purchase of Foreign Government Bonds

For many years Japanese life insurance companies, Trust Banks administering funds, managers of investment trusts, and private investors have been persistent purchasers of US Treasury Bonds. So great has been the demand that in one morning an entire issue was bought up by the Japanese. In this way they have regularly funded the unchecked US budget deficit. This has been a costly experience in view of the dollar's loss of value in yen terms since 1986. The question is whether there will be more interest in European issues. This has already begun to show and it was with the intention of promoting sales of sterling issues that the Japanese securities houses were pressed to become primary dealers in the London gilts market.

Corporate Bonds and Loans

Foreign corporations remain eager applicants for Japanese funds in these forms, both in the Eurobond and Samurai markets and through loans from Japanese banks.

Portfolio Investment

Although the proportion of shares on the London and New York Stock exchanges held in Japanese hands is still small, it can grow rapidly as trust funds, pension funds, and investment trusts begin to buy more foreign equities. Portfolios can also, of course, include property investments, and these are increasingly popular.

Direct Investment

This is the most difficult field and the one in which resentment is most easily aroused. Acquisition by takeover bid is particularly likely to be badly received, as Sony's acquisition of CBS and Mitsubishi's of the Rockefeller Center have shown. The British and the Japanese are now both very active purchasers of under-managed companies and this is arousing a lot of hostile comment in the American press and in Congress, with demands for protective legislation. Much less opposition is aroused by new, green-field investment – indeed, this can be greeted with enthusiasm. It is ironic that the Japanese destroyed the original British television industry but have been welcomed as the builders of a completely new one. They appear to be half-way through doing the same to the British car industry.

Development Aid

The announced intention of the Japanese government is to spend $50 billion on overseas aid programmes during the five years from 1988 to 1992.[5] This is commendable, particularly as a high proportion of the grants and low interest loans are to be untied. But no matter how free this aid may be, a very great deal of it seems to be spent with Japanese consultants, contractors, and suppliers. In spite of all the inter-governmental negotiations and agreements on 'credits mixtes', any British consortium tendering for an overseas project knows how difficult it is to secure a contract against Japanese competition – their offer always seems to contain an irresistible aid titbit. Increased aid from Japan to the Third World means increased competition for Britain.

It can thus be seen that there is no present difficulty about recycling the Japanese trade surplus to those countries in which it is earned. Indeed, Japan's exports of capital very much more than cover the gap. The question is whether the recipients, and particularly the United States, are satisfied to let things continue indefinitely in this way. They are certainly not satisfied, but they have not yet suggested a reasonable alternative.

THE YEN AS AN INTERNATIONAL CURRENCY

In chapter 13 we discussed the attempts made by the Americans to encourage the use of the yen in international trade. In 1986 only 3.5 per cent of exports and 0.6 per cent of imports in the IMF were financed in yen. In the same years and in the same IMF area, the aggregate proportion of the reserves of all the members, including Japan, held in yen, was only 6.9 per cent in 1986 and 7.2 per cent in 1988.[6] These are extraordinarily low figures for a currency which, being that of the world's strongest economy, should by now have become (or be about to become) the world's major reserve currency – or so conventional theory argues.

Neither the Japanese nor anyone else is behaving as if they intended that the yen should assume this role. The Americans continue to act as if the problems of the dollar were only a temporary aberration and the Eagle would always be king. That appears still to be the assumption of the Group of Five, and the main international use of the yen is to support the dollar.

Furthermore, as the IMF figures show, the Japanese authorities have done nothing to ensure that foreign holdings of yen are of sufficient size for it to be used as a reserve currency. By the end of 1988 they had not removed all the old restrictions. There were still restrictive controls on the issue of Samurai bonds. Permission was still required from the Bank of Japan to obtain yen for investment outside Japan. Foreigners were discouraged from holding Japanese government bonds by an interest-withholding tax that is hard to recover. No doubt they have it in mind to change these rules before long, but they have not said so.[7]

The official Japanese comment is that they are moving towards a 'multiple key-currency system'[8] in which the yen would share reserve burdens with the dollar and the Deutschemark. It is doubt-ful whether this elegant phrase represents a planned policy; it may mean no more than that the Japanese expect to see use of the yen gradually increase, both as a means of exchange and as part of the central reserves of other countries. Meanwhile, if capital exports continue to exceed Japan's surplus of current account at the present rate, five or ten years should see an enormous increase in foreigners' holdings of yen and the currency will move towards its new role. It is, after all, by the export of its capital surplus that a country first establishes its money as a reserve currency.

NOTES

1 GATT Annual Report, 1989.
2 Japan Ministry of Finance.
3 Figures supplied by British Invisibles.
4 Figures from the Japanese Ministry of Finance.
5 Japan's Official Development Assistance (ODA), Vol. I.
6 IMF Annual Reports, 1987 and 1989.
7 H. Flight and B. Lee-Swan, *All You Need to Know about Exchange Rates*, (Sidgwick & Jackson, London, 1988), pp. 162–3.
8 Yusuke Kashiwagi, 'The internationalization of the yen and the Tokyo financial market', *Speaking of Japan* (July 1987).

18

FUTURE

THE STATE OF JAPAN

Making predictions about the future is a waste of credibility but talking about the future can be interesting. For at least twenty years now there have been Western writers predicting that as the Japanese economy grew the nature of the Japanese people would change. Men and women, it was argued, would work less hard, would lose their intense loyalties to their companies, would shift restlessly from job to job, would lose respect for the seniority principle, and would generally behave like managers or workers in affluent, consumer societies in America or Europe. This would appear to be a thoroughly Marxist argument, accepting that there is a scientific law of history whereby the social and cultural 'superstructure' inevitably reflects the state of productive evolution. As the writers were usually anti-Marxists, this was odd. In any case, the predictions have not been more than marginally realized up to now.

What does need to be examined, on the other hand, is whether the major macro-economic fact of this stage of history, the existence of the chronic Japanese trade surplus, will continue for as long as can usefully be thought about, or whether it is seriously on the turn. This is a very important consideration because if the Japanese surplus will have disappeared by 1995 there is no point in taking drastic measures which risk upsetting the whole world's joint economic progress in order to counter it now. But if it is set to go on until AD 2050 unless a stop is put to it, then the sooner that action is taken to modify it the better.

Until recently, apart from the theoretical, sociological speculation of the kind already discussed, opinion has been that the
overwhelming tide of Japan's industrial supremacy, reinforced by
its financial supremacy, will continue to sweep on until some
distant time in the twenty-first century. However, the opposite
view has been put with great clarity and cogency by William
Emmott, Business Affairs Editor of *The Economist*.[1] This argument deserves careful attention; it is briefly as follows. The
Japanese surplus in physical trade has already been effectively
curbed by the revaluation of the yen, by the stimulation of
domestic demand, and by measures to encourage the import of
manufactured goods, and it is set to decline further. The surplus
of invisible trade or trade in services has failed to materialize,
because expenditure on travel, shipping, etc. is rising faster than
dividends on exported capital. Therefore, the external generation
of surplus capital is waning and may dry up at any time after
1995. As for the internal generation of surplus capital, it is
suggested that this too will dwindle, since the famous Japanese
high rate of saving is already falling and will do so even faster as
a new generation of young, high-spending consumers replace
their conservative elders. It is said that the policies required of
Japan today, such as a massive round of corporate investment
and the further stimulation of domestic demand in response to
foreign pressures, will mop up most of any available surplus.
Finally, based on a study produced by BZW,[2] it is argued that
demographic changes, which will leave Japan shortly with a
higher proportion of over-age people in its population than any
other leading industrial country, will require enormous expenditure on health and pensions and that this will finally wipe out the
surplus and produce a deficit. The essay concludes with a view of
the year 2010, taken from the BZW paper. By then, it says,
'Studies of Japan's high savings rate will be of only archaeologi-
cal significance.'

The trouble with this intimidating analysis is that it is based on
flat projections of present trends. It appears to assume that the
Japanese either will not or cannot react to the situation and alter
the factors in any way. A major theme of this present book,
however, has been that Japan is an intensely reactive society.
Faced with any historical predicament – military defeat, earth-

quake, depression, 'oil-shock', currency revaluation, or other imaginable challenge – the Japanese react at once with study, discussion, new ideas, new efforts, joint decision, and action to produce fresh circumstances and the most favourable outcome. Moreover, in the background, there still lurks and will always lurk the fear that Japan is a poor nation without resources that must fight every inch of the way. It is impossible to imagine a Japanese government, the officials of MITI and the Ministry of Finance, the Keidanren and the Nikkeiren, the business community and the trade unions, standing by and watching the achievements of the last four and a half decades being dissipated, without an enormous struggle. Their aim is to maintain in all circumstances a comfortable surplus, but on a more modest scale than in the past in order not to attract excessive hostility. Mr Emmott quotes a member of the Liberal Democratic Party as saying: 'Japanese industry would be destroyed if the yen–dollar rate were to fall as low as Y135.' This is a very striking quotation because, as the author acknowledges, the rate passed well below that without the predicted results, thereby once again demonstrating the ability of the Japanese to deal with forces to which other systems would probably succumb.

There is, of course, one factor over which the Japanese have no direct control – the demographic one. Undoubtedly, they will soon have the world's highest proportion of pensioners. But this subject requires a great deal more study than it has been given before projections are made. In particular, fresh thought is needed about the level of work-force required in the productive industry of a nation which also has the world's highest proportion of robots. With the development of Japanese 'biomimetics', the relationship between population, employment, and production could enter a new phase.

The argument should not be left without a word on the breathlessly awaited, youthful, high-spending class. According to *Japan Echo*,[3] these are already active as a group and have been dubbed *Shinjinrui*.[4] They are, as predicted, undoubtedly throw-away consumers. However, their function in the economy at the moment is to assist in switching part of economic growth from export-led to home-led production. This does not mean that they can be considered as a runaway force.

There is another consideration of major importance when speaking of the future. This is the fact that Japan has risen to its present position with a minimum expenditure on defence. If, for political or strategic reasons, Japan were to raise its level of defence spending per head of population to that of the European members of NATO, she would have to quadruple the annual amount; if she adopted the American level, she would need to increase it eightfold. This would certainly knock a large initial hole in the capital surplus, but the decision would no doubt be accompanied by removal of the present ban on the export of arms so that Japan would become a major, if not the major, seller of arms. Indeed, it is already apparent that Japan is building up a major armaments industry. That is not surprising. There is no reason why Japan should for ever depend on the Americans to equip its Self-Defence Forces, why they should not wish to develop defence technologies useful in non-military fields, or why individual companies should not exploit loopholes in the law to manufacture and export components not classified as full weapons. But that does not mean that the no-war clauses of the constitution are about to be repealed, as some Western journalists suggest. There is, as yet, no reason to reject the conclusion which has been put forward by Paul Kennedy that Japan has no present wish to become a Great Power in the politico-military sense and that it would require some important and unpredictable shift in the military stance of America, Russia, or China to bring about such a change in Japanese policy.[5]

Whatever view one takes of all these matters, by 1995 Japanese overseas assets will be more than $1 trillion and still rising. They could be very much more. A higher proportion than now will be tied up in industrial investment of various kinds – infrastructural and extractive investment in the Third World designed to ensure a supply of raw materials; productive enterprises in Newly Industrialized Countries (NICs) to export heavy or environmentally 'dirty' industry from Japan, with the advantage of cheaper local labour; production of high-quality consumer and capital goods in the United States and the European Community behind any tariff barriers or restrictions which those countries might be tempted to raise against imports from Japan. Britain is likely to go on receiving a large share of the third category. Very big sums of money will remain free, however, for investment in government paper, corporate bonds, equities, and more ephemeral investments, much of which will continue to pass through the City of London.

1992

While the world thinks about the future of Japan, the Japanese are thinking about the future of the European Community, and particularly about the formation of a Single European Market (SEM) in 1992. Until recently they have found it difficult to understand how much real substance there is in the European Community. They have thought it easier to deal with individual European governments (and sometimes to play them off against each other in the process) than with the European Commission. Their voluntary restraint agreements have been with the individual governments, though exceptionally a price and volume agreement on VTRs was reached with the Community as a whole. The Japanese dislike the Commission's exercise of its powers on anti-dumping and the fact that it instigated proceedings against Japan under the GATT rules. None of the relationships with the individual European countries could ever be as important as that with the United States, while that with the Community as a whole has seemed to lack reality. Japanese like to illustrate this by saying that the world is a steel triangle: one thick bar joins the United States and Japan and another thick bar joins the United States and Europe, while Europe and Japan are joined by a thin bar.

A different note was heard for the first time when Prime Minister Takeshita visited London in 1988. In his speech at the Mansion House on 4 May,[6] the Japanese Prime Minister opened with a few courtesies to his British hosts but then proceeded to speak only in terms of Japan and Europe. Japanese officials, bankers, and manufacturers have followed the negotiations for the Single European Market extremely closely, constantly asking detailed questions about such matters as the recognition of standards, residuary quotas, and government procurement. As usual, they will be fully ready to deal with the new challenge of the

SEM when it comes into being. It is, after all, partly their own creation. Both the pressure on private industry to enter into pan-European or inter-member mergers and acquisitions and the pressure on governments to make the political decisions to create a Single Market are in great part a reaction to the extreme competitiveness of Japanese companies, both within Europe and in Third Countries. Little progress was made in these directions until the weight of the deficit with Japan was felt. For the first time in history, Japan is playing a role in the internal evolution of Europe.

The Japanese are well aware that many Americans in the US Congress and administration hold the view that the SEM will be the cover for a protectionist 'Fortress Europe'. They have had reason to fear that, in the prolonged and difficult years of negotiation, the more intransigent and protectionist French might win out over the economically liberal Germans and British. Progress so far belies that fear. The last decisions will be the most difficult and will exact the greatest compromises, but nothing in the agreements already reached shows signs of any departure from GATT principles or contains any new barriers or discriminatory provisions. Nor is there any indication that those features of Community (and British) regulations which the Japanese so much dislike—anti-dumping proceedings against manufactures and components, determination of country of origin, setting of exclusive high-tech Standards, etc.—will be intensified. While real problems will undoubtedly arise between Europe and America over agricultural exports, Fortress Europe is still only a shadow cast by American perceptions of the weakness of their own industry and Japanese fears that their trading surplus will not be tolerated for ever. Neither Americans nor Japanese seem very impressed by the fact that, while neither of their Constitutions makes any mention of free trade, the Treaty of Rome is founded on it. The pressures exerted by the Europeans on Japan are light indeed compared to those exerted by the Americans in the current Strategic Impediment Initiative negotiations.

In the financial field the Japanese have studied the negotiations particularly intently. The two most important drafts under discussion are those for the Second Banking Co-ordination Directive and the Investment Services Directive. The first of these would allow a credit institution which is authorized in one Member State to establish a branch in, or provide cross-border services to, any other Member State on the basis of its home-country author-ization. In fact, a licence from its own home-country supervisor will serve as a single licence for a bank to provide its whole range of financial services anywhere in the Community. The draft assumes that two related directives will lay down harmonized standards for such matters as minimum capital requirements (5 million Ecu) and minimum capital/equity ratios. The draft Direc-tive on Investment lays down very similar rules in the investment field.

Both the above Directives will allow Japanese and other non-EC financial institutions to operate in exactly the same way throughout the Community as native banks and securities houses, either through a locally licensed subsidiary or by taking over an existing credit institution. However, in the original drafts, this could be made subject to satisfactory reciprocal facili-ties being given in the country of the applicant. These are almost the only draft Directives in the whole complex for the SEM which contain legal requirements for reciprocity. Such provisions are unlikely to appeal to the main Central Banks in Europe and may not therefore be adopted, but if they do become part of the Community law they could cause some problems for the Japanese. From the point of view of non-EC financial houses, it would all be much easier if a Community Central Bank were created to act as the sole licensing and regulatory authority throughout the EC, but this solution has been made impossible, for the time being, by the refusal of the British government to contemplate it. The rather complex regulatory arrangements which will have to be introduced as a result may cause quite a few difficulties. However, the fears expressed by some Japanese that the SEM will exclude foreign investment or make it much more difficult are not at all supported by the draft directives or any other indicators.

FINANCIAL RELATIONS

This book must end with its proper subject, the financial rela-tions between Britain and Japan. Is the talk about Global Finan-cial Markets just fashionable jargon of the day or does it describe the future?

There is no single answer to this question. Asset management is increasingly planned on a global basis in that many portfolios consist of assets in different countries and in different currencies. Second, many operations can be carried out at any time within the twenty-four hours by going to the appropriate time-window. The instant availability of information provided by electronic communication makes a view of a situation or transaction available globally at any moment in time. On the other hand, this time-function of individual markets itself guarantees their separate survival. Each one will also retain a special character because of its relationship with the area in which it is situated and each one will develop special activities or services to offer to the others. In other words, it is unlikely that there will be any great changes of structure. However, if any point of decision is to be able to have its requirements met instantly at any other point of its choice, there must be a totally free flow of services. If not, the system will not work and there will be no 'global' reality. Or to put it another way, as Mr Yusuke Kashiwagi, Chairman of the Bank of Tokyo, has said: 'If Japan is to grow as an international financial market, it must formulate rules applicable internationally.'[7]

Japan, having finally chosen the end, must will all the means to get there. Cultural differences, though they will always exist, are not a justification for refusing reciprocity of opportunity. Japan, after all, underwent astonishing cultural changes in 1868 and again in 1945, and both provided the foundations of success.

As for the British, it has to be hoped that not only bankers and workers in the City but also politicians, civil servants, and industrialists will remember how nearly London ceased to be an international financial centre in the 1950s and will be determined to maintain and strengthen an institution which provided the framework for a surplus of invisible earnings in 1988 of £11 billion.[8] To preserve the position of London may require two developments. First, the procedures and machinery of the various markets and exchanges will need to be made more efficient, speedier, and cheaper. For example, the cumbersome and expensive arrangements for settlement on the Stock Exchange, whatever their antique virtues for dealers, need improving in the interests of investors, who can obtain better facilities in Paris and

New York. Second, government needs to decide whether it really wishes to intervene to the point where the balance between the Bank of England and the institutions is disturbed and legislation replaces the free market. There is, of course, a direct link between the conduct of companies and the effectiveness of their self-regulation in the City and the degree of government intervention. Too many scandals breed too many interventions. Government also has the duty of developing its relations with Europe in such a way that Britain is not left stranded after 1992 on the margin of the Community's financial activity. 1989 was not a good year in this respect, but so long as these problems are resolved or prevented from arising the City of London will remain the focus of the Central Zone of the global financial markets and Japan will remain a major operator within it.

NOTES

1 William Emmott, 'The limits of Japanese power', *Amex Bank Review*, 16 (Oct. 1988).
2 Peter Morgan, 'Last of the big savers', BZW, Japan (Oct. 1987).
3 *Japanese Embassy Bulletin* (London), 459 (24 Oct. 1988).
4 From '*Shin*', meaning 'new', '*jin*', meaning 'man', and '*rui*', meaning 'race' – 'new human breed'.
5 Paul Kennedy, *The Rise and Fall of the Great Powers* (Unwin Hyman, 1988), p. 470–1.
6 Supplement to *Japan Embassy Bulletin* (London), 410.
7 Yusuke Kashiwagi, 'The internationalization of the Yen and the Tokyo financial market', *Speaking of Japan* (July 1987).
8 Figures provided by British Invisibles. These differ from the figures provided by the government which employs a different method of calculating net banking returns.

BIBLIOGRAPHY

ADAMS, Thomas, and HOSHII, Iwao, *A Financial History of Modern Japan* (Research Japan Limited, Tokyo, 1964).
—— *A Financial History of the New Japan* (Kodansha International, Ltd., Tokyo, 1972).
ALLEN, G. C., *A Short Economic History of Modern Japan* (Macmillan, London, 1985).
BARR, Elizabeth, *The Coming of the Barbarians: The Story of Western Settlement in Japan 1853–1870* (Macmillan, London, 1967).
BEASLEY, W. G., *Select Documents in Japanese Foreign Policy* (Clarendon Press, Oxford, 1967).
—— The Banking System of Japan Federation of Bankers Associations of Japan, Tokyo, 1982.
FELDMAN, Robert Alan, *Japanese Financial Markets: Deficits, Dilemmas and Deregulation* (Cambridge, 1986).
FOX, Grace Estelle, *Britain and Japan 1858–1883* (Clarendon Press, Oxford, 1969).
FRANKEL, Jeffrey A., 'The Institute for International Economic Policy', in Policy Analyses in International Economics, 9: *The Yen–Dollar Agreement Liberalising Japanese Capital Markets* (MIT Press, Washington, Dec. 1984).
—— *Banking in Modern Japan* (The Fuji Bank, Tokyo, 1967).
FUJIOKA, Masao, *Japan's International Finance: Today and Tomorrow* (The Japan Times, Tokyo, 1979).
HALL, Ivan Parker, *Mori Arinori*, Harvard East Asian Series (Harvard University Press, Harvard, 1968).
HORNE, James, *Japan's Financial Markets: Conflict and Consensus in*

Policy-making (George Allen & Unwin in association with the Australia–Japan Research Centre, Australian National University, Sydney, 1985).

HOSOMI, Takeshi, *Tokyo Ofushoa Shijo: Sekai Sandaikoku Kokusai Kinyu Senta no Tembo* (Toyo Keizai, Tokyo, 1985).

INOUYE, Junnosuke, *Problems of the Japanese Exchange* (Macmillan, London, 1931).

—— *Jardine Matheson ... a Historical Sketch* (Jardine House, Hong Kong).

JONES, H. J., *Live Machines: Hired Foreigners in Meiji Japan* (University of British Columbia Press, Vancouver, 1980).

KAMIKAWA, Hikomatsu, *Japanese–American Relations in the Meiji–Taisho Era* (Pan-Pacific Press, Tokyo, 1958).

KING, F. H. H., *Eastern Banking* (Athlone Press, London, 1983).

—— *History of the Hong Kong and Shanghai Banking Corporation* (Hong Kong).

LANE-POOLE, S., *The Life of Sir Harry Parkes* (Macmillan, London, 1894).

LOWE, Robert, *Great Britain and Japan 1911–15: A Study of British Far Eastern Policy* (Macmillan, London, 1969).

—— *The Mitsui Bank: A History of the First 100 years* (The Mitsui Bank, Tokyo, 1976).

MORGAN, Peter, 'Last of the Big Savers' (BZW, Tokyo, 1987).

MYERS, R. H., and Peattie, M. R., *The Japanese Colonial Empire: 1895–1945* (Princeton University Press, Princeton, 1984).

PEATTIE, M. R., et al. *Nippon Ginko Hyakunenshi*, Vol II (Bank of Japan, Tokyo, 1984).

ORBELL, John, *The History of Baring Brothers to 1939* (Baring Brothers, London, 1985).

PORTER, Robert, *Full Recognition of Japan* (Clarendon Press, Oxford, 1911).

PRINDL, Andreas, *Japanese Finance* (John Wiley and Sons, New York, 1981).

REED, Richard, *The National Westminster Bank: A Short History* (NatWest Bank, London, 1983).

SANSOM, Sir George, *A History of Japan* (Cresset Press, London, 1964), Vol. III.

SAYERS, E. J., *History of the Bank of England* (Cambridge University Press, Cambridge, 1976).

STORRY, Richard, *A History of Modern Japan* (Penguin, Harmondsworth, 1983).

VINER, Aron, 'Inside Japan's Financial Markets', *The Economist* (London, 1988).
WILLIAMS, H. S., and NAITO, Hiroshi, *The Kamakura Murders* (n.p., 1971).

INDEX

Index compiled by Mary Madden